MW00989900

HOPE FOR ALL

Three Principles
Interviews and more from the
Front Lines

– with a special section on –

A Guide for Realizing Community and Organizational Change from the Inside-Out

Updated excerpts from
Prevention from the Inside-Out: The New Paradigm

Jack Pransky, Ph.D.

CCB Publishing
British Columbia, Canada

Hope for All:
Three Principles Interviews and More from the Front Lines

Copyright © 2019, 2003 by Jack Pransky
ISBN-13 978-1-77143-372-3
First Edition

Library and Archives Canada Cataloguing in Publication
Pransky, Jack, 1946-, author
Hope for all : three principles interviews and more from the front lines
/ by Jack Pransky, Ph.D. -- First edition.
Issued in print and electronic formats.
ISBN 978-1-77143-372-3 (softcover).--ISBN 978-1-77143-373-0 (PDF)
Additional cataloguing data available from Library and Archives Canada

Cover artwork by Eden Rose August Rain

Editing by Lisa Stevens and Mick Tomlinson

Extreme care has been taken by the author to ensure that all information presented in this book is accurate and up to date at the time of publishing. Neither the author nor the publisher can be held responsible for any errors or omissions. Additionally, neither is any liability assumed for damages resulting from the use of the information contained herein.

All rights reserved. No part of this book may be used or reproduced, stored in a retrieval system or transmitted by any means, electronic, mechanical, photocopying, recording or otherwise without written permission from the author, except for brief, credited quotations embedded in articles and reviews.

For permission or information address
Jack Pransky at: jack@healthrealize.com

For information on lectures, seminars, workshops, trainings, counseling, coaching or mentoring with Jack Pransky, please see:
Center for Inside-Out Understanding
www.insideoutunderstanding.com

Publisher: CCB Publishing
British Columbia, Canada
www.ccbpublishing.com

This book is dedicated to the wonderful souls who contributed interviews to this book, originally through *Prevention from the Inside-Out*, and equally to Sydney Banks, without whose enlightenment experience and willingness to share it with the world none of the stories behind these interviews would exist; therefore, the interviews themselves never would have happened. The same is true for Dr. Roger Mills, who pioneered this work in Modello and several communities where many of these interviews took place.

A very special thank you to my granddaughter, Eden Rose August Rain, age 13, for the cover painting and design. I gave her two words, "hope" and "community," and what appears is what she came up with.

AUTHOR'S NOTE/PREFACE

My least known and least popular Three Principles book, *Prevention from the Inside-Out*, has languished on the shelves since 2003 when it first came out. I don't blame people for not buying it. I wrote it specifically for those working in the field of prevention (of all kinds of problem behaviors), almost as a textbook or guide, with lots of academic stuff (for lack of a better word); the volume was big, heavy and expensive. I knew it would not be a big seller, even among those involved with the Principles.

The thought kept nagging at me: "There's too much of value in there to simply be lost."

Mostly the incredible interviews I'd conducted with people on the front lines. Three Principles people must see these! They're so different from most available interviews because they delve extensively with great detail into the behind the scenes inner workings of the mind and how inside-out change is created in communities and organizations. I hadn't seen these interviews for a while; when I recently read them I became touched all over again.

For the last five years I'd been wondering what to do about this.

Then I heard the Center for Sustainable Change—the primary Three Principles organization dedicated to promulgating community change via Three Principles understanding—had been forced sadly to close its doors for lack of funding. I thought, "Now there is such a gap in helping communities know how to go about creating change from the inside-out. I wonder what I can do to help fill the gap?"

It came to me! I could combine the two. I could republish these amazing interviews for the general Three Principles public and at the same time include the portions of *Prevention from the Inside-Out* most helpful as a guide for Three Principles change agents working in communities and organizations.

Perfect.

Jack Pransky
Boca Raton, FL
September 2018

CONTENTS

INTRODUCTION FOR PREVENTION AND COMMUNITY WORKERS

[*Note: You don't have to read this section if you're not one of them.*]

Twelve years after witnessing the astonishing results achieved by Roger Mills in Modello[1] and well after alerting the field of prevention[2] [simultaneously with Bonnie Benard[3]] to this new, inside-out approach, in 2003 with the publication of *Prevention from the Inside-Out* I unequivocally heralded the Three Principles [a.k.a. Health Realization] as an entirely new paradigm for the field more efficacious than traditional outside-in approaches.[4] Fifteen years later, few in the prevention field have taken notice.

In some ways this is puzzling, for anecdotal and empirical results demonstrated by this approach have been at least very promising, if not well beyond what the field is used to seeing from outcome studies based on traditional approaches. Since the prevention field claims to be most interested in outcomes, why has the field not rushed in to see whether these impressive results can be validated or replicated?

In other ways it is not puzzling at all. Around the turn of the century the prevention field became enamored with scientific, evidence-based, peer-reviewed studies that could be replicated in other communities. This left little room for a new paradigm that did not have the funding for such required, extensive controlled studies, and available money has since become even more scarce. The field also became enamored with

---

[1] Pransky, J. (2011/1998). *Modello: A story of hope for the inner-city and beyond.* British Columbia, Canada: CCB Publishing

[2] Pransky, J. (2001/1991). *Prevention: The critical need.* Bloomington, IN: AuthorHouse

[3] Benard, B. & Lorio, R. (1991). Positive approach to social ills has promise. *Western center news* (June); Benard, B. (1994). The Health Realization approach to resiliency. *Western center news* (December).

[4] Pransky, J. (2003). Prevention from the Inside-Out. Bloomington, IN: AuthorHouse

credentialing prevention practitioners, and all training programs and all test questions for credentialing were based on prevention from the outside-in.[5] Besides, it is difficult for a new paradigm to be accepted because it is typically seen through traditional paradigm eyes; a new paradigm doesn't make much sense through those eyes. A new level of consciousness via new insight is needed to see it.

Thus, this new inside-out paradigm has been very slow to catch on. But I remain undaunted. I remember when I used to be a die-hard prevention-from-the-outside-in guy. I believed in changing conditions first. I had become fairly well-respected in the prevention field, especially after writing one of its first prevention books. When I saw the incredible value of prevention from the inside-out and switched to this new paradigm, suddenly I dropped off the prevention field's radar.

I remain undaunted, because when one sees the truth of how all the behaviors we're trying to prevent are truly created from within and we understand what makes those behaviors change, it is very difficult to turn away. I am even more confident now that one day—I have no idea how long it will take—prevention from the inside-out will become the norm. Why? Because more powerful changes happen in more people's lives and at a more accelerated rate, and it is based on how things really work, not just on how the field thinks it works. All I hope is this makes people curious enough to read this book and decide for themselves. Meanwhile, the approach now most often called the Three Principles (formerly Health Realization) is working one person at a time, one community at a time, one organization at a time, as anecdotal, unscientific results continue to mount, and as scientific results are finally beginning to trickle in. It is only a matter of time.

What is most difficult to refute is found in the interviews herein from some people who experienced firsthand how a deep understanding of the Three Principles changed their lives, and those who were on the front lines applying these Principles to community work from the inside-out.

---

[5] Note: Some material from my original pre-Principles prevention book, *Prevention: The Critical Need* even appeared in the State of New Jersey's credentialing test, at least.

Excerpt from the Preface to *Prevention from the Inside-Out*

In November 1987, an event of enormous magnitude occurred in the field of prevention—only no one knew it. Dr. Roger Mills began a new experiment. He attempted for the first time to affect community change from an entirely different direction—from the inside-out… Results showed that two low-income housing projects replete with violence, drug gangs, shootings, crack addicts and alcoholics, child abuse and spouse abuse, were completely turned around. In 2½ years they became healthy communities. Many residents' lives were completely altered. Unfortunately, the quality of research left something to be desired, went unpublished, and very few took notice.

Yet Mills had proven something. He demonstrated that in fact it was *possible* to achieve community change, reduce problems and improve well-being by taking a completely different approach. Not only was it possible, it looked quite promising. This was not a new program; this was an entirely new way of conducting prevention. Mills took an enormous risk. People called him crazy, stating that trying to point people inside themselves when they are surrounded by massive and overwhelming external problems not only would never work, it was insulting. But Mills proved them wrong. And, he'd attempted this in some of the most difficult and problem-laden environments. If it could happen there, it could happen anywhere.

I am grateful for Mills paving the way. Since then, similar results from this inside-out prevention approach have rippled across the country, changing thousands of lives and improving scores of communities and organizations.

Another Excerpt from *Prevention from the Inside-Out* —just to set the stage

...two critical elements I realized I [and the entire prevention field] had missed entirely, and these, to me, are what the Three Principles of Universal Mind, Consciousness and Thought are all about:

1) ...no matter what terrific things we do in the name of prevention, even if precisely researched-based, **if people's *thinking* does not change, their feelings and behavior *will not* change**...

2) ... ***when* people are connected with their "Health" or internal well-being or "spiritual essence" they do not commit the acts we are trying to prevent**. Now I see that everyone has within them all the wisdom and common sense they will ever need to overcome any problem behavior or difficulty they encounter. Instead of doing all these things from the outside in hopes it will strengthen them on the inside, we could help them realize the inside directly—help them see they already have all the resources within that they will ever need to make it out of their plight. We could help them *see* their innate essence that provides automatic strength and hope and what separates them from it, so on their own they would be guided toward Health and well-being and away from problems.

The significance of these cannot be overstated.

Though this book is written primarily for people familiar with the Three Principles, if this is a reader's first exposure it would seem wise to write something briefly from my perspective about what the Three Principles are and how they work together to create our experience. "Principle" means fundamental truth about the way things are. Simply put, ***Universal Mind*** is the formless energy and intelligence behind all life, including the "life force" within us; ***Consciousness*** is the ability to experience life and be aware of that experience; ***Thought*** is the power to create and form thoughts. It works like this: In the outside world some situation or circumstance occurs or someone does something to us. Whatever happens, we don't take it in directly; it *always* gets filtered through our own thinking, and we make meaning of it for ourselves. Out of *All* possibilities inherent in Universal Mind, a thought somehow comes to us. We often don't know we're thinking it or what the thought is. This thought instantaneously is picked up by our consciousness, which sends it right through our senses and gives us a "real" sensory feeling or experience of whatever we're thinking. We *really feel it*; it looks and feels so real! But nothing in the outside world can *ever* make us feel anything. Only our own creative thinking about it intermingled with consciousness can make us feel any particular way. So what we believe is reality or truth is really only an illusion of our own creation. We could see the same situation from many different levels of consciousness; in fact, we do see it differently at different times. Lucky us, thought changes on its own and when it does we get a new experience, a new feeling. Furthermore, Universal Mind, as pure energy, also has the inherent quality of pure peace, pure love and pure wisdom—the essence of who we are, because we are a tiny part of the One. The only thing that can give us the illusion that we're not is our very own creative thinking. When people truly realize this at a deep level, lives can change. Think of all the problem behaviors we try to prevent where someone acted from what they would call "reality." If they saw it as merely an illusion of their own creation they would not have to "go after" it. If they allowed themselves to be guided by wisdom, they would not go after their compelling emotions. The implications are enormous—not only for perpetrators of problems but for us all. For more on this I recommend *The Missing Link* [Banks, S. (1998). Renton, WA: Lone Pine Publishing], and *Seduced by Consciousness* [Pransky, J. (2017). British Columbia, Canada: CCB Publishing].

PART I.

THE INTERVIEWS

1. HELEN

Interview with Helen Neal-Pore (Ali). *Helen is a miracle. Abused, depressed and suicidal one day, overnight she became happy and peaceful—a completely new person. Changes of this nature are rare; they are not the norm. This shows the possibility. It raises the question, "How could this happen?" Some shift of enormous magnitude must have occurred. Here is Helen's story. I interviewed her at her home in Tampa, Florida in November 2001.*[6]

LIFE BEFORE UNDERSTANDING

JP: What were you like before you got involved with this understanding?

HNP: I was very nervous and very insecure. I had very low self-esteem—felt real bad about myself. Back from my beginning I thought there was something about me that wasn't right.

JP: What made you think that?

HNP: Well, I was born into a home where there was a lot of violence. My parents were very hard workers, so I always was kind of comfortable that way, but no hugging, no time, no loving. My father was a weekend alcoholic. Friday was payday and my dad would come home drinking. Now he's going to be gone for a whole weekend, so then my mom would start, "You go every weekend, you've got to stay home," and here it go. My mom was very verbal, and she would just tell him off, so the only way he knew to shut her up was to start punching her. And that would give him an excuse: "See what you made me do? Now I've got to leave!" And then, maybe Sunday we'd see him again, and then he'd be sobering up for work, and when he sobered down everything would be real quiet. Even as a little kid I took responsibility for them and for

---

[6] After this interview, Helen wrote up her story in the book, *OK Forever: A Book of Hope,* now available in its 2nd Edition from Amazon.com.

their happiness. So on Sunday I would grab my dad's uniform, boots and hat—he was a heavy construction equipment operator—and put it on, and I would come in the living room where they weren't even speaking to each other, and I'd just sit there. And all of a sudden they'd bust out laughing, and I would break that cycle of quietness and silence in the house. Then things would be normal until Thursday. Then my mom decided to go to work early so she would not be abused over the weekend. So then I was dropped here and there and went to feeling like I wasn't wanted at an early, early age.

And then, when I was real small, probably between five and seven, my older cousin molested me. And he made me feel like it was my fault, something that I did, and that I couldn't tell anybody because I'd get in trouble. So I kind of held that in for a lot of years, thinking that there was something wrong with me.

Then the very first boy I liked when I was about fourteen and dated for four years, ended up rejecting me right prior to our marriage at eighteen. He just kind of disappeared—

JP: You mean he left you at the altar?

HNP: A month before—and I had no idea why, other than there had to be something wrong with me. I thought maybe it was because I was heavy, so I just had these very insecure thoughts.

Then I kind of flipped the switch and I said, "Okay, I'm going to make people like me." I thought, maybe if I just do whatever people ask me to do, just run myself raggedy, then people would like me. So I was trying to buy my friendship, with girlfriends too. If they needed a ride I'd take them; if they needed money I'd give it. It wasn't working [laughs].

JP: When you say, "It wasn't working," what do you mean?

HNP: It didn't make me happy. I started feeling, "Now they just using me. The only reason they like me is because I have a little money, or I have a car, I can take them places." So nothing I was doing was working. But being black, we never think of psychologists or going to get help. This was normal. My cousins were the same way, because the same thing was going in their home. You know what it was, Jack? I was always there for everybody else, even the adults in my life, so I wondered, where was my person?

JP: So what happened after being left a month before the altar—

HNP: I was so angry because I wanted to get back at him. I was the admission clerk at a hospital and this cook in the hospital was my friend, and we started hanging out together. She was just doing things that I would never be bold enough to do, like going with other men and partying, and it wasn't good stuff [laughs]. It was not the typical Helen.

So I met a guy one night and we danced, and the next day he called me, and I had to go to work, and he said, "Can I borrow your car?" And I was naïve and not smart at all, and said, "Sure." So he picked me up that evening, and I said, "Where do I need to take you, because I'm really tired, and I want to go home and go to bed." He said, "Oh you're my bitch now. You belong to me!" And I'm going, "Excuse me!?" So then he smacks me. That was my first experience with domestic violence. And he goes, "Yeah, I've just moved into your house!" And he moved his stuff into my apartment. And when we got to the apartment he was like, "Well, come on in!" And I was, like, "No no no," because I didn't want him to rape me. I didn't know what was going to happen—I was scared. So I said, "I need to go somewhere. Just give me my car keys." And I took off driving. And I was wanting to go to my parents but they're going to want to kill me because I let this guy have access to my whole apartment, everything.

And I drove around and went by this filling station where me and my friend would stop and get gas. And this guy was there, and we'd seen him but I didn't know him, and I told him what had happened. And he said, "Don't worry, I'll get him out of there. I'll help you out. I'll pretend I'm your big brother." And when he got off work he went and he beat this guy up and threw his stuff out of my house. And I was so grateful! Somebody cared about me. So now I'm in *love* with this guy, I thought, not knowing him.

We dated for about a year, and then he asked me to marry him. He was from a different kind of life-style. His family lived in, like, really the predominantly ghetto-kind of area where there was always drug-dealers on the street, always stuff happening, the police was always there, and he wanted to move on that side of town. So he found a duplex, but it was in an area that wasn't safe, and it wasn't anything that I was used to. But he knew the lady and her little kids next door. And I said, "Well, okay, they're always home. They'll watch the house."

So two weeks after we got married, one day I was at home, and he spent a lot of time with that woman and her three kids. I was thinking this was a friend, no big deal. And his phone rang, and it was his mother, so I went over to tell him that and knocked on the door. The little kids were sitting there, and I said, "Is my husband over here?" And this little kid said, "Oh yeah, he's in the bedroom with mom." So now I'm like, "Oh God, he's moving next door to his woman!" So I busted in the bedroom, and to my surprise she was shooting him up with heroin. I'd married a heroin addict.

That day I got beat so bad I didn't recognize my own face. Now that I knew his secret, every time he'd think about me busting into that room he'd just beat me for no reason. And then right after the fight, or when he'd go to sleep and wake up he'd say, "What happened to you?" He didn't even remember abusing me. About two months of him was about all I could take.

After that I moved away for a little while, then came back and met my next husband. He was a honky—handsome, tall, big and really cute. He'd asked me, "Will you go to church with me?" And I was, like, "*Wow!*" Nobody had ever asked me to go to church. So we'd party on Saturday and go to church on Sunday. [laughs] But when I got pregnant I didn't want to go out any more. Then I started listening in church, and I'm finding out about Jesus, and it took me to a level that there was a peace, and I didn't want to go out partying anymore. My husband and I had been together four years and we had a wonderful relationship, or so I thought—because one day he came home one day with a woman in the car and pulled into our driveway and said, "I don't love you anymore, because you love God and that baby more than you love me. I'm leaving you." I'm going, "What?!" I mean, we never had a problem before! So now I'm rejected again, and it was devastating. I got real depressed. I lost a lot of weight, wouldn't eat, and just took care of my baby—he was probably the only reason I wanted to live. I even thought suicide and had a handgun. Then one day my baby picked up that handgun, and that was the last day I ever had a gun in my house, period.

So I let a year or two go by and I'm really praying that God's going to bring him back. I was doing all this praying and feeling real low in myself. I was a real good Sunday school teacher—I was so good, Jack, for everybody but me. I could get in that church and I could teach, and I would get this energy from somewhere that was just so great. But then I'd get home and I would just cry. I had a good 38-year pity-party [laughs] before I got into this understanding. (But now that I look back and know what I know now, I was in my innate wisdom when I'd do other things for other people—but I never pulled on that for me.)

Then I met this guy who was not attractive, glasses taped together in the middle, wore really old clothes, stuff like that. So I thought, "I don't want him, so maybe nobody else is going to want him either." [laughs] But we got to talking. It was more like a friendship, and it went on for about four years. I had told him that I was still waiting for my husband to come back (of course, my husband is probably on woman number six by now and he wasn't heading back my way no way.) [laughs]

Then this guy decided that he wanted to be intimate. I wasn't attracted to him, but we start a sexual relationship. And the first time I got pregnant. So the right thing for a Sunday school teacher to do is to get married. So I married someone I wasn't in love with, just so other people wouldn't think I was this person who did something that she shouldn't have did. [laughs] So in this relationship I wasn't as intimate as a wife should be to her husband, and I just wasn't doing what he wanted. And he just got really ugly, verbal abusive, and started calling me names, and I had my own business at that time, I had my own company, and I started losing everything.

JP: What was the business?

HNP: I had a boarding home where I took care of elderly people. I had a four-bedroom house with a couple of apartments in back. And I was able to be home with my son. This guy had helped me for four years with this business, but when we got married he said, "These people got to go." And I'm saying, "This is my income! I make good money." I mean, I was going on cruises, living a good life. I said, "I don't think we can live off of your paycheck. I don't think you make enough to take care of me or this household." But he thought he could. So I quit my job, and that's when the verbal abuse really started, because then it became a financial strain on him. So now he wants me to work. So I had to go off to work. Then he'd say, "You don't spend enough time with the boys!" So then I'd quit that job and stay home and then he'd say, "There's not enough money to take care of you. Go to work!" And I was trying to be what I thought at that time in my religious beliefs that I had to be a perfect wife and submissive to my husband. So being submissive to my husband caused me a couple of nervous breakdowns [laughs].

JP: You're talking nervous breakdown, literally?

HNP: Literally. Mental hospital. I had had these episodes where I would cry and couldn't stop, and then I'd feel like something was crawling all over me. It felt like bugs were in the top of my head and then crawling all over me. Then my children would play, and it would just sound like a freight train coming through the living room. And I would be, "Just shut up!" I couldn't stand to even hear them laugh. And they would then cry because they didn't know what was happening. As soon as they'd get quiet I would kind of calm down.

Then it got so bad this one particular time that I woke up and just started crying and I couldn't stop. So my mom took me to my doctor, and he sent me to a psychologist. And I'm going, "Oh my God, I'm crazy!" Now this was really validating everything I had thought in the past that something was wrong with me. So I go telling him how I was feeling but I never related what was going on in my relationship: My husband would play mind games with me. He'd say things real nasty, like scream at me, "Iron my shirt!" And I'd say, "Well you don't have to talk to me like that." And then he'd go, [real sweet voice] "Well, all I said was would you please iron my shirt. You make such a big deal out of little stuff." And I'd go, "Okay?" And the next thing you know I'm ironing his shirt, and I'm going, "That ain't what I heard." Then he'd go, "You just crazy!" He'd say that all the time. It never dawned on me that I'm getting mentally and emotionally abused.

The doctor put me in Memorial Hospital, and when this man took a key and unlocked that door, it hit me, "I have a mental problem, and I'm going into a *psych ward*!" And when he closed that door behind me I really cried then. I mean, I broke down and I *cried*.

And then all of a sudden I looked up from my tears and feeling sorry for myself and I saw all these people, and they were looking so out of it. They were just zonked out, and the women's hair was just a mess like it hadn't been combed and nobody had took care of them. And my nurse instinct just jumped in there immediately and I wanted to take care of these women. And I started doing their hair. And in two weeks my doctor said, "You are doing so much better I think I'm going to let you go home." Now I was feeling good about myself, I was away from my husband and all that chaos and taking my Xanax and Tofenel as prescribed. Then I went right back into that relationship. And then everything just started all over again. Then I had a second breakdown.

JP: What do you remember about that?

HNP: My third husband has a stepdaughter. One night we were home watching a movie, and we were laughing and just having a wonderful time, and he came in and started screaming at both of us. And it felt like those things were just crawling all over me again. I mean, it came to a point where I was just like [sucks in breath] speechless. I couldn't talk. I have never had anything that severe happen to me. It was such a panic. Then I started having panic attacks. I'd get real scared—it was just like jumping. And it got to the point after that night I just would jump at the least little thing, like if somebody would walk up on me.

JP: How long were you in the hospital this time?

HNP: Probably four weeks. But I had a horrible dream one night that I shot him. It was so real. I shot him for every man that had ever hurt me in my life. Then I knew I couldn't be in that relationship. I knew that when he did get violent that I was capable of doing something like that, and I had to be out of it. I couldn't be in an abusive relationship.

JP: How long from the time you got out of the hospital until you left him?

HNP: A few months. What happened was, my younger son wanted to go to a birthday party that my older son was going to, and he went to screaming. And my husband went to grab him and was shaking him: "You ain't going, so just shut up!" And he had never went off on the kids before. So when I grabbed my son to take him, he grabbed him and threw him on his bed, then he went to choking me. So my older son runs to a neighbor's house and calls my parents. And the police came, and I told them, "Make him give me my car keys. I'm trying to leave." We had two cars and his car was there, plus he had a truck. And the police officer said, "Is his name on the title?" And I said, "Yuh." And he said, "Well, then we can't." And I said, "He just abused me, he choked me." And they go, "We don't see any bruises." So they told me that I could leave, but they couldn't make him give me my car keys. So I left there walking with one child on one hip and dragging the other one behind me. And my parents pulled up and we got in the car with them.

I had heard about The Spring, which was a shelter for battered women, and I called them. I said, "I have to feed my kids and I only have $35 left and I have nowhere else to go to." I felt really bad because for so many years I had helped so many people, and everybody that I called, Jack, turned me down because they didn't want to get involved in our business—all these friends that I had housed and given money to and took places. Family members too. So the Shelter told me they had a bed for us, and me and my sons went to the shelter. And they got me clothes. I was able to go to work as a Kindergarten teacher at my Church school. I was there twenty-one days.

And I met my [future] daughter there—she and her mom were my roommates—she was three years old at that time, and we kind of became friends. Then after me getting out of the shelter, we still kept in touch and the little girl became my Goddaughter. The next year her mother got back into her bad relationship and ended up shooting at the baby's father. The police knocked on my door at 3:00 in the morning with her, because the baby told them, at almost three, she goes, "Don't arrest me. I didn't do nothing. Take me to my Godmom's." This little baby showed them where I lived, and she's been with me ever since. I've adopted her since. She's thirteen now.

So now it's me and my three kids now, and we're living in low-income housing on welfare in the projects in Tampa, and I'm feeling really low. In

1993 I decided to go back to the shelter to say thank you for what they did for me and my kids. They said to me, "Helen, we need you to go and speak, we need a survivor, someone who's gotten out of a bad relationship and has made it for herself and her kids. I didn't think I had made it; I'm still on welfare and feeling sorry for myself, but they thought I had made it just because I'd gotten out of the abusive relationship. And I said, "No, I can't do that. I'm not a speaker. You got the wrong person." So then they sicked Mable Bexley on me. I admired her highly because she was the woman that started this shelter. Then I felt obligated because I owe Miss Mable.

One day I was on a panel in 1996, and Jeannie Williamson—who at the time was deputy director at Bay Area Legal Services—she saw me speak. Somewhere in my talk I had talked about my "stinkin' thinkin'," and how I was making these bad choices, and that I have a choice to make better ones but I didn't choose to do it at that time in those relationships. And she came up to me afterwards and she said, "Oh my God, you were awesome!" And I said, "Really?" I didn't think so. I was getting ready to get to my car and get back to my Xanax so I could calm down [laughs]. So she says, "There's going to be a Health Realization training. Elsie Spittle is doing a training, and I would love for you to come." And I said, "How much is it?" "And she said $250 for four days, and I said, "Oh ma'am, I'm sorry, I'm on welfare and I don't have any money." And she said, "No, we'll take care of it. Bay Area Legal will pay for you to go." And I said [under breath], "Oh shoot, now, she's going to pay for me to go, like I need something else." I'm already seeing my psychiatrist, I'm taking Xanax, I'm seeing a counselor, I'm taking my Tofenel, what do I need with a Health Realization class?" I was not happy about this. But I'm a people-pleaser, so the first thing that comes out of my mouth is, "Okay." [laughs]

The day before the class started I had to go see my psychologist, so I thought the best way to get out of this class is to go ahead and have another good breakdown. So I go in there remembering all the things that happened to me from my birth and examining my life and these marriages and how awful they was, and I was really in a bad, bad space.

JP: This was when you were talking to the psychologist?

HNP: The day before. I was doing a reminiscing. I was going down memory lane [laughs]. So by the time I went to see her, I am a nervous wreck. I'm crying, snotting and everything. I was just out of it. So she thinks I'm having another breakdown and starts calling around trying to find a bed. Couldn't find one! And this was my seventh psychologist, by the way. Seven years of therapy with seven different people. And they didn't find a bed, so I might as well go to this stupid Health Realization class.

THE INSIGHT

So I go in there the next day, and I was the only black in the audience. And I felt, "I'm in the wrong place. There's nobody my color here." There were two black ladies but they were presenters: Theresa Roberson, from Tampa, and Cynthia Stennis [from the Modello project (Pransky, 1998)]. And Elsie talks with this soft voice.

The other thing about them was, I had never seen so many happy people at one place—all of the presenters: Jeannie (the lawyer that introduced me), Elsie, Theresa, Cynthia and Reese [Coppage]—they had this peace about them that I had never experienced and never seen. And Elsie went to talking about how that we all had this innate wisdom, and that we were all connected to a greater source, greater than us—which immediately, because of my religious background, I thought of the Holy Spirit and God—yeah, okay I can buy that; I'm okay with that part. That's cool.

And then she started talking about Thought. How our thoughts create our reality. And I was lost there. I didn't understand that. And then she drew the thought cycle, where she says a thought gives you a feeling, and then you get a behavior, and then you get a result. And I'm like, no, it's what I'm feeling that make me think about stuff—I thought it was the other way around: because I'm feeling bad, I think bad. But when she went through it, the way she did it, it was so powerful that I knew that it was something to it. But it was too easy. When she was saying that we could let go of that stuff, and everything that had happened to us in the past was past, it was just memory, it was just thought, it was no longer alive, and it was only when we start validating it and accepting it that it becomes alive. And it was weird to me, very weird. It was too simple. She couldn't tell me that I could just start thinking better or I can start looking at things a different way and then feel different. It was just too easy.

So the first day I was just doing a whole lot of head-thinking, not saying anything, but one thing I wanted to do was make this little lady out a liar. That was on my agenda. Because I had a thirteen-year-old son, and we have not gotten along, and he wouldn't even move unless I'm screaming and hollering at him. Nothing's working. So after the end of the class this day, I just had to prove that this couldn't work. I was going to go home and try this out, and then I was going to come in the next day and tell her how this didn't work.

So I thought about my boy coming home from school when I'm not home, and he drop his book-bags in the middle of the floor, the remotes would be everywhere, he would make a mess with the food, whatever. So I would have to go in and scream at him. So I said, "No, I learned this new stuff, I'm not going to scream today. I'm going to do like Miss Lady said. I'm going to be nice and quiet and calm, and I'm going to see what happens." So I go in and sure enough everything was a mess. So I go, "You know, Shevon, this is your house. I went to this class today, and I learned that this is my baby's house, and I would love a nice living room for people to come walk into, but you live here too, and it is your responsibility to keep your living room clean too. But if you don't want to, that's okay. When people come in I'm going to tell them that this is my baby's living room too, and if he wants a messy living room then it's all right by me." So I went in my room and started putting on some more casual clothes to do dinner, and all of a sudden I heard his door slam. So I came back out and I went in the kitchen, I looked in the living room and the remote controls were all back in the thing, and his books and stuff was up. Now, before I would have had to yell, "*Pick up your stuff!*" and he would have picked up one item and *slowly* took it out, then I'd have to scream again for the second item. So I said, "Wait a minute, this stuff works! This lady's not lying." You know? He didn't change. He didn't go to that class. *I* went. *I* did something different. I handled it a different way. She's right, we get what we give. If I give out love and kindness, it's going to be different.

Then I knew if I passed this next test, this stuff was good. My ex-husband calls my son every day. He has always been a good father. But usually when he calls, I'd throw the phone: "*Your daddy want to talk to you!*" I just didn't even want to hear his voice, I had so much hatred for him because I felt like I had lost everything—I had lost my business, I lost my home, I'm on welfare—and it all was because of him! So he called, and I answered and I said [cheerfully], "Hi!" And he's, like, real quiet on the other end of the phone. I had never in 5 years said hi, not in that tone of voice [laughs]. So he was like, "Hello? Is C.J. there?" And I said, "Yes. I went to this class today, and it was really nice, and I realized that we will never be husband and wife, but because of C.J. we need to be the best parents he could have. We need to be the best for him. So I think we should just get along, for him, what do you think?" And there's silence on the other end of the phone. This man is just, like, speechless. And he says, [meekly] "Okay." So I say, "Well, hold on, let me get C.J." And it was the first time that it felt like these weights just lifted off my shoulders, with this person.

Then I remembered her talking about this innate wisdom that we all had, and that night I started thinking about that even more in my bed. I went to looking back over my life and I realized, my dad was only doing the best he could with what he knew. He saw his dad come home drunk and abuse his mom. My mom wasn't rejecting me, she was just trying to be safe. My cousin molested me: He took advantage of me. That was not my fault. The boyfriend that left me, I had no idea why, but he had came back into my life by then—

JP: The first guy who left you?

HNP: Yes. A year before getting into this understanding, I was living back at my parent's house because they had bought another house. And he had came knocking on the door looking for me when his mother passed away. And he said, "Are you married?" That's the first thing came out of his mouth. And I'm going, "What do you mean I'm married?" And he says, "I came back to marry you." And I'm going, "I think you're about twenty-some years late on this marriage thing. [laughs] Why did you ever leave me?" And he said, "Do you remember when I used to come visit you, and on Fridays your dad would wave the gun at me because he'd be drunk, and he'd be cussing and going and fighting your mom?" And I said, "Well, yuh." And he said, "Well, I got scared and I thought if I married you, your dad would shoot me one day." And I said, "Well there was no bullets in the gun!" He goes, "What do you mean? " I said, "Because on Thursday night we'd take the bullets out of the gun, because we know he's going to come home Friday and swing the gun. And on Sunday before he comes home we put them back in there because we know he's going to clean his gun on Monday." So this guy left me and I'm thinking "rejected," and getting into all these relationships trying to get back at him. And it was all because he thought that my dad was going to hurt him.

JP: Well, he could have told you.

HNP: Yuh. I agree. I would have at least known what was up. But he didn't. He said, "I didn't want to hurt you." "But you hurt me worse by not telling me, because then I had to leave it to my own imagination to know why!"

JP: So back to that night—

HNP: I'm going back and reevaluating my whole life. Then I realized that, wait a minute, he was just doing the best he could at the time. He was scared. I jumped the gun and went to thinking something else. Then I went to thinking about giving that guy my car keys—I allowed him to take advantage of me because I turned over my car keys. And then this other boy, I saw that there was abuse in his family, and I still married someone that I saw abuse in. And I took for granted that those things on his arm were whatever lie he told me—I bought into it. And the other relationship with the husband that ran off with this woman: Well, when his mom got saved, his mom and dad separated, his dad ran around a few years, then he came back home. He thought he was going to run around for ten years like his dad did and then come back home. Then I was thinking, he was husband number two, and I was looking for husband number three [as in "strike three"]. And with husband number three I married somebody that I wasn't really in love with. And it finally dawned on me when I went to this Health Realization class that day, because Elsie said something like, "Even if you got into a relationship with someone that did something to you or hurt you in some way, there was something about that person—everybody has some good inside of them—and there was something good about that person that attracted you to that person in the first place, even before the dislike or the disagreement happened." So I went to thinking about this last husband, and he was a good father, and what I didn't have was a relationship that him and his daughter had. Then I realized why I couldn't be intimate with him. I wanted him to treat me like he treated his children. He was looking for a wife, and I was looking for a father. And it was just so eye-opening for me that, wait a minute, the reason this relationship didn't work was because we were looking for two different things. You don't be intimate with your father! So I didn't want to be intimate with him. That was just so relieving—I was just having one insight after another—

JP: While you were lying in bed.

HNP: Lying in bed! I mean, I was just like, "*Wow!*" [laughs] I just had one insight after another and I just kept cleaning up my life. And then the nervous breakdowns and the abuse and all this other stuff, by me thinking that this was my last chance at marriage, I was the one that stayed in that abusive relationship, and not really knowing that emotional and mental abuse is abuse. I didn't learn that until I went to the battered women's shelter when it got physical. So I realized all that stuff is just *thought* because it's not real anymore.

And that night [pause]—now I get teary-eyed because this is the turning point in my life—that night I made a promise to myself [emotional pause] that nothing, no matter what episode happened in my life [pause], would ever have as much control over me as the last thirty-eight years of my life had. And I vowed that I would take one day at a time. And when things happened to me and when people did things to me, I knew that they had this innate wisdom, this innate health that Elsie was talking about. And I would always, no matter who I was dealing with, no matter how poor they were, no matter who they were, no matter what problems they had, I would always speak to their innate wisdom. I would never look at the person and judge another human being in my life. And it was *powerful*! I mean, it was a wake-up call for me. And I now knew that I had the person to make me happy [pause], and that was *myself* and my connection to the spiritual whatever-she's-talking-about. [laughs] I didn't know what it was [laughs]. But I knew that if I could tap into that for everybody else, now I'm going to start tapping into it for myself. And that was my flip. I was always there for other people, I've always had that gift, but I never had that gift for me—to love me. It wasn't important anymore to think of what anyone else thought about me—how fat I was or how ugly I was or however unwanted I was, *I love me*! Right where I was. And I knew from that day forward, laying in my bed that night, that this was something that I was going to do for the rest of my life. Because I knew there were a lot of Helen's out there that were feeling like I was, and no one was telling them that they were *one thought away* from being healthy—mentally healthy.

By the time I got ready for that class the next day, I was just so sold on this stuff. I'm lit up like a Christmas tree. And Jeannie noticed right away that there was something different about me. But it's like that one night I shedded thirty-eight years of Hell. And I just let it all go.

JP: Incredible.

HNP: Mm hmm and took it for what it was—it was just *Thought*. But no one had ever told me that. Elsie used that circle, and I *saw* it. I saw how I was thinking. And I saw that things are going to happen to me, people aren't going to like me and it's just what I think about it that matters. And when I catch myself I can just recognize that, "Wait a minute, it's just that my thinking is off, and I don't have to deal with that right now. It's going to be okay." Ain't that *powerful*?

JP: I'll say!

SHARING WITH OTHERS AND LIFE AFTER

HNP: So the second day of class I came and I shared the experience and how it felt like a ton of bricks had just lifted away from me. By the third day I was just glowing, and by the fourth day, Elsie hired me as a trainer.

JP: [laughs]

HNP: And I started working with her company, which at that time was Life Core Consulting, or something like that. And they were doing a program in a housing project with some residents, working with the children and the older ladies, but no one was touching the teen moms. And I said, "Why don't I start teaching this to the teen moms?" And Elsie said, "I don't have any money to pay you." And I said, "Oh, I don't need to get paid, I just need to do this." So I would get my food stamps and I'd buy a bottle of coke and chips, and I started meeting with the teen moms. And soon that group grew tremendously, and six months went by, and I told Elsie, "OK, I'm ready to start my company now. I want to do what you're doing." And she first said, "Helen, it took me twenty years to really get to this point." And I'm saying, "That was you."

JP: [laughs]

HNP: "I'm ready!" I think at first she was thinking I was kidding. Then the opportunity came where she was moving to California. And I said, "I want you to do this for me and help me through this before you leave." And she helped me get Life Changing Consultants started. And that's the name of my consulting business.

And my life changed. The first thing that happened was that a week after that first training I had gone to, I went up to my psychiatrist and I said, "I'm through with taking this medication." And she said, "What do you mean?" And I said, "I don't need it any more. I'm free." And I've been off it to this day. Never even thought about needing it again.

JP: Wow!

HNP: Then I wanted to do something different. My first real job was at Alpha House, which is a home for pregnant teen moms. These ladies were at the same training, and the lady that ran the housing part of this saw how I changed immediately, and when they told her that I had started a company, they were my first paid job. In March I learned my understanding, and in September I started my company, and by November I was working for Alpha House doing groups with the teen moms, teaching Health Realization.

JP: Amazing.

HNP: It was! The next year was kind of slow. I gave back to The Spring, the battered women's shelter. Then by word of mouth people went there watching me. Then some of the same clients I was working with went to drug rehab' and went to telling that Miss Helen was doing great things and would come and do groups. So I started doing three different sessions for the drug rehab, the moms and infants' group, and then I stared doing their men, and then the residential. And it just has flourished from there.

JP: Did you start seeing changes in the people you were working with?

HNP: Oh yes! Especially after I started Life-changing Support Groups [with help from Reese Coppage]. Then in there, I saw miracles happen.

JP: Give me one example.

HNP: One day we were having a group, and one of the guys who was driving the residential treatment van—he had been going to commit suicide when he first came into the group, and he's now in the Health Realization and living a good life, just got married, just bought a house, doing wonderful—so he was driving the van, and there was a homeless lady sitting on the bench outside the church, crying. He sees her and he goes over to her and he says, "You need to come inside and see Miss Helen." And she says, "No, I'm gonna kill myself." And he says, "Yeah, I know the look, I was going to do that last year, but now I'm doing good. But you need to come in because I was feeling this way almost a year ago." And she said, "I don't want to see Miss Helen or nobody. I don't want anything." So I went out, and she was a bag lady—dirty, smelly, the whole nine yards. And something just said, "Hug her. She just needs you to hug her." So I thought, "Oooo, I'm going to hug her," and then all of a sudden the odor went away. It was like somebody just took their fingers and plugged up my nose, and I just laid her into me and she just cried on my shoulder, and I just hugged her. I said, "I love you. I don't know why, but I just need to tell you. I don't know who you are, but I love you, and I want you to just come inside and get you some food and get you cleaned up, and we here to help you. This is a support group." So she came in, and we went to talking about Thought, and she went to sharing about how she had been molested as a child, and how her mom didn't like her, and she had been a school teacher, and after her husband had died she got into a relationship with someone on drugs, and it just kind of pulled her down. And she had been on the streets for the past seven years, had lost her children, and she had just given up hope. And she started coming to the group and started dressing better and the next thing you know, she had a job back in the school system. And she rented this apartment that we're in right now and stayed here for a while. And she went back and forth and back and forth, but I was always there for her with unconditional love. Now she just bought a condominium and she's working for the State. Now she's totally drug free. She's not doing any crack or anything now. She's been totally clean for the past year and a half. Isn't that great? I mean, I've seen miracle after miracle. She walks in the door now and people don't recognize her. She's become so pretty—a beautiful African woman, and she's my best friend. And she's just one of the many, many stories.

JP: Thank you! Well, this was great.

HNP: Good [laughs]. This life is so great. I'm just so grateful for Jeannie—I'll be forever indebted to her for the rest of my life. And now I'll share it with anybody who will listen. Anybody that wants a new life, I have the key to open that door [laughs].

2. MISS BEVERLEY

Interview with "Miss Beverley" Wilson [Hayes]. *Beverley Wilson is one of the most powerful people I have ever met. She has a look that can cut through you like a razor. Beverley became one of the best at doing whatever she felt she needed to do to survive on the streets. She became one of the best and meanest of addicts. She became one of the best at throwing herself into recovery. She became one of the best at seeing from the inside-out, then in conveying this understanding and drawing it out of others. In a way, this interview contrasts the difference between what often occurs when traditional programs affect people from the outside-in and what can happen when people are affected from the inside-out. Miss Beverley never ceases to touch my heart. I interviewed her at her home in San Leandro, California in May 2001.*

LIFE BEFORE UNDERSTANDING

JP: What were you like before you got into Health Realization?

BW: I guess a good word would be *intense*. I was three-and-a-half years sober, going to a lot of AA meetings and just doing that 110%, and part of the AA program is that you get a sponsor. So for me, being the oldest in my family of seven siblings and always having a lot of responsibility and being kind of a leader all my life, this was a time when I really surrendered my life and kind of allowed this woman that I was with to show me some things about life.

JP: The woman you were with?

BW: Her name is Jewel—my sponsor. We had a job working for the County in the community trying to get people into recovery. We'd go up under the bridges and out to the public housing developments, on the streets, on Skid Row—we'd go everywhere. I knew all the people because I was born and raised in the town. Jewel had been sober, like, ten years, so she had the sobriety, and I knew all the little cuts and the underground paths to the community. So I really got into the mode of following, and I needed to do that because I really had never did that. I followed this woman, Jewel, for a long time, but about three years into it, I just started getting this feeling like, "This is too hard!" We were working seven days a week, from 7:00 in the morning often until 11:00 at night, every day of the week. And our work life and our volunteer work life was enmeshed, and it was non-stop. You get on this drive of helping people, and it's *intoxicating*—just keeps your adrenaline pumping. You're always looking out for people to help. You always carry a bag with stuff to give them. I mean, it was just intense [laughs].

I just kept getting this little gnawing feeling in my gut, like something's wrong with this picture, but I didn't know what. I was staying sober, coming from experiencing heroin addiction, twelve years on methadone and all that stuff. To be living this life was certainly much better than what I had, right? So I just put my heart and soul into it, but after a while I noticed when I went to the gas station early in the morning, I'd give the woman my money, and she'd throw money at me in the change machine. And one of the things they teach you is to act as if you're okay, especially in trying times, so I had gotten to be pretty good at this, but on the inside, I'm like "Rrrrrrrr!" I'd be wanting to bite her head off. So, one day it was like, "I don't like this feeling. I'm tired of acting as if I'm okay." I'm looking good on the outside and I'm doing all these wonderful things, but on the inside I'm taking all this medicine for my stomach, and I'm just all like full of knots. And I was asking people about it. And it was like, "Well, Beverley, you're going good. This is great," and dah de dah de dah.

So I had formed a habit of praying and meditating, so I got talking about this with God that I was tired of looking good, I wanted to *be* good, you know? It's something wrong with this woman in this box at seven o'clock in the morning throwing the money at me—how do I deal with that? How do I deal with when I'm in the supermarket and I specially picked out all these luscious nectarines and some really soft bread, and I get to the stand and they throw stuff in on top of it? How do I deal with this? And so to me it was presented in my mind like a big old question mark in the sky. How do I reach the people that don't even want to hear about God, because everybody doesn't want to hear about Twelve Steps and your Higher Power? And I resented—but I could never admit to it—the fact that I needed a sponsor and I needed to go to meetings all the time. For me, there was something wrong with that.

JP: It was like a dependency on it?

BW: Well, it just didn't seem right. It seemed kind of like being a Catholic the first five or six years of my life, you couldn't talk to God directly, you had to go through a priest, and I didn't like that. I wanted to know how could I do this on my own. Another thing that popped in my mind was I get good feelings from going to meetings—don't get me wrong, I had nice feelings—but what I wanted to know internally, how do I create this feeling that I get in a meeting on my own? And that was the same question I was asking the priest in catechism a long time ago in church. "I want to talk to God my own self. How do I do this?" [voice deepens] "No, no, you can't talk to God. Who do you think you are?" It's always like you go through a middleman. Even on the street with the drugs, I hated middlemen. I always tried to get around them. And, like I said, the question in my mind was, how do I reach the people that don't want to hear it?

About six months I had this with me, but I didn't have no solutions. I'd got sober and moved to a nice neighborhood, but where I grew up at there was no services for people coming out of treatment. So I asked my agency, could I start a group out there? I had this ex-convict guy that was tattooed from his neck all the way to his ankles. He drew me this beautiful picture of a horizon, with the sun and this beautiful sunrise, just before the sun comes up, where the rays peek up over the hills. And that's when I named the classes, "The Sunrise Look into Reality." This group became very, very popular. It was like a wellspring to the people in the community. People was waiting for me at work. They'd be sitting there like it was a haven, because they knew on Tuesday, at 12:30, I would be there.

JP: Besides, you always had a way with people.

BW: Oh, I always did, yeah. I went on to another job but I kept doing that group, and my boss who I worked for at that time never forgot that. So Stockton, where I lived at this time, they had twelve international visitors from South Africa come who were on a tour around the United States. So the mayor and the community activists had, like, a town hall meeting for these visitors, and one of the places they wanted to take them was to a grass roots effort, and guess where they chose to bring the international visitors? To my group! So, man, I'm getting all this attention from the people over at Department of Drug and Alcohol Services, my ex-boss and stuff. So when they got to my class, I was really kind of nervous, because it was so important, and who am I? I'm just this little peon out of the community doing this stuff that I'm doing. But here they come! I asked the class permission for them to sit in. I told the visitors that they could stay on one condition: "You have to participate in the class." So the same assignment that I gave to the class that day I gave to them, and it was some kind of handout that talked about how we shrink when we get in front of people and don't say the things that's really on our mind because we feel intimidated by this or that person, and how to really look inside and envision yourself moving past that—something to that effect. And one of the women had a life-changing experience in the class—

JP: One of the women from the class?

BW: No, one of the international visitors had it! And let me tell you how it looked to me, Jack. When they got through with the assignment, it was their turn, if anybody wanted, to voluntarily share what they had found out. Well, a few people was real enthusiastic. They just shared what they got and they were so gut-level honest. And one of the visitors raised her hand and I saw tears streaming down her face, and, oh my God, inside, I got so scared. I was like, "Oh no, she's crying!" When people cry, it meant to me that I had did something to them, you know? So I was *nervous*. She raised her hand, and I'm just holding my breath, but on the outside I'm looking cool—because I know how to act. And this woman, she begins to talk in broken English, and she said she was a pharmacist, but all of her life what she really wanted to do in her heart was work as a public servant in the community with people. But because of where she came from, everyone was in the field of medicine and professionals in her family. Even before she said it, you could feel the power coming from her. So she said, "I'm going to speak to you, I have never spoken before." The way she said it, you couldn't understand what she meant, because she spoke broken English. So she took a deep breath, and the tears were still streaming down her face, and she said when she gets around her father and her two brothers, all doctors, she never, ever has spoken that she really wanted to get out into the community and work with people. But she looked inside herself and saw that when she got home she was going to see about changing and working in the community. It was just powerful. And so, they left. The class was good, we all had a good time, but I was glad it was over, and I went on about my life.

About a week later, I get a call from Robert Graham—he forms small businesses in foreign countries like Honduras, and he was one of the people that was on that committee with the international visitors. I had told him that I wanted to start a consulting business but I didn't know how to start it, and could he help me? So he contacted me and he said, "Beverley, I wanted to tell you what happened the other night with the international visitors." I said, "Really?" "Yeah," he said, "they had a big dinner that night, and all of them met back up and told what they had experienced in our town." So that African lady told about what she'd discovered about herself in that class. Another African lady jumped up and says, "All we want to know is, why do you have Beverley Jones [my name at that time] out here in this little, small building, doing this work that she's doing? Why don't you have her somewhere where she can effect world change!?" And everybody was, like, whoooo, what happened? They was just saying all these things about me. I didn't know none of this was happening. So he told me he thought that I was doing a thing that they was calling, "Psychology of Mind," and he wanted to send me to a six-day conference. He had talked to my boss about it, and if I was willing to go, he would sponsor me to go there.

JP: He said he thought that you were doing that?

THE INSIGHT

BW: He said, "There's a conference where I think what you're doing naturally is the thing they're calling 'Psychology of Mind.' I'd like to arrange for you to go check it out." That's where I met Roger Mills, Elsie [Spittle] and the girls from Florida [the Modello project], and that's how I got into what I'm doing now. That was my beginning.

JP: Do you remember what your experience was at that week-long conference?

BW: Well, this was 1991. I went up there with Manzell Williams and we missed the first day of the conference. So on the second day I'm trying to be all inconspicuous and find out what this is all about, because I'm suspicious as hell. I just was checking everything out.

Then an interesting thing happened for me when Roger spoke about a quiet mind. I started hearing scriptures out of the Bible. Like he would say, "We've got to have a quiet mind and connect with this thing inside of us," and I would hear, "Be still and know." At this time I didn't know anything about scriptures, but he would say one thing and I'd hear something coming from inside of me—something else. So I'm wondering, how did he do that trick? I thought it was some kind of trick. So I'm sitting like in the back, and I said to myself, "I got to get up here closer so I can examine him." So I got up there closer, and then he appeared to me to be cutting up everything that I believed in, because he was talking about Twelve-step programs and how you could peel the onion layer by layer if you wanted to, or you could learn this and it was like having a knife cutting in you straight to the core. So I was, like, "Who in the hell does he think he is!?" Because I'm 110% into AA and NA

[Narcotics Anonymous], and he's telling me stuff that's shaking everything that I believe in. So that was the stuff that I had to get through the first day or two.

But the interesting thing was, I was sharing a room with Laura Graham, Robert's daughter. And they were saying, "Just start playing around with this right away," so I started playing around with it. The thing that really got me was what they called "quiet listening," but when they said, "quiet listening," I heard "listening softly." You know that song? [sings] "Killing me softly with his song, killing me softly," and I would hear [sings] "Listening softly to this song," and it was just like something magical was happening inside me about the listening piece. And I started trying it out on Laura in the room, and we got to be really, really good friends, and she got some insight about some stuff that had been troubling her a long time. And I knew I was onto something, because that question mark that I had in the sky about something that would help humans that was not restricted to just one little group, it answered that question for me. So that was very exciting to me. It was like, "Now, I want to know more about this!"

Plus, I wanted to start a business, and I was in a thing called Women Entrepreneurs, and one of the things my teacher had talked about, Roger kind of validated. She was talking about working smart as opposed to working hard. Some people are taught to work hard, and they think the suffering and the hardness all that hard work is good. I'm always looking for a way to get stuff accomplished, but I really would like to know how to get it accomplished in a smooth way, you know? So when they was talking about how we stay so busy, and we run so much, that we can't even see how to make our lives work—and I learned from that conference that that was true. Because I had been so busy—I was on a hot-line list for five years that was twenty-four hours a day, so I'd get suicide calls in the middle of the night—plus I had four kids still at home. I just had this crazy, no-stop world, and I wanted to get off this world, even though I didn't know where I would go from there because it was the best thing I had. But I started getting an idea that if I learned more about this Health Realization, that I'd be able to accomplish some goals that I had. And around this time that I was learning Health Realization, I was developing my idea about being an international motivational speaker. I wanted to do that for a living. And Jewel had an idea that she wanted to open up halfway houses. So something in me told me that whenever you want something to happen good for you, help your friend. So I helped her start this house, and that took seven years to get the house really established. In my heart of hearts—I didn't speak with no humans about this—was when the house got established and was self-sustaining, I'd go pursue my little idea about starting this consulting thing.

So I started following Roger around. Wherever Roger was having a training that was in California, I'd ask him, "Could I come?" Or I'd just show up. I had back surgery around this time and I was off from work for a year. So that year I'd just followed Health Realization around and cut loose a lot of the work because my back was hurt. I was really slowing down a lot and deciding to do some things on my own.

JP: Did you feel differently at all during that time?

BW: Yeah. I felt scared. I felt real scared.

JP: How come?

BW: Well, you get dependent—but you don't know you're dependent—on a system. In AA and NA they're telling you that if you don't do this system exactly the way it's laid out, you're going to get drunk again, you're going to die. I had all this conditioning. I really believed, and it was working for me a long time. But this other thing was springing up in me—that I didn't really trust—telling me there was another way. This other was good, but it wasn't really me. I was going along with something. I lived in this real protective world of AA for four or five years. I met Roger when I was about three-and-a-half years sober, but I stayed in this world. I didn't do no functions outside of this world until I took that course in Women Entrepreneurs and went to that conference where Roger was at. I was afraid—but he was teaching me how to recognize my thoughts, and pay attention to that, and then quiet myself. So I saw that I had this fear that they was going to make me think something that would get me drunk. I kind of always walked with that trepidation, you know? I'd do it, but I'd have to walk through *trembling* inside. I'd be trembling inside, but I couldn't *not* do it. Something was drawing me to this. You feel me?

JP: Yeah, I do.

BW: So I couldn't really talk to nobody about it, because everybody I talked to believed like I did. The motto was, "Meeting makers make it." I still was doing a lot of meetings, but now I had these two worlds going. After I went through Women Entrepreneurs, I decided on a salary that was double what I was making. At that time it was audacity to even *think* that I could make $15 an hour, but that was my ideal salary. I was grateful for the $8.16 I was making, but while everybody else was happy to be driving County cars, that wore off for me in about three months. I mean, let's get real, we're still on poverty level, we still need food stamps, we still aren't making enough to even live. This is *poverty level*! So I saw that I needed to make $15 an hour, and I stuck to it. I'm a stubborn old fool! [laughs]

And another interesting thing that was happening, Jack—and this is the part I really want to somehow blow up because one day I'm going to write a book about it—I was a heroin addict of the worst kind. I had been on methadone for twelve years. Most people that stay on methadone that long never get off. They're deemed doomed! And they kind of get this thing in their head that they're going to do this "'til the wheels fall off," because it's legal, you can stay loaded, and all this stuff. But one day I looked around, and I was like, "*Hell, no!* I don't want to do this 'til no wheels fall off. I'm sick of this!" I just got tired of it. Something happened and I got off the methadone, and I went into a program and stayed sober for a year. But at that time they had all these incredible hurdles, and my four kids were in foster care, so you had a reunification thing but it was so tough hardly nobody made it. But I made it! I wanted to get my year pin, and I wanted my kids back. I loved my kids, even though my actions and behaviors along the way didn't always reflect that—but in my heart, you know? So whatever they told me to do, I did it.

And when I came back and got my year pin, this got the attention of the Welfare Department and the Methadone Clinic. They sent the top administrator to have a little meeting with me: "How come you're the only one out of eighty people in your class that came back to get your year pin? What could we have done to make that easier for you? If you could design a program, what would it look like?" I said, "Number one, I wouldn't have it so you have to go so many different places"—you had to go to a parenting class for your reunification, you had to go to four meetings a week, you had to get a job because you didn't have no welfare check anymore and the job is going to be minimum wage, you had to go and find a place to live that you could afford, you had to get back and forth to work, and you didn't have a drivers' license. So I told her, "If I was going to do it, I'd have all those services set up in one place, and I would really want the people to get training *with* their kids—provide a way that they could come and bring their kids, because they was teaching me stuff in parenting that I had never learned." I was honest, and I was able to put words to feelings—raggedy, it was rough—so I was straight, direct, to the point, but it was knocking people's socks off.

I started crying in one parenting class—they was talking about teaching your kids socialization skills. Usually when I start crying I'll get mad about something and I would leave because I'd be embarrassed that I didn't know, because something in me thought I'm supposed to know all this stuff. So one night in the parenting class, I just got overwhelmed from what they was teaching us, and I'm supposed to remember it and do it when I get my kids back! I realized that they was telling me to teach my kids something that *I* didn't know, and that angered me. I was also learning that anger was motivated by fear—and I was afraid I was going to learn all this stuff and *still* be inadequate at parenting. And I told that to the teacher. And when I said it, about four or five women and men started crying and said the same thing. Some of them was ready to exit but had been feeling these feelings for months and never spoke. I was new.

LIFE AFTER & SHARING WITH OTHERS

So big things started happening for me. People started coming asking my advice and asking me how to put something together. The very first program they opened was FOCUS—Families Overcoming Drug-Using Situations—where they had everything that me and Bonnie Butz had talked about in place. And they hired me as the first drug counselor to come there and teach the classes. So that was my first experience. This was like my dream job, because it was working with women who were drug using, or who had babies and got those babies taken because they had been under the influence.

About four or five times I'd be asked to help them design these programs, but I'd still be the lowest person on the totem pole. I'd still be the drug counselor. Roger pointed out to me in the Health Realization classes that something's trying to tell us something on the inside, but we're so busy we can't even hear it. And when I slowed down and had that year off from work, I was able to really start considering some things. One of the things I was feeling was, it looked like injustice: They was asking me a lot of questions, taking my ideas and formulating them into programs and giving me a little slot in that thing. I had a funny feeling, like, if they're asking me all this stuff, maybe what I know is important.

By the time I was work-ready again, the County called me back. "Beverley, we want to start a program called AIM—Allegiance of Infants and Mothers. Can you show Janet how to start this program?" I said, "I don't know. What would my job title be?" "Oh, you'd have your same job back as a drug counselor, but she doesn't have any idea how to start this thing, and you know everybody. They're going to come if you're there. Can you start it?" And I said, "I don't think so. If I do this, I want to earn $15 an hour. Can you pay me $15 an hour?" She caught her breath. She was like, "I barely make $15 an hour." I said, "Then I'm sorry, I can't take your job." And I'm telling you, at this time I didn't know *nothing*! I was, like, crazy, but I hung up the phone, and I felt weird. But I just had made up my mind that I'd just stick with the unemployment and the workman's comp until I got what I needed.

Here I am telling people that they can come out, but I'm really living and working on poverty level. So that was screaming in me.

About two or three days later I get a call from Marta Obekowski at East Bay Community Recovery Center, and the mayor wanted them to start up a Health Realization Project in a place called Sixty-ninth Village in East Oakland, and she wanted to know could I come there and help them start this program. I said, "I'll come if you'll pay me $15 an hour." She said, "We were prepared to pay you $13.20." I said, "I'm sorry, I can't take it," and I thanked her for considering me, and I hung up. About twenty-five minutes later, she called me back. She said, "Beverley, I talked to my bosses. If you come, we'll pay you $15 an hour." I said, "I'll be right there!"

I was scared of driving on the freeway, but I was tired of being afraid of driving on the freeway without alcohol or drugs in me. So this job gave me that opportunity, because I knew if I ever got a chance to drive on the freeway that I could learn, and that if I kept doing it I would do it well. That was my thinking. So I did. I took the job in Oakland, and the rest is history…

COMMUNITY WORK FROM THE INSIDE-OUT

JP: How did you end up working with the Coliseum Gardens project, to start it off?

BW: Well, they was paying me $15 an hour, number one [laughs]—I didn't care what they wanted me to do. That was a dream come true. How I started working with it, it was me and Ron Pellum, who was an African American male—Ron, he's a knowing person about street stuff, but he's not really a street person. He's what street people would call a square, but he's hip—he's a hip square, but he ain't really been out there. And Lisa Allen was a white woman—me and her was about the same age. She had the prettiest green eyes, and she was full of spunk. She was real intense, real intense. She was always moving, always going, and she loved people. That was her gift. And Ron could fit in anywhere. He was just a mellow dude. Lisa was a real go-getter, just finished her Masters in psychology. What I brought to the table was that they needed somebody that was African American and knew Health Realization, and also knew the language of the people.

JP: These two other people didn't know Health Realization?

BW: No. Well, Lisa knew Health Realization; she was at that training in Vallejo with me. But I had followed Roger [Mills] around for a year, so I really had the most experience out of anybody there as far as knowing the model. And Ron had little or no experience.

JP: What year was this?

BW: This was in '92. So we started going into Coliseum Gardens in East Oakland.

JP: Did you get any direction about what you were supposed to do?

BW: We flew by the seat of our pants—that's what we called it—but what we were supposed to do was go and see the Health[7] in the community. That's what we were looking for. We was looking for the Health in the people that we knew was there. So our first six months was basically going from door to door, getting cussed out, slammed doors, sometimes making a hit, and doing the same thing over again the next day. So that's what we did. We built rapport one person at a time for six months. Lisa had a passion for the adolescents, and I liked the adults. And Ron just kind of got along with everybody.

The agency that I went to work for, they wrote a simple proposal for some grant money, and they got it. That made a big difference, because it kind of gave us free rein to go in and assess the situation and find out what we could and could not do. At that time at Coliseum anybody just couldn't go up in there. It was like a desert. They had no services. If a person had a heart attack and needed an ambulance, if that ambulance couldn't get police escort to go in there to serve that person, it was tough-titty. They just couldn't get services. They didn't have maintenance services. They didn't have cabs—that was unheard of—cabs did not go in there. Pizzas, cable TV, none of that stuff was in there. And the place was guarded by sentries—little kids. It's one way in at Coliseum and one way out, and the little kids would stop you and ask you what was your business there. "What are you doing here?"

So, when we first went out there, our first day we were received like, "You guys got to be crazy, coming out here! These people don't want no help." That was an Oakland Housing Authority police officer speaking to us. "You guys are crazy. You done lost your minds!" "What, you think you're going to come up here and set out a table and hand out little pamphlets?"—we had little papers about health issues. We just started with whatever we could and try to get in and meet the people.

---

[7] Often I capitalize the word "Health" in this book when I refer to total mental, emotional and spiritual Health.

But first we had to get through these little kids blocking the entryway. So I handled that situation when we got up there. They said, "Who you coming out here to see?" I looked at the little boy—I looked him up and down and I said, "I might be coming to see you! You sure got on some cute tennis shoes." He looked at me, and he looked at the other guys, and he said, "Oh, man, she crazy!" See, I knew it was a good thing to be considered crazy in the ghetto. So they let us come on in.

We told them we was coming out there to work, and we just was going to try to start some empowerment classes and get to see if anybody was interested in going. We set up a table. Some people was curious and came by and talked to us, and stuff like that. And after we went around the whole development and kind of talked to people for about two or three weeks, we decided to start a class.

The first class we had was, "Girl, Let's Talk!" We set it up for women to see if women will come out. We just got a handful of people, and that went okay. Nothing was going real fabulous. We still had to go back and back and back, over and over again, back and forth to them doors, and every time we see the people, just treat them kindly and really ask them important questions like, "How are you today?" and remember their names and stuff like that. We just chatted with them. We got the kids interested in Girl Scouts. I was a Girl Scout leader, but my task was to teach Health Realization in the Girl Scout classes. And I was good—

JP: I'll bet you were!

BW: The kids, they catch on so quick. But at first it was real trying. One day, I asked them to draw something, and what they drew was tombstones and guns and Uzis—all kind of stuff. It was just sad—that was sad to me. When I drove home that night I was thinking about it. I didn't understand what I needed to do but having that hour-and-a-half commute was really good for me because I could kind of sort stuff out. And it occurred to me that instead of asking them how their community was, maybe I should ask them to dream of what they wanted their community to be like. And that changed the whole flavor of the class. And this time when they did the drawings, they drew fruit trees. What the kids wanted was, they wished there was trees out there that had fruit, where they could just go in their yard and pick the orange or a plum or a peach or something like that. And they wished that they had equipment where they could play on. They had sandboxes and stuff, but all the toys had been tore up years ago. Some of them wished they had grass and flowers in there instead of the dirt. It was just like barren dirt. You ever been out there?

JP: I never have.

BW: Oh, I wish I could take you out there one day. Anyway, so that's what they dreamed of and that was a good thing, because later that came true. It really happened! If you go out there now, it's trees, fruit trees. It's still got patches of dirt, but it also has grassy areas, too, where before there was none. But that's kind of how we got in with the kids. So the kids started to go home and do their homework, and they would voluntarily ask to wash the dishes, and their mothers got interested in what we was teaching them. And finally we got a big class started, for big people.

Coliseum was mostly Asian Americans and African Americans, but what happened was, I found out from doing the door-to-doors that the Asian people were already organized. They met in family circles and group meetings in their homes all the time, so it was about finding out who was the leader. They won't really say there was a leader, but it was this one guy named Chi. And Chi had his people organized. When I met him, we ended up becoming close because he told me a story that was so powerful I was stunned. I was just stunned. He told me about his journey from Cambodia to here, what he went through, what it was like for him growing up. He told me stuff that just really opened my eyes, because I never personally talked to anybody—I'd seen a lot of immigrants in my town, but I never really, personally talked to any. And he told me a story that was so moving that it just stunned me. I mean I was in a daze for about a week. So I was telling Ron and Lisa, "We got to figure out how to get the African American people together, just to tell their separate stories!"

So what we discovered from doing our outreach was that the Asians had some preconceived ideas about the African Americans, and the African Americans had some ideas about the Asians, and everybody's assumptions were off, you know what I'm saying? So it was so good when we first got this little core group of people. We had twelve Asians, because Chi would organize the Asians. It was so sweet, because he'd come and his people would come. The African Americans, on the other hand, were filled with apathy and mistrust, because so many times people came out there to work and they said they'd stay for five or six months, and it looked like they just left in the middle of the night. So they were reluctant to join anything because they had always saw that people would bring them a false sense of hope, and they'd be telling them what they should do, and then they'd leave. But we wasn't telling them what to do. We was actually telling them that we was there to listen to their ideas and to be the bridge between them and Oakland Housing Authority. And I told them I was out there to work myself out of a job, because I really wanted to be an international motivational speaker, and I really meant that. I'd just tell them that all the time.

And it was so funny, after a while we got a little core group of African Americans, maybe ten, and four of them was out of the same family. But the people that we got was so key, because they were like the matriarchs of that community, you know? Because we got Mama Smith and her two daughters, Adelle and Ruby, and then maybe one of Ruby's daughters would come every now and then, so we had like four generations out of one family. Then we got this other lady named Alice that liked to feed the homeless, so she was like a powerhouse in their community, and she would come. And then we got a few other people that were just interested in getting things for their kids—the kids that had been in the little Girl Scout classes.

JP: Did you go out of your way to go after folks like that, or did it just kind of happen?

BW: In a way, yeah, you're looking for leaders. My ideal was that we were going to go in and this was going to become a self-sustaining community, but I didn't know how long that was going to be—if it was two years or five years, or how long, we didn't know.

JP. How long did it take you to even get this core group?

BW: The core group probably took about six to seven months. Yeah, we had just the little group of people and that built over time, because that core group really bought it, you know? We taught them about separate realities. And at this time, the relationship with the police department and the relationship with Oakland Housing Authority was torn, it was ripped, it was really bad. The Oakland Housing Authority police could not come in Coliseum without being escorted by the Oakland PD. They could not come out there, because the people would rock them and bottle them, and the way the Coliseum is set up, it's like a fort. It's one way in and one way out. It's only two entrances and exits, and it's a high-rise, and they would get on top of the buildings and rock and bottle the police, and they couldn't see who was attacking them so they wouldn't go in there.

So through having the classes the people bonded. They told each other their stories and found out they had a lot of misconceptions, and they were laughing at them. An example of that is that African Americans thought that the federal government had a warehouse where they was giving the Asian people new cars, so they was mad at them—every time the Asians got a new car, when they come outside they cut all the tires. In their minds, they're thinking that these people are being treated privileged, and they've been here all their lives and they ain't never gave them *nothing*! So what Chi was able to do was tell them that when Asian families wanted a car, five families would get together, or three families, and what they'll do is buy a hundred-pound bag of rice. Wherever Asians have dirt, they're going to make vegetables, they're going to plant stuff. So they said they plant their vegetables, and they buy these big, large bags of rice and big bags of potatoes. They buy in quantity, and they split this stuff up among the families, and they stay out of the grocery stores as much as they can so that their money don't go for food, and they save their money. In three months' time, they can go and purchase a car. All five families will use that car, and they'll repeat the process until the next family gets a car, then they'll do the same thing until everybody in their group has a car. Then they'll start eating. So when they was talking, Ruby asked, "You mean you don't eat no meat?" And Chi said, "Very seldom." And she looked over at Adele and she said, "Girl, we ain't gonna do without no meat!" It was like they never imagined that these people had a system—they was systematically accomplishing these things.

And the Asians' misconception about the African Americans was what the general society thinks, that these people are lazy and shiftless, they been here all their lives, and they don't want nothing, they ain't gonna never want nothing, and that's why they ain't got nothing. So they told some of their stories about how they came from the South, and it never occurred to the immigrants from Cambodia that African Americans have migrated from Alabama and Louisiana and all this stuff and came here and thought that they was going to get—to them California was the land of milk and honey, not just America. They wasn't free where they came from. They told about living where blacks didn't drink out of the faucets. They just told their stories, and it was just bonding. We had an interpreter in those classes. These classes, they were very slow, because the interpreter would interpret what the Cambodians who couldn't speak English would say to us. After a while, we got so good, we were so in tune with each other that they would be telling a story, and we would be crying, and we don't even know what they was saying yet. We were so connected we could feel the emotion of each other, and it was happening the other way around, too. That's the invisible stuff that's happening within the group.

One day I was teaching about separate realities—and when we're connected to our intuition, we know what to teach—and one of their big barriers was going to the welfare office. The Asians and the African-Americans would have this trouble, because they always felt talked down to. So they go in there with an attitude. The attitude was like, "*I need these food stamps!*" or whatever, but it was always meeting this resistance. So we was telling them about Mind, Consciousness, and Thought—how our thoughts create our reality—and helping them see that behind that desk this welfare worker is just a human being. They function just like you do. They have high moods and low moods and all this stuff. And the judge, behind that robe, is a human. They function just like you. But that day we was talking about a judge and a police officer, seeing beyond their roles, their roles in life, and seeing that a person really existed in there, and to stop approaching the robe and instead approach the person—go to the heart of the matter, and kind of talk about what comes from the heart reaches the heart and ways that we could do that. And some of the ways they had tried that didn't get them the results that they wanted, like cussing the woman out—"You just think you something because you working in this office. You could be out here in this line!"—and all that stuff that didn't work. And we was taking a look at it, just knowing that if they quieted down when they felt themselves getting angry, maybe step back from the situation, and then approached it different, they might get different results.

So the day that we was talking about the judge and the police officer, in walks this little, frazzled police officer! And right away, when he walked in the room, you could feel the energy shift. Just for a moment, there was a dead silence. But around this time we had been having a class of about eight or nine weeks now—

JP: Meeting once a week?

BW: Once a week. But we see the people every day, you see what I'm saying? So we get personal contact with people every day, but we had a formal class once a week. So in walks this police officer. And he looks like, I swear, you know how the Indians, when they had the forts and the messenger would come with the mail and he had arrows sticking on his back, and he'd rush in the door? So this police officer, he just looked like he got arrows sticking out of him and everything [laughs]. I turned around and I look at him, and I'm fascinated because I can't believe my lucky stars. Here I am, teaching the class about taking the uniform off the police officer and the judge, and getting to the heart of the matter, really finding out who this person is and, like, out of nowhere, in drops this frazzled-looking police officer. So just for a moment, there was a little stigma. And I looked at him, and I said, "Welcome. Hi, my name is Beverley Wilson, what can we do for you?" And he said, "Well, I'm here because I got to do some community policing in this area, and I need to learn to work with the community." And he was just saying all these things, and so it was like, *wow!* I said, "Well, it's good that you came because our class today is about separate realities." And because I had listened to them very softly, and I could hear the things that troubled them, I was able to articulate to him what they was saying, and they was just sitting there nodding their heads.

One of their complaints with the police department was that their kids and grandkids would be sitting on the porch—it didn't look like they would be doing anything—and all of a sudden a police car would pull up and they'd arrest him. And when they came out of the house to ask them what was going on, they'd tell them, "Shut up! Go back in your house or I'm going to arrest you too." And that made them very mad, made them want to throw bottles at them and rock their cars, and run them out and protect their kids, because it didn't seem fair. So I said, "Maybe this is what they're concerned with." I spoke for the people, because they had just told me all this stuff. So then I said, "Maybe you could give us the separate reality for the police officer. What does it look like for a police officer coming in here?"

And Jerry [Williams], he looked around—I mean, this took him so back, number one that people was on the edge of their seats waiting to hear his response. It was dead quiet. So he said, "Well, one of the things that happens is that we get insecure"—because he had heard me talking about insecurity. He said, "When we're making an arrest there are certain things that a police officer has to do to secure his area—it's a procedure that we have to do to make sure that we're safe and that what we're doing is safe." And he just kind of laid down everything that a police officer goes through. And so Miss Smith, one of the matriarchs of the community, she said, "Well, some of the police officers are really rude!" He said, "I know that's true, but I'm here hoping that if you can tell me some of the complaints, and that you could tell me some of the problems, and that I could sit down and listen to more classes like this, what you guys are doing here—if you just allow me to come in and just learn, hopefully I can do something about it." So they considered that. It still was a little tense.

And at the end of class that day Miss Smith asked, "Could we end the class in prayer? That we could pray for peace in the community, and for better relationships with the Oakland Police Department." And that's what the prayer was. So the next thing you know she held out her hand and she grabbed Jerry's hand, and it just hit her. She said, "I can't believe it. Here I am holding the police's hand." They *hated* them! And that was like the beginning of a long process.

JP: Jerry must have felt like he was walking into a gold mine.

BW: He did! Well, it was interesting. What we didn't know, he had just left Lockwood Gardens. Coliseum and Lockwood are across the street from each other. They're two different communities and Lockwood is, like, the better of the two as far as society is concerned—and Coliseum is like the stepchild. So he had just went to Lockwood, and he walked in on a meeting where they was getting all their frustrations out. They was talking about the problems in the community and they needed to get their anger out and discuss the problem. Then he walked in, and they turned around, and they said, "*There's the problem there!*" [laughs] And the lady that was having the meeting said, "You better leave." So he got run out of there. That was his frazzled look. It was like, "How am I supposed to work with this community? I've been working on them all these years, now you want me to work with them?!" He felt like somebody had given him a bad injustice, like somebody didn't like him in his department. He thought he was a good cop! And then he got to walk into this other meeting, what we was doing. And we didn't have no way of knowing that, but that's what happened.

So what I suggested to him was that he come and take the class. Everybody agreed that he could come if he wanted to. So for about the next six months, Jerry came into the Health Realization class on Thursdays. And he gave everybody in there his pager number, his beeper number, and they started paging him and all kinds of stuff. He really made my work a lot easier. And I made his work a lot easier, because the gift he said that I gave to him, and I know it's true, is that I taught him to look beyond the role that the person had chosen—because people in the community have roles, too, you know? And to be able to see that.

Like, one of the things he thought was that heroin addicts were just sitting up nodding, that they just sitting there doing nothing. And I told him, "Oh, no. Why don't you go ask her what she been thinking about when she's doing that?" I said, "She could be tap dancing, she could be dancing with Fred Astaire, she could be on a slow boat to China. Because a person on drugs—I know this from my own personal experience—you'd be dreaming about stuff, but you don't call it dreaming. You think that you living in an unreality, you know? You just create a world inside your head, but it's very real. That's why you want to go back there so much." So he got so curious as to what was really going on with people. And he was so humble, because he didn't get it. It took Jerry about six months before he ever understood our thoughts create our experience, and his thoughts was creating his experience too with the people. But because he had decided to come to the class he had kind of suspended his judgment. He was trying to create something, so he had to abandon everything that he knew.

Then one night I did a talk down at a college for NA, and Jerry came. It was like he was looking for answers wherever he could. At that time I probably had been sober five years, and Jerry had just came out of being an undercover cop five years before, and we was the two most unlikely people to team up: An ex-undercover cop and an ex-recovering addict, you know what I'm saying? [laughs] But we was so good for each other, because I could tell him things he would never think about, and he taught me stuff that I would never think about that gave me empathy and compassion for the role that he chose in life. Police officers have a hard role, and their lives are always on the line, you know?

And so he came to this big old thing I did down at this college. I was, like, the Unity Day main speaker, and Jerry sat there and counted two thousand people, and when it was over he waited for me. And he had to wait a long time because it was lines of people waiting to talk to me. And he said, "Beverley, why isn't the media here?" He was so excited. He thought that people was on drugs and didn't get off and they was bad people and they died or they went to prison. He didn't know that there was this whole other world. So that made me very rich. I introduced him to stuff that he didn't even know about, which gave him a lot of hope. He started seeing hope in the people, and it was a fun thing.

JP: So did you feel the understanding coming alive in you during this time?

BW: Oh yes! All the time! We didn't have no set agenda for our work. We created the agenda at the end of the week. We looked back and saw what happened, you know what I'm saying? [laughs] We didn't never know what was going to happen. But we knew that if we were quiet, that intuitively we would know. And we knew that our job was to find the Health in the people—that's mainly the main thing—and to hold it up so that they could see it. We couldn't give it to them, but we could hold it up so they could see it, hold it up in a way that they could see it their own selves. And that's what we were able to do. Sometimes Roger [Mills] would come. I think Roger came up there about three times, did about three two-or-three-day classes during this period, and I ended up working out there five years. But in two-and-a-half years so many changes had happened between the African Americans and the Asian Americans and the relationship with the Oakland Housing Authority Police Department and some of the relationships with Oakland Housing Authority that people start coming from all around the world to find out what was going on there.

They sent these two reporters out there, and this reporter, she stayed for two months interviewing all the people. She wanted to know what had happened that was causing the peaceful times that was happening out there, so she interviewed the people, one by one, for two months. And when she got through writing up her story, the editors named it, "A Miracle on Sixty-Sixth Avenue." It was a twelve-page article in the *Oakland Express,* October of 1994[8]. And I tell you, after that article went out, people started to come out—even before that people started coming, like John Wood from Australia, and Linda Washman from Minnesota who works at the senator's office. They came out. They wanted to see the people and talk to the people and find out what happened that brought about this change, where people were planting seeds, flower seeds, fruit trees. And you'd see an African American digging the dirt, and you'd see an Asian person putting in the seed, and an African American watering, you know? They was just like, "What brought about this unity in the community? What happened?" What happened was, we just talked to people about their thinking, taught them Health Realization.

JP: That answers what I was just going to ask you: What do you attribute the change to?

BW: And I attribute the change to a bunch of people that I worked with, like Lisa and Ron and myself, and then Jerry coming on board, and then us being able to recognize a couple of residents like Vivian and this other guy that we got on as part-time employees and taught them the Health Realization model. And Chi, the Asian guy. Those people loved us. I mean, they loved us! You see, I didn't know when I first went out there that African Americans wasn't supposed to talk to Asian people. I didn't know that. That was good, because I just talked to them. Even though they didn't speak English I just talked to them. I said, "Well, you know 'Hi!'" I was just speaking to them and shaking their hands. And, if something really happened good—like I had three Asian girls in my class, and them little girls loved me, and so their parents started loving me because the kids didn't want to go home, you know? There'd be all this different interactions, relationships-building. So it was just a good thing.

MORE ON SHARING AND LIFE AFTER

JP: During those five years you worked at Coliseum Gardens, what was happening inside you?

BW: Oh, I was beginning to dream great dreams—that dream of being an international motivational speaker was really, really in me. Because now I'm making enough money to go in the store and put stuff in the shopping cart and

[8] "Miracle on Sixty-Sixth Avenue" (1994, October). *Oakland Express.*

at the checkout stand not have to put six things back. I'm feeling good. I'm long hours on the freeway, because I had a three-and-a-half-hour commute round-trip some days, but I'm making my life work. And by me getting away from Stockton working for East Bay Project—nobody who worked there was in recovery. Nobody! Matter of fact, the first dinner we had, everybody ordered drinks. So I really had to make up my mind what I was going to do, because I was outside my web of security. So I'm getting stronger and stronger, and not so much into this life that I had known. I'm exploring new territory. I'm starting to build friendships here. I plugged into AA down here, but it wasn't no-ways like when I went to seven to nine meetings a week. When I got here I would go to a meeting because I'd be shaken up from driving on the freeway, so I'd go in and get centered.

But I still had that big question of how do I create what I get in the meetings when I'm in the car or in the gas station or in the grocery store? I was starting to get a sense of how you do that, because I got none of these safety nets over here that they said I was dependent on. I had to learn to be there for myself. And then what I was learning—and the more I taught it, the more I learned it—was that our wisdom is inside of us. The piece that was missing that they never really talked about was *that we think*, and that *our thoughts create our reality moment to moment*. And *being okay when I'm in a low mood*—I don't have to be terrified about that and run nowhere—that I could be okay if I just had the understanding that I was just in a low mood, it would pass. I didn't have to be frightened by it or terrified by it—just be still for a minute, reconnect to myself. Because the help is in the understanding that I'm in a low mood. I don't have to be in a high mood all the time, or way up there. The fact that you're in a low mood, enjoy it. I really was learning all this stuff and I was sharing with people, you know? I was real open about the times I wasn't in a good mood. I made up a little signal with them. I said, "When I get to working and I'm off-base, I'm going to let you know. I'm going to tell you, 'Lilly's loose.' Just give me a little time, I'll make my adjustments as I move around." Because I would get off balance; it was like I was crooked, you know? But if I just acknowledge that and let everybody know to give me a little space, then I could feel myself self-correct somewhere.

JP: Was there any point, either during the Coliseum Gardens phase, or afterwards for you, where you really felt like you made a major shift?

BW: Yeah. It had to do with a tragedy. In February, two important things that I had always dreamed of happening were about to occur. I got asked to speak at the annual conference in Burlington, Vermont.

JP: Where we met.

BW: Yeah, where we met. That meant I was going on a big airplane. And at the same time I was asked to do a world conference meeting at a thing called a "Mountain Miracle" for NA World Service. So that was going to be taped, and the tape would be distributed around the world. That was two major things leading me to my goal.

And they were, like, scheduled three weeks apart—both in the same month. And I had been telling Vivian [a co-worker/resident in Coliseum Gardens] and Jerry [Williams] too, "Oh, we got to keep learning this, because there's no telling where our life is going to go." So the day I came and told Vivian that we were going to Burlington, Vermont—she was doing outreach, and I went and found her. "I have our tickets to go to Burlington, Vermont." She said, "What?" I said, "Girl, I got our airline tickets right here!" She just fell over backwards on the grass, because I had been telling her for months to hold on to her seat belt, because we was going somewhere. This was big, because I could just *feel it*.

But let me tell you what happened, Jack. I was excited. Everybody in my family was excited, because I got asked to talk at the Vermont conference for Psychology of Mind. And my mother, who I had a new relationship with for six-and-a-half years—I'm six-and-a-half years sober by now—my mother was excited, because I'm telling her I'm going to be an international motivational speaker. I don't know how it's going to happen, but I'm dreaming. I'm saying stuff and it's coming out of my mind into reality all the time—little bitty stuff, then big stuff, then bigger stuff. Going to Vermont is like flying all the way across the map! I had a map showing them how far I was going to fly. Everybody was excited. I had my bag packed for weeks! And my sponsor bought me a camera and three rolls of film. So I said, "Hmm, I got two trips planned, and she bought three rolls of film, I guess one event is a surprise." I knew intuitively that something else was going to happen that was unexpected, and I never thought anything more about it, and pretty soon it was July.

And on July 10th, my sister Elaine called. She said, "Beverley, they say Mama's at the hospital, and she can't talk!" And I don't know why, I just felt this paralyzing, gripping fear run through my body like a cold, icy finger go down my back. I just fell on my knees, and I laid flat on my face on my bed. And I just started praying again that God's will would be done in me, that I would be still, quiet. And for some reason I had calmness about it. And I got up and my daughter, Mary, went with me. And I was kind of driving a little bit fast, but I was real still inside and driving with precision. Then all of a sudden something occurred to me, and it said, "Drive the speed limit. It's over." So I was, like, "Hmm," so I slowed down. I got to the hospital, about eleven miles from the house, and one of the nurses I had went to grammar school with saw me and knowing I'm the oldest in the family she said, "Beverley, go in there and tell your sisters and brothers to quiet down. This is a hospital. And tell them to stop beating your mother and shaking her like that, because the mortician is going to think that somebody beat her!" So I can't believe what she's telling me. I said, "What are you saying?" She said, "Your mom passed away."

Now my normal response to that, Jack—I really need to tell you this because this happened to me in 1975: My brother died, and my ex-husband—my husband at the time—came to me and said [gruffly], "I just came to tell you that your damn brother is dead." And I just went *off*! And that's when I had started on a downhill spiral in life at that time, because of my inability to accept reality—especially the way he told me. In my mind it was like, "If you were going to tell me that, why didn't you tell me in a nice, calm way?" Well, people tell you in a way that makes sense to them in that moment. And again, here was this woman telling me the biggest thing that could ever happen to me—my worst fear in the whole world was the death of my mother—and she is telling me to go in and take care of my sisters and brothers. I felt just assaulted. I just felt hurt. [emotional voice] Right away I wanted to get so mad at her, but I realized—because I knew Health Realization—that wasn't the real issue. So I asked myself, "Beverley, baby, what are you afraid of?"

And I walked down there where my mother was, and I walked in the room, and my seven brothers and sisters was in there and some of my nieces—and at this time everybody was still on drugs; I was the only one that had gotten out. It was like I was the survivor off a wrecked ship. And there I saw—my niece was beating her head up against the wall, my other brother was standing at my mother's feet, just shaking her, trying to wake her up, and my little brother who's 6'9" had called the doctor and told him with a look of death, "You better wake her up!" And I'm looking at everything that's happening in this room, and then I looked inside me, and I understood the meaning of the Serenity Prayer so deep that day. I'd been saying it for over six years, but that day I *saw* it with a striking clarity. It said, "God grant me the serenity—to accept the things that I cannot change—courage to change the things I can—and the *wisdom* to know the difference." For some reason that prayer *split* from me that day, and I understood that this was a situation that I could do nothing about. So something inside me said, "Just quiet down, calm down."

So I had the most beautiful thought in my mind, and I couldn't tell nobody in the room this thought, but I imagined my mother in a spirit form just floating up in the air, turning flips backwards. She was so free. My mother was crippled and had diabetes, she was very sickly. And in my mind's eye I saw that she was free. And something in me said, "She done shed this body and jetted up on out of here, on to a new adventure." And to me that was a warm, comforting thought. But the reality was that my mom, when I went over and looked at her, I could see something was missing. My mother was not there, and it was so final for me. It was in that moment I just embraced that reality. It was, like [softly], "Bye, Mama. You're gone." And I turned around and looked at my sisters and brothers, I said, "You guys, she is not here! And this is a hospital. Deal with your hurt the way you got to, but there's other people in here that need help"—or whatever I said to them. And then, I knew what to do. Something told me to go call Jewel, and go call my daughter who's waiting at home, and make a couple of phone calls. That's what I did. The next thing I knew, two or three people from the fellowship of Alcoholics Anonymous came into my mother's hospital room and sat in there with me until the coroner came to take her body away. But me having that calmness was like a tuning fork to my brothers and sisters. What I said to them was in such a quiet, certain way, and at the same time it was so respectful of where they were at that they just responded to it, you know?

Anyway, that was four days before July 15th when I was scheduled to go to Vermont. I had never done a funeral before. And I walked in a kind of quietness, because I knew about this inner chamber in me, this innate Health, and I kept tapping into that. And I was able to make my mother's funeral arrangements, got my crazy brothers—my seven brothers and sisters who were drug-addicted at that time—to sign over parts of their insurance money, because we didn't quite have enough money. They all agreed to give up $150, $100, $50 off their insurance policies! These people were *hooked* and alcoholic, and they didn't ask for no money! They didn't even think about it because there was such a hush and such a quietness surrounding this whole thing. And we buried my mother that Wednesday. And that Thursday, at 4:00 in the morning, I drove from Stockton to San Francisco and caught the biggest airplane I ever caught in my life and went to Burlington, Vermont with the freshness of my mother's burial and death still in me. But I knew that this was one of the price tags, or one of the omens or challenges in life that I had to walk through to get to my dream. And how I knew that I'll never know. But I went there and did that. I was there for four days. I came home, and then got ready for the Mountain Miracle picnic where I was supposed to speak. And I just had a strength, an inner-knowing—an inner strength that I had never experienced before—

JP: You moved me big-time that day when you spoke at the conference.

BW: Oh, really? Well a tape came out of that other experience, the name of it was "A Mountain Miracle," and to this day it is the most widely sold tape in Narcotics Anonymous. That tape almost got me to Paris, but I didn't make it. The tape went to Paris; I didn't. But it was a masterpiece—I knew when I was doing it that *I* wasn't doing it, but I knew that it was deep. That was the time when I knew, when I walked in the death of my mother and I wasn't in my conditioned habit of being in my AA meetings supported by the people, because when I went to Vermont I was around no one. And I knew that something wonderful and powerful was happening inside of me. It was with me 24-7—and that was the best news I had even gotten in my life—that I was very capable of dealing with life as it unfolded, no matter what happened. Because if I could walk through the death of my mother and stay sane and lead my brothers and sisters through that, then I could do anything!

JP: So, in the few minutes we have left, what else do you want to make sure I get in here?

BW: Well, I just want to speak to the people that look like they're caught up in a cycle. I'm a behind-the-scenes person, and I like that role. I like when there's something that I can teach people that when they learn it they feel like they got it from inside of themselves. It's almost like I'm invisible. But it carries a certain weight when you're working in a community or when you're doing work in a thankless job. The main thing I want people to know is to look for the hidden justices in life. Look for hidden justice! Because the hidden justice carries the payment. It's the thing that *lifts* you up when you want to give up, or it *lifts* you up when someone else might get credit for some work that you feel like maybe you should have been at least mentioned in. And it's always present if we look for it.

JP: What do you mean by hidden justice?

BW: I mean that every time something happens, and it may not look like it's right, *know* that even though it looks like it's out of order, it's in order. There's a bigger picture. There's a bigger message. There's something much bigger going on than what our sometimes-finite mind can see. There's infinite possibilities of reward, but they may not come in the way that you think. And if you keep your mind focused on the way you *think* it should look, you'll never see the reward that's there, every step of the way, all the time! Because the greatest gift I've learned out of every time I thought there was an injustice—even when I was starting all these programs and they was still giving me the same job and it gave me a feeling that I didn't like that. And when I learned Health Realization, they let me know that people wasn't doing things to me, that I had the power to let life go *through* me—not happen *to* me! And if I feel I was being victimized, it couldn't happen unless I participated. If I felt like I was being stepped on, then I needed to stand up! There's a bigger picture than what we can see. Always! Especially when it's something that feels like it's not right. When it feels like it's not right, *know that it's right*. The way I'm looking at it can be seen so many different ways. If I know that, even if I can't see it, just knowing that there's a different way gives me leverage in life, and it gives me the ability to navigate through life. And even if I can't *see* the hidden justice, I know it's there! So having the ability to just know that it's there and move on—go on and do what makes you feel good and let peace of mind—having real peace of mind and feeling good from the inside-out—be your reward. And then what you do is you turn around, and you look one day and you see countless things that sprung up out of that, that you never would have been able to see if you hold on to the idea that people are doing something to you. And a lot of people walk with that feeling of injustice, like they can't get anywhere because somebody's got their thumb on them. The only person that has their thumb on me is what's going through me in my mind and working through me, coloring the world that I see. You feel me? So the most powerful gift I've been given is having the ability to know that I could have anything I want. I'm Beverley Wilson. I can do anything I want!

The last thing I'm going to show you is what the lady that knew me the longest—one of my sponsors, who was also my methadone counselor—at my going-away party when I was moving to the Bay area, she wrote this poem about me. I want to read it to you. It's called, "Why did you call her a lady?"—because they called me *Miss* Beverley. That's my new name. It says:

> She lives in the darkness. She's OUT of her mind.
> Obsessed with drugs. Surrounded by thugs.
> She SCREAMS, yells and curses with a stare in her eyes.
> She despises the world, pegs in her head

(That was me she's talking about!)

> She's CRAZED with no rhyme or reason, no purpose, no plan.
> NEVER a kind word or gesture in mind.
> She's sad and she's lonely, CONFUSED and out of control
> Her children are scared, all tattered and torn.
> She's LOST and astray. Most said she will never find her way.
> But I said to myself, No addict is without hope.
> So you can say, then, Why do I call her a lady?
> Because today she's REBORN. A bright, shining star.

GLORIOUS, a winner. Spiritual and fine.
She's clean and she's sober. God's in her life.
She's got dignity and pride. Friends all around her.
She's talented and blessed. Her children have blossomed.
They're happy, they're wholesome. Their mother's a mom.
She's black and she's beautiful. She's one of a kind.
She's joyous and free, and best of all, my sponsee.
A gracious lady, Miss Beverley.

Written by Pam H. [laughs] Whooo! Every time I re-read it I'll be, like, dang, she really saw that in me. Because this was really who I was! She was my sponsor the twelve years I was on methadone, coming in and out, crazy as hell. She knew me good! You feel me? [laughs]

JP: Ah, that is really beautiful.

BW: You want one more thing somebody else wrote? My daughter just wrote this to me. I got to read this to you. My daughter's twenty-five. She wrote,

> As I write this letter, a sense of self-trust overwhelms me. That self-trust assures me that no matter what I write here, or decide to write, God's will and His favor accompanies me wherever I may go. It leads. I follow. And who taught me that truth? You, Mom. Who taught me to soar when I left the nest, unsure and afraid of the fall? You left the house with wings. I know it's true, because as I teach my two kids to soar, what you have taught me comes up more and more. If you felt unappreciated on Mothers' Day, know that the appreciation is in the day you received your first breath. You have been a counselor, a mediator, a devout mother, a father, a friend. There are just so many things to me that you have been. I could go on and on, telling all these nice things, because you are worth it, but I truly need to thank you for following God's words, hearing His voice, heeding His call, oh, because by your example, you have taught me it all, just by saying Yes to the Master's Will. I understand that you are at a place where the last child is leaving the home, and thirty-two glorious years of mothering is about to be done. But as you experience that, know that I truly believe I stood on the edge of time and chose you as my mom. Only you could have executed, from the ups and downs of life, a landing so smooth under the command of God. Mom, you did

> that. I love you, you strong, beautiful, spirited mother. I salute you. Your daughter, Monique."

JP: Brought tears to my eyes.

BW: [laughs] That's what my girl wrote. Ain't she something? Ain't this girl something!? That's my *girl*! She read this to me. I spoke just this last Saturday night in Stockton for the treatment center that I went through fourteen years ago, at their annual dinner, and she had arranged with them to read me that after I spoke the other night. There wasn't a dry eye in that place. She knocked me out. That is my girl. And *all* my kids are like that.

3. N[9]

Interview with N*. When I first met N she looked mighty grim, tough as nails, impenetrable, her face hard as a rock. Everything about her looked hard. She never smiled. By the time of this interview N had become soft and sweet, having undergone a massive transformation. She had been addicted to alcohol and pills, then became free—not "recovering," but recovered and free. I have tremendous respect for N's intelligence and abilities. Unlike Helen, it took N years, but the change is no less impressive. I interviewed her at her home in May 2001.*

LIFE BEFORE UNDERSTANDING

JP: What were you like before you discovered this understanding?

N: I was working at a drug and alcohol treatment center for women, a very large facility. I had a huge caseload. I was overwhelmed, and personally I was functional in my life but not very happy. I felt like everybody else lived kind of up here [raises hand], and they would drop down if something really bad happened—a death, or a huge disappointment—they'd get sad for a while, and then they'd come back up. But I knew I wasn't like that. I thought I was somehow organically different, in that I was mostly down here [lowers hand], unless something really good happened outside of me—like if I met someone, got a new job, got a new car or something. Then I'd go back down again. And after struggling with being down for a long time—after working on myself, after reading 1500 self-help books and trying everything—I decided that the best I could do was accept that I was different than other people, that my home base was sort of down, and if that's the way God made me, I would just have to accept that that would be my lot in life.

JP: So you weren't happy.

---

[9] This person requested that her name be removed, so I changed her name and eliminated other identifying information.

N: No. I would have temporary happiness, but it was always contingent.

JP: Did you know why?

N: I would read books or I would go to therapy or I would go to support groups, and they would all say, "This is why you're unhappy." And by the time I looked at everybody's opinions about why I wasn't happy, I was studying so much unhappiness it's no wonder I wasn't happy. That's all I was looking at! But it seemed no matter how earnestly I considered that, I would be more informed about why I didn't feel better, but it didn't help me get out of it. So I had a lingering feeling that perhaps I wasn't getting to the bottom of why I was feeling bad.

JP: Can you give an idea of what your life had been like before this time?

N: Well, as far back as I can remember, I thought I wasn't good enough, and I didn't know why. My strategy for dealing with that was to hope nobody noticed, and try to convince them by overcompensating, overachieving, being on the honor roll in school, getting involved in a lot of activities, trying to get outside acknowledgment. People would tell my parents how pretty I was, how brilliant I was, how gifted I was, how smart I was, but no matter how much people told me that, I had the feeling that if they really knew, they wouldn't say all those nice things. So now I had everybody fooled and I had all this tension around being found out.

Anyway, I got accepted to every college I applied to, and I didn't feel comfortable going to any of them. I just didn't have that kind of confidence or security to go out on my own. So I started working and went to a junior college and stayed in school and moved out on my own and just felt resigned.

And I found that by drinking I could get a break from all that. So on the weekends I would go out with my friends and get really drunk. And I didn't think that was a problem because I was the least drunk of all my friends. They would get so much more intoxicated that I'd end up taking care of them. I was the one who would clean everybody up and make sure they got home. But I couldn't get free of the alcohol—that would be the place where I could get a little break. It felt like the one thing I did *for me.*

As I got older my body started to hurt physically. I had been in a dance academy when I was young, so I had some physical issues. The older I got, the more physical pain I had, so I would go to the doctor and they would give me pain pills. I would drink on the weekends and take the pills sporadically during the week. I was not doing it in a way big enough to really catch much attention, but feeling more and more as time went by that if I didn't have those things I was in trouble. I knew more and more that I needed those things to be okay, and that made me feel even worse. Now not only was I not good enough, but I couldn't even be in the world without this help. I was in therapy, and I showed up one day at the therapy session, and it had been two days since I had taken anything, but I was still kind of really groggy and just out of it—

JP: What drugs are we talking about here?

N: Opiates. Pain medication. I showed up at this therapy session, and she took one look at me and knew I was out of whack. And she said, "You really need help with this." And I said, "I can't give up the pills because my body hurts too much!" And she said, "Well, don't make any decisions about what you can or can't do." And she also said something really neat. She said, "Don't label yourself as anything. Don't make any permanent decisions about anything. Just go to this center and have an assessment and talk to these people. These people understand about chronic physical pain and they can help you with that. But they can help you do it without drugs."

JP: How long were you on these pills at this point?

N: I went into treatment when I was twenty-two. I didn't get medication until after I was out of high school. But the alcohol started when I was—well, on occasion I used to sneak drinks at a very young age, about eight or so, but I started really drinking when I was a teenager. And again, the people that I'm checked in with at this hospital, their substance abuse was so much more exaggerated than mine that they kind of laughed at me. They thought I was cute. At that point I had the sense that if I let it get fully out of control, that would be one more example of how I couldn't do anything right, so I kept kind of a tight lid on it. But I was getting that feeling like, "I need it." I would make sure I had a couple pills in my purse everywhere I went, even if I didn't take them, just so I had them. And I would look forward to the weekends when I could drink. The physical piece was one thing, but the psychological insecurity was driving the whole thing.

So I had this assessment, and they said, "You need to check in." And I said, "That's crap! I'm not checking in. That's too big of a commitment." I mean, it scared me, really frightened me, because they wanted to take away from me the thing that I thought was helping me make it through each day or each week. So they called in the big guns, and this doctor shows up and he says, "So why don't you want to come in?" And I said, "Well I just don't think I'm ready. I need to think about this." And he looked at me out of the corner of his eye and said, "You know, you're the kind that'll probably go try everything else first, and then you'll be back," And he got up and walked out. I was so angry! Somehow I had the sense that he was onto me, and I really wanted to kind of stay in control. That was the thing I was holding onto, the idea of control, to compensate for all that insecurity. I didn't like that he saw me so clearly—somehow that made me feel like he knew, he had control and I didn't. I left the office in defiance and went home and called a friend and just started crying hysterically, "I don't know what to do. I'm a mess!" And she said, "It kind of sounds like you need a place where you can just sort of fall apart and chill out for a while and figure out how to feel better." And I thought, "Well, that's what this place is. Why am I not doing it? Life's got to be better *than this*." So I checked in.

That was actually a really great time, the five weeks or so that I was there. I felt better there than I had felt all my life. I had people teaching me how to deal with my body, and there were a lot of really fun people there, and I connected with people, and it was the first time I came out of my own head and was more connected to other people than to my own insecurity. I had this tremendous relief, but I was frightened to go home. And they made a big deal out of going home: That's when you have all this risk for relapse, and they have all kinds of labels for what I was going through and who I was now. Somehow, even though I had joined that recovery culture—where you label yourself as an addict or an alcoholic and do all this work on yourself and go to meetings—in the back of my head I still had those words from that therapist: "Just go see what makes sense, and don't identify with any one thing."

JP: How long were you in that world?

N: After I got out of treatment I went home and I crashed and burned. I mean I got swept right back into my head and was horribly depressed. I tried to work. I got a job, and I went to work for two days—and every break I got, and at lunchtime, I went out and slept in my car. I could not stay present. A couple of days later I walked into the human resource department and just quit.

JP: What year?

N: 1990. And I ran to that doctor and said, "I can't function anymore. I can't work." He put me on disability. I was on disability for eleven months. Most of that eleven months I didn't get out of bed. It was a big deal if I could get up and do one thing. I would get up and go to therapy and come home and go back to bed. I would just lay in the bed and stare at the ceiling, lost in thought. I didn't know anything. I just knew I couldn't move. And the therapist I was still with at the time was very anti-medication. She wanted me to look at my past, look at my family, so I followed her recommendations for a long time, and after eleven months I still couldn't function. Eleven months sober and I was feeling worse and worse. So I went back to this doctor and said, "I don't know what I'm going to do because I can't function, and my disability is going to run out. I think I need to apply for SSI"—which is Federal disability. It's a more permanent disability status, meaning you'll probably need subsidy for a while, or forever. He said, "I think you should try to work before you do that. If you go on permanent disability that's going to be on your record for the rest of your life, and that may impact the way you want to live your life." And I'm really grateful that he said that. So I did.

I decided that I was just suffering too much, so I wanted to go check out medication. And at the time medication was still pretty controversial in the recovery community. "Don't take nothing, no matter what" was the attitude. I was very proud that I was off all pain medication and managing my physical issues holistically. But I kept getting that nagging feeling. "There's got to be something more to life. It's got to get better than this." So I went to another addiction medicine doctor who was a psychiatrist. He put me on Prozac. I had mixed feelings about taking a medication for depression, but it helped me. I could get out of bed. I could go to work. I could maintain a conversation with people. Before, even talking to anybody was too much effort. I remember driving over the Santa Cruz Mountains one day, and all of a sudden the trees were green. They had not looked green to me before. And I was relieved that I was depressed because at least I knew what it was now. People were giving me names for my problems, telling me, "It's because you have a chemical imbalance." In kind of a backwards way it got my confidence up that it wasn't my fault. I had so much insecurity that everything I did was an obvious symptom of my own inadequacy, and I couldn't do anything right, so to get these diagnoses in a way was kind of a relief.

But my body was still hurting and I was doing the best I could holistically, so I went to another doctor, and he said, "You have chronic fatigue syndrome." Again, another diagnosis, and initially, relief. I thought, "Maybe it's not me. I just have these things." So now I have this disease of addiction, and I have this disease of depression, and I have this disease of chronic fatigue syndrome, and it's not my fault. That took a lot of pressure off me.

I decided I would pursue my first love, psychology. I got a job working in a treatment center, and I got a degree in Behavioral Sciences with advanced certifications in addictions studies. I was still taking depression medications to help me, and it made a big difference. I could function. I could hold down a job. I could be consistent. But medications have side-effects and I suffered with those, and over time the medications became less effective as my body got used to them. So the doses would go up. At one point I got to a high enough dose on Prozac that I got really flat. While meds can take you out of depression, high doses can take you out of other feelings too. Then my dose had to go up again. All of a sudden I was angry. Finally I got so angry I wanted to run someone over with the car. I called the psychiatrist and said, "I wanted to run somebody over with the car today. I don't think that's good." At that point the dose was high enough on the Prozac that it would keep me up during the day, but I couldn't sleep at night, so then I had to take another medication for that—

JP: What year are we at now?

N: Oh, 1993. So they switched me to a different medication. I was still reading self-help books, and I was going to support group meetings and getting more and more dissatisfied. It seemed like my whole life was working on myself, with this nagging feeling that it wasn't going to quite get me there, and that if I stopped all this working on myself, I was going to sink right back down. It was as if all the alcohol and the pills were replaced by this intensive work on myself, and I still wasn't happy.

JP: Were you still on pain medication?

N: No. I was "clean and sober." I was taking medication for depression and high doses of antivirals for chronic fatigue syndrome. I got promoted to a position as counselor, and my job was to help the women on my caseload understand that recovery was hard, and they had a long road ahead of them. I couldn't understand why when they left treatment, they would get loaded again and come back. So I would tell them again, "Recovery *is* really hard and you need to work really hard on yourself, and we all have to do that." I was definitely in the popular recovery world, but it bothered me inside that over the years the same women that had previously received treatment returned again. I was discouraged. I saw they weren't happy either. I knew that I was only just a little bit ahead of them. They were very hopeful about what I could offer them, because I wasn't relapsing. To them that was a big deal. But I wasn't happy. And I had been trained in a way of helping people with chemical dependency that was very confrontive, very in-your-face, so I was that way with them—

JP: I'll bet you liked that, too.

N: I did and I didn't. I mean, that was what I learned, to be hard on people, confront them, break those walls down and get through to them. The training was that the disease of addiction is extremely powerful and the only way you're going to help people is to break through all that—really nail people. By then we were experiencing more and more women coming into treatment from the criminal justice system, and these women were even tougher and more manipulative. We learned techniques to get through all that criminal thinking. I proceeded to just get tougher and tougher. I prided myself on being a real bitch on wheels. And the more my clients disliked me the more I thought I was doing a good job. Nobody was going to get over on me! But inside I was not happy. I knew my clients weren't happy. And I just thought, "This is life. It's hard." And I watched my colleagues in the field and would sometimes hear things like, "So and so's back again," and people would sigh, "Oh, she's a tough one. Well, she never really worked the program, she doesn't work on herself, she needs to work her steps, she needs to go to meetings." But I was going to meetings and working on myself and I wasn't happy. I felt like we were blaming the clients for something that they were coming to us for help with, and underneath, it just didn't sit right.

So I don't know why but it occurred to me if we were still using the computers made in the 1970s, that wouldn't make sense. Technology evolves. Why is it that we're using therapies that aren't evolving? Why are we using therapies that are 40, 50, 100 years old with people? What's new out there? I decided to start looking around. I started going through the training catalogues, thinking there's got to be something else, and I went to a number of different things and dabbled in them, and then I went to a Health Realization training in the fall of 1994.

THE INSIGHT

JP: How did you run into it?

N: What happened was that, Bob Garner, who is the Director of the [Santa Clara] County Department of Alcohol and Drug Services, had encountered Health Realization. I was working for a private non-profit agency that contracted with the County to provide services. I loved what I did, but I was miserable. [laughs] So Bob Garner liked Health Realization, and he brought Mark Howard and Joe Bailey in. He thought, "Let me do a half-day orientation, and people can get a little feel for it and see if they want to sign up for this four-day training."

Some of my colleagues went to that orientation—I didn't go—and when they came back they were violently opposed to it. They trashed it because they listened through all their beliefs about addiction. I mean, one of the really important things for the recovery community is this idea of a power greater than yourself, something bigger than you are. We used to say things like, "Your best thinking got you here. Your best thinking got you loaded." So you didn't want to trust yourself. You didn't want to trust your own thinking. You didn't want to trust your head. You wanted to trust something bigger than you. So it was really important that you were connected to some kind of spiritual power bigger than you, and you could define that however you wanted, but it had to be more than just you. So my colleagues listened to the idea that people had Health in them and they could trust it and it came from within you—they listened to that idea through the lens of, "You can't trust yourself. You have to trust something bigger than you, or you're going to get loaded and die!" I mean, they had such a negative reaction to this overview, they felt like it was really dangerous for recovering people. And I can understand that, because we did lose clients. Clients would come in for treatment, and they'd leave and relapse and die. And when you're working around that, you start to gather a lot of pressure in your own thinking about getting people well before they kill themselves, either directly or indirectly.

Anyway, I wasn't going to go to this training because I heard so many bad things about it, and the people who had mentored me and trained me thought this was the worst thing they had ever heard. Bob Garner had sent around this glowing, supportive letter introducing it, and I looked at it and I thought, "That's unusual." But couple of days before the training this clinical supervisor for the County came to our agency—Annette Graff. We had our meeting with her, and she was on her way out the door, and she said, "Oh, are you going to the four-day training?" And I said, "No. I heard really bad things about it and I'm not going to go." She said something like, "That's surprising to me. I've been involved with it for a while, and I've seen things from this approach that I never would have believed. I've seen people who are literally still under the influence sit on the edge of their seat, wanting to understand what this is, and I've seen people get well." And it wasn't so much what she said, but it was the way she said it. I didn't feel pressure to go, it was more like hope. I heard hope, and I got curious. So I said, "Well, can you still get me in?" She said, "Absolutely." So I went.

It was a huge training with about 150 of us, and Joe Bailey had come in from out of town and was teaching with Mark Howard, and the two of them had never taught together before. They did this four-day course. And I remember the first day, they spent the whole first morning from 8:30 until noon talking about how to listen. I don't know what they were doing, but in my mind at that time they were doing something to us. I didn't know what they were doing, but I knew I felt excited. They were going to tell us something, I had that feeling. And I just wanted them to get on with it. I was tired of hearing about listening. I felt like, "I got it already. Tell me what this is!" And the feeling that the two of them were in I had never been around anything like that. They were so light that I got giddy. I got high just being around them. And I thought I knew what they meant by listening, and I wanted them to just tell me what it was so I could listen to that, but in retrospect I realize I didn't hear anything. I wasn't listening to the piece about listening. But I knew I was excited. I loved what they said, and I wanted to be around them. I got such a good feeling those four days—that feeling changed my life.

I came back from those four days and I ran into my executive director after the training—because I would go to the training and I would go back to check on my caseload after hours—and she said, "What is with you?" And I said, "I feel like I've been on retreat!" Keep in mind though, because I didn't know how to listen I also heard everything Mark and Joe said through my own lens, which was the whole recovery culture, but I didn't hear anything that conflicted. I heard things that were the same, but the feeling was better, and I knew I just wanted to be around this. So there were maybe four or five of us that would meet every once in a while to read Joe's book, or watch a tape, or somehow try to keep what we'd learned alive. And pretty soon Bob Garner brought Roger [Mills] down to do more training. He sent out a flyer to everybody who had gone to the training that said, "If you'd like to stay involved in this, Dr. Roger Mills is going to come into the County and we'd like to get a nucleus of people together who'd like to stay connected to this."

So I went to that, and Roger started using us as facilitators for his training. I was willing to do anything that they wanted me to do. I just wanted to learn more. And everybody I met that was connected to this was in this feeling, and I wanted to be around them because I had never felt like that before in my life. I knew when I got around them it rubbed off on me, but I couldn't sustain that on my own. I couldn't maintain that feeling when I was away from them, so I just wanted to be around them. Thank God for Roger, because he wouldn't settle for that. He would not let that be okay. He would challenge us and talk about how the feeling didn't come from us being together. He would say it came from me, and I didn't understand that. And he would say things that at that point I didn't agree with. Roger would put it right out there. He said things that were very contradictory to what I believed in terms of keeping myself clean and sober and in recovery, and even though he said things I thought weren't true, and that he didn't understand addiction, I didn't care because I just wanted that feeling. So the feeling really hooked me.

So I followed Health Realization trainings everywhere. Anywhere Roger was going to be, I showed up. I didn't care if I was invited or not. I worked overtime like you wouldn't believe, just to be able to take time off. I used vacation time, anything. Later, Roger offered an advanced class and I didn't know how I was going to get the money to do it, but the money came through. I knew I didn't know how to live this, but I knew I wanted to. And because I wanted so badly to understand I would argue with Roger and Mark. I told Mark Howard he didn't understand women's issues, and I told Roger he wasn't an alcoholic so he didn't understand that. And the two of them were so patient with me, because I argued from my intellect about everything. But underneath I knew there was something that was true, and I wanted to understand it. Roger was the first person that told me, "Inside, you're not different than anybody else. You're just like everybody else, except for your thinking—except for the way you think." I thought I was different. I thought I had a chemical imbalance; I have these diseases. So I argued with him. But I wanted him to be right.

Roger would talk about Thought, and I didn't hear "Thought," I heard "thinking." So I would work on my thinking. For a year and a half I put everything I heard into my intellect, and I *worked* on my thinking, because that was what I knew. You work on yourself. Roger would talk about the difference between cognitive psychology and Psychology of Mind, and I didn't get that. In my own defense I see why I didn't connect to it, because one of the things that I felt, and what I've seen with other people who suffer with depression, is that sometimes thinking can be so heavy that it manifests itself physically—that's where there's a real disconnect. I was at one time so cut off from myself that I couldn't see myself thinking; all I knew was my feelings. It was like there was a wall. I didn't see myself as a thinker, creating. It was like fuzz. It was numb. I was not at all aware that I created a constant stream of thought. I just couldn't see Thought. So all I knew to do was to try to think right, try to think positive—I didn't see all the insecure thought that I created. I just saw myself trying to correct my thinking.

After a year and a half of doing that I was exhausted. I was so profoundly tired that I could hardly move. But it wasn't the same kind of lethargy that I had had with depression. I didn't feel hopeless. I didn't feel lost. I just felt tired. And right about that point Roger nailed me on my thinking about being "depressed." I asserted that I had chemical imbalance and did not have mental health the way other people did. I felt that this "innate health" concept was a great idea and if people could believe it it would be wonderful, and maybe people could talk themselves into it, but I did not have Health the way other people did. And he looked at me and said, "Why would you be any different than anybody else?" He nailed me. I don't know what happened, but I started sobbing in front of everybody. I just broke down crying. I don't know exactly what the catalyst was but right at that point, about a year and a half, I just felt too tired to work on my thinking any more. I didn't have it in me, so I finally let go. After a year and a half of being told, "You're okay, you have Health just like everybody else does, it will take care of you, you can trust it, if you start to understand the way you function and how your mind works, you'll be okay," I finally trusted it. Sometimes I felt a lot of fear that I was going to get horribly depressed again, that I was going to drink again. I mean, I just had all these fears—but somehow, eventually, I let them go. I started to see them as thoughts I created too. And I'm grateful that I was physically tired because I just didn't have it in me to do all that mental work. Actually, honestly, for a while I was so tired that I had to have people drive me places. I could not physically sit and hold still for more than fifteen minutes. If I drove for twenty minutes I was asleep at the wheel. I could not hold still without going to sleep. That's how tired I was.

JP: Were you still taking the medications at this time?

N: Yeah. I was still taking medication for depression. And after I started to shift I slept for about six months. I would go to work and come home and sleep. I slept twelve to fourteen hours a day. I was absolutely wiped out, but for the first time I wasn't worried about being in bed. It wasn't the same kind of tired. I felt physically tired instead of mentally tired. So I rested. I knew to rest, no matter what anyone thought. People were worried about me. Cathy [Casey] was worried about me. Cathy was in the advanced class, and we didn't know each other very well. I had been a little insecure, because I saw other people getting healthier much faster than I did. Their moods were better. They had that feeling that I talked about, that Joe and Mark and Roger had, and I didn't have that feeling yet. And Roger was using them to teach, and he was taking them to Hawaii and all over. I was working and sleeping and working and sleeping, and I got a little insecure about that. But then all of a sudden *I started to see myself creating insecurity*. It was like the window opened and I started to see Thought. I saw the function of Thought, and how it created all the insecure things I thought *all day long*.

JP: Do you know what made you see that?

N: I don't know exactly what it was, except I had been around this long enough and heard it, and I trusted the feeling of people I was around. I didn't always trust what they said, but there was something irrefutable about that feeling. So I started to get glimmers of my own thinking, and then I got curious about my thinking, and I started to see how much insecure thought I had. And at that point I did a lot of looking at the content of my own thinking, which is not something I encourage people to do, but that's what I did. And that was the proof for me. When I started to see what I thought all day long, I could see why I was so depressed. I saw why I thought I was never good enough, because all day long I thought I wasn't good enough.

JP: When you see what you're doing to yourself with your own thinking, that's helpful.

N: Yeah, that's what I saw. It helped me tremendously, and that built up my faith that every emotion that I had was my own thinking. I used to think my thoughts and feelings were two separate animals. I thought my thoughts came from my head and my feelings came from my heart, and there was a world in between the two, and a lot of times there was a huge discrepancy between what I felt and what I thought. Now I know what that is—it's what people would call mixed feelings. Mixed feelings come from mixed thinking, and I had mixed thinking, and I didn't know that. So when I started to get those glimmers of how I created this feeling for myself all the time I went to Roger and I said, "I think I'm getting worse, because I'm making this insecurity all the time." And he laughed. He said, "You're not getting worse. You're just finally seeing what you've always been doing. It's always been there. You're just seeing it now." And I said, "Well what do I do? I don't want to think like this." And he said, "You don't do anything. Your own Health will take care of it. The fact that you see it is all." At that point I trusted him so much that I said, "Okay."

I remember one day that old feeling of depression came back. I started to go down, and I started to get scared. I thought, "Oh, God, here we go. It's coming back! Maybe it really is a chemical thing or a seasonal thing." But in the back of my mind I heard Roger saying, "You're just going into a low mood. Don't worry about it. Don't try to figure it out. Just try to relax and your Health will come back." And I thought, "I don't think he really understands, but I'm going to try this shit. I'm going to try what he says, and I'm going to see, I'm going to try leaving it alone and we'll see if it passes." So I got ready for a three-day depression where you don't get out of bed, you don't go out of the house, you don't go to work, you're down. I got in the bed and I got books and I got magazines, and I got food, and all the cats and the remote controls, and I was going to bunk down. I got ready for the big one. I watched some TV and read a book for about three hours. And all of a sudden I thought, "Well, I'm bored. I think I'll get up," and that was it. It was done! And I didn't even realize it was done until I was already up doing the dishes, which used to be a huge thing for me, even to do dishes. And I thought, "Oh, shit," and that was it! I tested it and it was true. It wasn't just something people were saying. It was the truth that we all function this way. This *is* how it works! It's just a matter of fact. And from that point, I took off.

SHARING WITH OTHERS & LIFE AFTER

JP: So where are we now?

N: Maybe 1996 or 1997. We were still following Roger around, facilitating, and Bob was designing the training of trainers program, and I think Roger saw promise in me. So even though I kind of didn't connect as quickly as other people, he saw that I would connect eventually. He knew that the earnestness was there, that I really wanted to see it, even though I debated with him so long. So, then we started the training programs, got certified and started speaking. For a while, Roger would have me go in and talk to people about depression, addiction and alcoholism, and just tell my own personal story. That was kind of awkward because I never planned to be speaking in front of groups. I thought I would be a counselor in this rehab center until I died, I guess. I never saw myself being in front of the public, teaching, talking to the drug court, or a medical center. I didn't plan for any of this. In fact, ever since I really connected with this I don't think I've planned anything in life.

JP: So, when did you give up your medication?

N: I don't remember, 1997 or 1998, somewhere in there. Actually, looking back, I think I could have gotten off of it sooner, but there was something I didn't understand. I didn't understand that as I stopped creating all this agony for myself that my chemistry would change—that my chemistry was coming from how I created my life through Thought. It was just the residue of my thinking in my body. I started to get some side-effects from my medication, and I didn't understand that as your own body begins to heal chemically you don't need as much of the medication, so you experience more side effects and less benefit. I was experiencing more side-effects, like my mouth was so dry I could hardly speak. When I told my psychiatrist that, he said, "Well, sometimes this happens after a period of years on a certain medication, so what we do is we change you to a different one." So I switched to a different drug, and actually I think what was happening to me was my own Health was coming up and I didn't know that. Eventually I started asking my psychiatrist. He said, "I think there's an integral connection between the mind and the body, and I don't know if you can separate them." So when I said, "I'm doing pretty well, what do you think about my medication?" he said, "Would you like to try lowering the dose?" And so we started kind of stepping it down, and I would leave it there for six months, then I would step down again and leave that there for four months, and step down, and eventually I just got off it.

JP: How did you feel when you finally broke free?

N: I was a little frightened because I'd had so much thinking all of my life about needing something to be okay. I had that belief ingrained and didn't see it as Thought very deeply. I didn't know I had a belief about that. There was so much medical information given to me about chemical imbalances and reoccurrence and recidivism that it looked really factual to me that it might be more than my thinking. When I actually got off the medication, I had normal ups and downs like everybody else, but as soon as I saw them for what they were, they would shift.

JP: [laughs]. It's amazing how that works.

N: And I've just never had a problem with it since. It felt like such a natural process. I didn't get attached to, "Oh, I have to get off these medicines." I made a kind of peace with medications. I just let it be okay that I needed to be on them, and when I didn't need them anymore I got off them with the help of my doctor.

JP: When did you start speaking at the annual conference?

N: In San Jose. That was the first one. I was on a panel, and I just talked for maybe fifteen minutes.

JP: You were incredible!

N: I was so inspired. I was helping myself, I was helping the clients.

JP: Not too long after that I think, or just before it, we first met at George [Pransky]'s, at his "rigor" session—and you still looked like a real hard-ass to me.

N: It took time for me. I've seen some people jump! Like Cathy, when she heard the Principles, that was it! Day one! But it took me time. It just took time for me to see it, but I was slowly changing, and I was different with my clients in spite of myself.

JP: How were you different?

N: Well, the thing that stayed with me first was the idea that *people have Health in them*, I think because that was so profound for me personally. Then, that *we created our life*. At that point we didn't talk as much about the Principles, we talked more about Thought. So I would talk about Thought, and at first I did more of a memorized, canned thing, and that didn't go over very well with my clients, so I dropped that. But *I remembered that if they had Health in them I wanted to look for it*. Even though I didn't realize it, I was hanging out with my clients more, whereas before it was more working on them. And early on I was still big into accountability and responsibility and all of that, but at least I was connecting to them, where before I was very disconnected.

PERSPECTIVE ON TRADITIONAL DRUG AND ALCOHOL INTERVENTION IN LIGHT OF THE THREE PRINCIPLES

JP: At what point did you feel like you needed to switch what you did in your counseling?

N: It was a gradual thing because, early on, I still believed there was a disease, a physical disease, and that's a big thing in the addictions field. It's almost blasphemous to say anything else. Initially I was still going to meetings, and I believed in that. At some point—I don't remember when, I think it was probably around 1996—I started to do some reflection about the business of addiction. What I noticed was, we called it "the disease," but it didn't start out that way. It started out as "the disease concept." And "concept" by now was a familiar word to me. It was clear to me that a concept is something you create through Thought. It's an idea—it's a way of looking at something. It doesn't mean that it's a fact. It's a way of holding something in your mind. And as I did some research, I went back and saw how originally it was "the disease concept," and there's a reason the field created the idea of a disease concept.

Before the disease concept, addiction or alcoholism was seen as a moral problem, a character flaw; people were put away in asylums, they were shunned, people would think they had evil spirits in them, and really bizarre things happened to people who couldn't stop drinking. And so the world came up with this idea of a disease concept, like diabetes—that there is this thing in you that happened and it's not your fault, but it does happen, and you can treat it, and you're not a bad person. That was helpful to the world when that happened, because people didn't feel bad about themselves anymore. They didn't have all that awful thinking about themselves as a horrible person. "I'm not a horrible person. I just have this thing, and I can treat the thing, I can deal with the thing, I can work on the thing." So that helped the world so much, and I found new respect for "the disease," but I stopped seeing it literally.

We used to have discussions in Roger's advanced class about what would happen to somebody who had really connected to their own mental health and saw the role of Thought—what would happen if that person who used to have an addiction problem had a drink. We used to debate about that. And initially I argued, "Well, if they have this disease, the disease is going to take over," and he looked at me—because that was my big fear, that I would take a drink again—and he said, "You have come too far. You can't go back. If you were to take a drink again, I think you would pretty quickly realize what was going on and turn away from it." And I didn't know about that, but it made me think. I did *not* want to check it out, but it made me think.

Over the years I've become happier and happier and happier, and now I don't need to be around Health Realization people to feel good any more. I feel good on my own, and I finally saw that this wasn't something you supported or worked on, it was just truth about how you function, period. I feel so good I really don't want to drink or take anything that would numb this feeling I found within myself. Actually, I guess what happened is that I forgot about the disease concept. I didn't feel opposed to it, I just saw it as an idea that was helpful to the world at a certain point, a way of looking at it. And we've now evolved and see something new, and despite the fact that it's controversial and difficult for some people it's still true, and it makes sense to me.

You know what really helped me? God, it was probably 1998 or so, and we were all having dinner at a restaurant, and they brought the dessert menu in. It was in French or something, and I couldn't figure out what everything was, so I said, "Bring me this one." I didn't know what it was. So they brought it and I started eating it, and I wasn't thinking about it; I was just eating. I didn't know that this dessert had a syrup on it that was just loaded with liquor, and pretty soon I start feeling fuzzy—you know that feeling where you feel like you want to come back but you can't? I asked, "Does this have alcohol in it?" And the waiter said, "Oh, yes, it's got..."—I can't remember exactly what, but it had a lot of alcohol in it. I kind of started to freak out, because that's a big thing in the addiction field. You don't put any alcohol in your body because it triggers the disease and the whole thing will take over—and all those memories flooded back, and I was a little freaked out. So I had to get a hold of myself. It was like I was sitting there and kind of fuzzy, and the next thing that hit me was, "N, I can't believe you ever wanted to feel this way." I felt *so* bad. I felt so fuzzy and out of it. It just felt bad. I felt numb. And that surprised me. That was a huge revelation to me: "*This* is what you used to go through!?" It made sense, though, because I was so low in my feeling that numb was an improvement. But now I was up a lot higher, so numb was a big step down. I felt this instant aversion to it then. So that was helpful to me, because all the fears about relapse, or wanting to drink, or the something waking up inside me and taking over again were obviously not true *at this new level of consciousness*. Right then I knew I was safe. And I've never worried about it since. Nor have I taken a drink. Why would I want to?

JP: So what do you say to people now who are totally into AA—whose lives are still not that great, but who can't bear the thought of giving it up?

N: That's a tough one. I mean, I was there.

JP: Are you still going to meetings?

N: No. I did go, but about six years into my own sobriety—like around 1995 or 1996—it didn't feel right any more. I just could not get into it. I noticed that most people—not everybody, but a lot of people—were in a bad feeling at meetings. But the thing I appreciate is, I think when Bill Wilson started Alcoholics Anonymous—see, Bill had what he called a spiritual experience, what I would call a huge insight. He had a huge vertical shift, and that changed him. And that's what he called a removal of the compulsion to drink—it was taken from him. And he knew that that was not something he did personally. He didn't will himself to stop drinking. He had this spiritual experience, and it was gone, and when he talked to people and worked with people, he worked from that insight, he worked from that feeling. And I think in trying to help other people, you can't manufacture a spiritual experience. You can't manufacture a jump in levels of consciousness. You can't make that happen from the intellect. And so in trying to help other people, what he did was kind of devise, "Well, maybe if you do these series of things you'll position yourself for a spiritual experience," and that's what the Twelve Steps are. If you read the steps, the last step says, "Having had a spiritual awakening as the result of these steps . . ." In Bill's mind, I think he may have looked back and thought, "What happened to me before this experience? Maybe that was the groundwork, and maybe if people do that, they'll have the same experience that I did." The Twelve-Step programs came from that.

And over the course of years, I think the same thing has happened there that has happened to other movements: The further away you are from the original inspiration the more likely you are to find people following technique, following rituals that they don't really feel and understand. So I think there may have been a time where Twelve-Step was very different than it is today. I remember when I got sober the old-timers were different; they were different from the newer people. They had more of a lightheartedness. If you read the Big Book of AA, you hear some things in there that are very different from what modern Twelve-Step people talk about, but there are also some places where they were onto something. The old-timers were always really connected to the book, always really connected to how simple it is. They didn't do massive inventories on themselves where they looked at everything that happened to them and every feeling they ever had.

In the old days when Bill worked steps with people, they worked twelve steps in a series of hours, hours to days. It was like, "Okay, look. Do you realize that you can't control your drinking anymore? Are you getting that through your head? And what are you carrying around in your head? What are you carrying there? Who are you resentful of? Who are you holding on to stuff about, because you're probably drinking over that? Let's get that out. Let's get that out of your head. What do you need to do to get that out of your head? Well, you probably need to apologize where you were wrong, and let it be that other people have screwed you over, that it happened, and you're okay. And every day, why don't you try to live the right way, and get out of yourself and get out of your head and help other people." That's what the steps are. If you simplify them, there's wisdom in them. But now it's turned into *a thing*. People take years working the steps. They write small books. Bill didn't do that with it. It was a very matter-of-fact, kind of quick thing. Really what the Big Book of Alcoholics Anonymous says is that the point of getting sober is to go back to your life, go back to your family, go back to your community. They never encouraged you to spend your life in meetings and spend your life working on yourself. It's not about that. And the book even says that the spiritual power that's greater than you is inside you. It says that! It's deep in the essence of everyone.

JP: A lot of people see it outside of themselves.

N: Yes. As you get further in time away from Bill who had the original insight, what you get are followers. And they follow the ritual and they follow the doctrine and they follow the dogma and they follow the technique, and they're not connected to what it meant. So it's different now than it was, and even as different as it is, it's still saving people's lives. The nice thing about Twelve Steps is that it's everywhere. It's almost "twenty-four, seven." And you can find other people who are sober anywhere, anytime. When you're in that much psychological pain that you need to take something to feel better, you're in *a lot* of pain. And you're very disconnected and very isolated. I mean, I love the idea that other people are around, that they want to help you, that there's hope that you don't have to do this anymore. So I love those things. But I just don't know that they've seen the psychological function that creates the compulsion. They don't know about that. And in a part of the Big Book, it says science may one day discover a pill or some magic that will help us get past this, but it hasn't done so yet. Well, that was written when? Now we have that—not a pill, but this understanding—and I think that's just hard for them to believe, and they're frightened, and their life depends on not taking a risk that will take their sobriety away. I understand that. I've been there. I've seen people try to talk to Twelve-Step people about The Three Principles and try to rip the way they see sobriety away from them, and they get too frightened to listen. So that doesn't make sense to me.

I know what appealed to me—even though I was listening through the whole recovery culture—was *the feeling*. And the fact that no matter what I said or how much I argued, people like Joe and Mark and Roger didn't lose their bearings, they didn't lose that feeling, and they didn't lose rapport with me, they didn't lose faith in me. They just knew I was in the middle of learning and I didn't see it yet. If somebody had taken what I thought was my recovery on with me too soon, I think I would have left. The clients, on the other hand, for whom Twelve-Step doesn't make sense, who are having trouble staying sober, who have tried that and are not having success with it, they get this like that! [snaps fingers] They're happy to give it up. It's the people whose lives have been saved by Twelve-Step that have trouble hearing.

MORE SHARING AND LIFE AFTER

JP: Do you see this as magic—how you got better, how others get better?

N: Well, it's like it's magic, but it's science. It's like a magical science. By science I mean there are very specific laws that we now understand that can predict cause and effect. When people understand these laws, really feel them, it changes them in an amazing way that always still surprises me, even now. I had never before seen transformation like I've seen in myself or in my clients. It doesn't surprise me, but then again it does. I still kind of marvel at it every time.

JP: Do you remember at that next annual conference, when you spoke about rapture?

N: Yeah. Rapture. It's just an amazing thing that somebody has gone to sleep inside, and then— [pauses, long silence]

JP: When you talked about rapture, it was one of the most moving things I've experienced.

N: I remember not being able to find the right words for the feeling and going through a thesaurus looking for the right word. And I found "rapture." I was so hesitant to use that word because it sounded Biblical, or it sounded weird. But it was the right word. [grabs a dictionary] This wasn't the dictionary I had, but it's still close. [reads] "Ecstatic joy or delight, expression of ecstatic delight, a feeling, especially in religious ecstasy of being transported to another place or sphere in existence." That's close.

JP: Did you feel that within yourself?

N: Uh huh. I did. I would have moments of that. That's the place I had found in myself. I wouldn't say I was there every moment of every day, but for the most part, the world that I'm in is so light. I'm happy. And then I have these deep moments that just feel like they don't even belong to me. But in that feeling I feel so free, and I had never had that. I was surprised that my clients knew what that was. They would talk to me about, "That's a natural high," and I just didn't know that. I mean, in my life I felt like I had gone to sleep or been in pain, that when you come out of that it's just an amazing thing. And to not only have that for yourself, but to watch that happen to other people. It looks like their soul wakes up again, and I know your soul is always there, but I don't know any other words for that. It's just, people come back! And I've seen that all the way now from people in jail, to people in drug treatment, to people diagnosed with catatonic schizophrenia—people who come back. I've even seen executives come back! [laughs] I guess it would be like—I've never had a baby or seen a baby being born, but you know when you talk to somebody who has witnessed a delivery, it's as if there are no words for it, except that it's an amazing, amazing thing. That's the only thing I know that might come close.

ORGANIZATIONAL CHANGE FROM THE INSIDE-OUT

JP: How did it all get started at the treatment facility?

N: Well, I came back from that training with Joe and Mark, and I was different. I was not the same. I didn't understand the Principles, but I heard something that changed me, and I was in a better feeling, and my clients picked up on my mood because I was not in a great feeling before. I noticed they wanted to be around me.

JP: That was a switch?

N: Yeah, well, they normally wanted to run from me. I mean, when clients came in, the first thing they would do is find out who's who and what [section] they want to be in and who their best counselor is, and you didn't want to get assigned to me because I was tough. I nailed you on everything, didn't give a lot, withheld passes and privileges. I was big into the "being accountable" thing.

JP: So that's where you were working…?

N: That's where I was working, and I changed with my clients. They stopped feeling like my clients and I just wanted to go hang out with them. And I stopped trying to do a big clinical thing when we did group. I really didn't even want to know how they were doing and what was up. I just wanted us to get to that feeling. At the beginning I was still teaching some of the old stuff, and I tried teaching some new stuff but they just don't mix. I loved the idea that people had Health in them, and even if they couldn't connect to it they still had it. I loved that. And over the course of a couple of years, I kept going to trainings, kept going to trainings, and Roger used to tell us, "Don't worry about teaching this. Just talk from your heart. Just say what you know. Say what's real to you." So I guess I was just doing that, and I didn't really realize I was being different that much, because it wasn't something I was *trying* to do, be different. One day I got a call from my boss at our work, a "Come to my office" phone call. So I walked up to her office thinking, "What'd I do? I don't even know what I did." And I sat down and she said, "You know, I have noticed that your [section] doesn't take a turn anymore."

JP: A turn?

N: At the treatment facility the clients live in these [sections], and there are three primary [sections] and a detox [section]. There were three counselors, and every counselor had a [section]. Every morning we would sit at staffing, and staffing consisted of the night shift reviewing everything that had happened since we left. On Monday morning that was a long thing. They'd tell us who did what, and everything that was happening. Of course the clients would spend their time acting out as soon as the counseling staff went home because nobody was on them anymore, so they would gear up. We used to spend our time containing them, and as soon as we'd leave they'd explode. So morning staffing was the report out of who did what to whom, who's fighting with who, who had a breakdown, who got suicidal, who came back loaded, and who was in the bushes with whom—all that happens at every residential facility. There's this contagion effect. For example, if one person started stealing…then everybody became suspicious, which bred hostility then anger then fighting, and then somebody was drinking or loaded—it was like a nuclear bomb would go off…. It would take maybe a week or so and you'd finally get the whole thing settled down. Then the same thing would happen in somebody else's [section]. So it just rotated. It was kind of like, "Whose turn is it now?" And your job as a counselor was to try to get that under control. So when my boss called me up to ask me about my [section], that was a big deal. She said, "Your [section] doesn't take a turn anymore. I don't hear about your [section] in staffing anymore. They're not fighting. They're not sneaking their boyfriends in. Their tests are coming back clean. They're completing treatment. I just realized your [section] hasn't had a turn in a long time. What are you doing down there?"

I remember I was in a horrible mood that day, and I knew I was in a low mood and so I thought, "Oh, my God. They want to know what I'm doing, and here's my opportunity to say something about Health Realization, and I feel like shit." And I thought, "Well, you know, it doesn't matter. The door is open, just walk through it." And so I said, "Well, I learned this new thing, and it's called Health Realization, and it's based on the fact that everybody is healthy, and that sometimes we're connected to it and sometimes we're not, and whether we are or not depends on how we're using our own functioning, and once you know about that, you can navigate it better." I don't know if I said it like that but it's an approximation of that in my own simple language at the time. She said, "You're kidding." I said, "No." She said, "You've got to tell [the executive director] about this!" So she kind of drug me by the hand and put me in front of her and said, "You've got to hear this!"

And I remember I was feeling so bad that day, I thought, "I just don't have it in me to do this again," but I did it again. And [the executive director] got so excited. She got so excited! She is an incredible person, because she is always only interested in what is best for the clients. And she said, "This sounds like it's really good for the clients." And I said, "Yes, I think it is." She said, "Well, do you think you could teach this to the other staff?" I said, "I don't know how to teach this to the other staff." And she said, "What if we get you more training?" And I said, "Well, I'll try." So she paid for some training for me. Then she created a position within the agency for me—I think I kept some clinical work at first, and I did a staff group at that facility, and then the next contract year she created a pure training position for me, and I traveled around to the different facilities within [the company]. I did some training at [the treatment facility], and I did some training at the other sites too and started working with staff. That came out of nowhere. That position did not exist. She created that for me. And then the County wanted to borrow me, so I split my time between the agency and the County. Eventually, [the executive director] asked me to train the executive management team for [the company]—so the Principles became a top-to-bottom understanding within the agency.

JP: So it kind of gradually took over the place?

N: Yeah. Their position at the time I was still working there was that all staff were asked to check out Health Realization. They were asked to attend a core course. And a lot of the people after the core course would attend my ongoing trainings. Or sometimes they would sit in on my ongoing trainings and then get interested in going to the core course. And that's where the momentum came from. I learned a lot doing that. It was a huge transition for me to go from working with the clients to working with staff, because in my mind staff were different. I could see the utmost innocence in a client that threw a hissy fit or stole food or got loaded or hit somebody else—I mean, that was very innocent to me—but when my boss would ask me to sit with a colleague who had been screaming at clients and telling the clients to "fuck off" and "go pack your fucking bags," I didn't see that as innocent. I had a lot of judgment about my colleagues because I had an idea in my head that they ought to be in a certain place, because they were staff.

JP: That seems to be true for a lot of us.

N: I didn't know how to be with that, and I struggled with it for a while, and I remember kind of running to Roger. "Roger, what am I going to do? Some of them are hurting the clients and acting like idiots!" And he said, "Well you've just got to see *them* as your clients. You've got to see them the exact same may you see the clients." Pretty quickly that part became easier because I realized, "Well, they're human just like the clients. It would be nice if they knew better, but sometimes they don't. They lose their bearings just like the clients do." So they became my new clients. Then I got frustrated with some people in my personal life. And then I saw, "Oh, this is the same thing."

And the insight was kind of like, "Oh, everybody's a client!" But not like I'm walking around doing therapy on everybody; it was like, "Oh, *everybody's just human!*" It's across the board, the human thing. You don't change up when you change roles. The rules are the same, and you stay the same no matter where you go.

The next big one for me, was seeing Health in systems, seeing the innocence in systems—because the systems didn't work the way I wanted them to. But when I sat and looked at it, a system is made up of people, it's group thinking, it's layers of thinking, and that's why it can get bogged down. When I would try to fight the system I would get nowhere. I would make enemies. I'd lose my good feeling. And I saw, "*Oh*, this is the same thing!" You don't go into a system and challenge the system and fight the system and take on the system—you look for the same Health that you look for in your clients and your colleagues. Then you draw that out and that gets the system moving. You don't work against it. So I saw that in kind of gradual layers.

JP: So is that pretty much how it evolved in Santa Clara County?

N: A lot of it was from the ground up. Some places you go, you go in top-down, but Santa Clara County has been more bottom-up. The first people to really appreciate what we were saying were the clients and the inmates.

JP: Is that how Bob Garner [County alcohol and drug abuse director] ended up hearing about it, and got turned on enough to want the training?

N: No. Bob Garner heard about this from his partner, Penny. Penny was into this, and she works for a business; she'd been into it for a while, using it in business as a leadership paradigm—and she kind of dragged him in one day and said, "You really have to listen to this." And he got turned on. Some of the stats from Modello got him curious. He talks about how he knew that the alcohol and drug system did the best it could by people, but the results weren't great. Bob is amazingly visionary. He was looking for something that would get results, more than something safe. That's why he threw this out in that huge training in 1994, and there were a handful of us that stayed with it. He brought Roger in, and we stayed with Roger, and he kept providing trainings, and we got enough of us that we started to be able to teach the clients. I was at the treatment facility, Cathy [Casey] was in the jails, various other people throughout the County within little, tiny pockets that you would think wouldn't impact a whole County, but we hit enough clients and enough inmates that they started saying to the judges, to their social workers, to their counselors, "I'm into this Health Realization thing. I see it's my thinking now.

I know I'm okay now." And then the social workers and the counselors would come, would want to know what it was, because their clients were talking about it. We'd have people come to our core courses and say, "My clients know more about this than I do. I need to know what this is!" So it really went up from the bottom, and now we're at the point where the board of supervisors has heard about it, and some of them have participated in the training themselves and see how helpful it is and support its use in different agencies. Social Services is now involved. It's really mushroomed.

JP: Was Beverley involved at all in training in the County?

N: Absolutely. The first time I met Beverley, Roger brought her in to speak at one of those trainings, and she was really helpful for those of us that were in recovery because she could speak so powerfully. So that made us all feel safer—there was somebody that understood. Beverley has so much presence. She's so dynamic that you can't be around her and not hear something. It doesn't really matter what Beverley says, you just change after you've been around Beverley. So, yes, Beverley was one of the people when I got ready to present this to the staff—we did a big presentation at the treatment facility—Roger came and she came, and she was hugely instrumental in people being willing to listen, because of the way she spoke. She just has that. She's still working miracles here, teaching in the jail.

ON PREVENTION

JP: Is there anything else you would like to say?

N: How this relates to prevention: I have never met anybody that works in the field of prevention that doesn't have a heart of gold, and really just wants to make a difference. Prevention people are so good-hearted, have so much good will, good nature. But I will be honest with you—I never saw myself working in prevention because, personally, I didn't have much faith in it—it hadn't worked for me. You see, I had been warned about the possibility that I could become easily addicted to substances. From that traditional prevention standpoint, people had warned me to be careful about that. They said, "These are the risk factors, these are the coping skills, these are the life skills. You want to watch out for this." People really tried to talk to me about it beforehand. This is just *me*, personally; I know there are prevention strategies that are proven effective. But what happened for me was that I still drank. The piece of it that was helpful was that, because people had talked to me about the fact that you could develop addictions, I knew that there were resources out there. I did know that, and I was connected to people in the community to get to those resources.

But *all the good information and skills in the world can't help you if you don't have the psychological functioning to support it.* I had really good information, I had skills, I was warned, but the level at which I functioned didn't allow me to make use of the good information and skills I had. When people are hurting, they just want a first step—they just want to stop hurting. And even if you know what you're going to use to help you stop hurting will hurt you even more, you don't really care because you just want to feel better. The worse the pain is, the less you care about the consequences and the toll it takes on you. It's a psychological survival issue. And the ultimate prevention can only be people understanding their own functioning, because it takes a healthy level of functioning to make use of good information and skills. And if people understand their own psychological functioning, they will be operating at a higher level and they won't need relief. But if you aren't connected to your own Health, if you don't feel well, then it's more important to feel well than to do the right thing. Think of all the people doing prevention work, intervention and treatment work, who are working so hard and feeling discouraged because it's hard work to make even a dent. This would be so helpful to them, because it would *move the clients into their own Health—that's the ultimate prevention.* And it would connect the providers to their own health more deeply. Professionals have to have their health too, so they can sustain their work. It's so important to me to have this understanding because I watch professionals wear down, and I've seen them discouraged, and I've seen them lose faith, and that's unfortunate. I'm so grateful for what I've found. I don't know how to express in words how truly grateful I am for what I know now.

4. ELSIE

Interview with Elsie Spittle*. As Elsie Spittle states in her book,* The Wisdom Within *(Mills & Spittle, 2001), "Ken [her husband] and I had known Syd [Banks] prior to his profound discovery about the nature of Mind, and we initially found it extremely difficult to accept the incredible change that occurred in Syd. That a man with minimal education and no psychological training could have an insight so transcendent that he could describe the relationship between Mind, Consciousness and Thought with absolute certainty was beyond our understanding. I became quite indignant whenever he would make such statements—I had no idea that this discovery had anything of value to the world." Eventually Elsie came to see a bit of what he had discovered, and it changed her life. She began to work with Roger Mills in his community prevention efforts, then became an excellent inside-out community prevention worker on her own. Today Elsie is a deep and powerful conveyor of this understanding who has touched many lives. I interviewed her at her home in Long Beach, California in May 2001.*

LIFE BEFORE UNDERSTANDING

JP: What were you like before you ran into this understanding?

ES: [laughs] Oh, this is wicked! I was really a pretty unhappy person. I liked to blame other people for my problems, and so I lived in a lot of blame. I lived in a lot of dissatisfaction. I lived in a lot of neediness, wanting more, wishing I had more, and it didn't happen. I came from a religious background and I thought prayer would be helpful, so I would have this kind of wishful prayer that I would use on Sundays to see if that might help change my life, and that didn't work very well either.

JP: Well it did work; it just happened later than you thought.

ES: [laughs] A lot later! Many, many years later. So that's what I was like. I was generally discontented and didn't think there was any way out of it. I thought that's just what life was like, because, frankly, that was the environment I was brought up in. That was how my family was, and it looked pretty normal, but I didn't like that normality.

JP: Were you married at the time?

ES: Yes. I had been married for eleven years. I got married when I was almost eighteen.

JP: Could you characterize the reaction you had when you first heard this understanding?

ES: My first reaction was disbelief—disbelief that we created our experience. Then came anger.

JP: Anger? Why?

ES: Well, when I think back now—I mean, then I didn't know; I just felt angry and I didn't know why—angry because I thought it was nonsense; I was just hearing nonsense.

THE INSIGHT

JP: What happened to change that?

ES: I had an insight about my anger, that *my anger was being created by the way I was thinking*. And that was really the start of my journey, where I realized, via insight, that it was an inside-out process that was creating my anger. You understand, when I was first introduced to the Principles, I had a lot of fear and resistance.

JP: Why do you think it scared you?

ES: Because it was the truth, and the message was pointing me to the fact that *we create our own experience*. If I bought into that, I would have to look at the fact that my life was a mess because of the way I was thinking and how I was living, and I didn't want to look at that. It was much easier, I thought, to blame—to blame my husband, to blame the children because they weren't behaving in the way I thought they should, to blame circumstances, the environment I'd been brought up in. It was much easier to blame everyone and everything else than to look at the truth, and that's what scared me. That's what really scared me.

JP: So how come you didn't run in the other direction?

ES: Where could I go?

JP: [laughs] Do you remember what you felt after your insight?

ES: I felt *such* relief. With the spontaneous release of the anger, I felt like there really *is* something to life, you know? There really is something to this understanding of how the Principles work to create our experience of life. And the overwhelming feeling I had was of relief.

JP: So from the point you had that insight, what started to happen to you?

ES: I started to listen more to my family. I started to listen more to myself, to the wisdom. I started to be more aware of my negativity and not go there—be wiser and not go in that same direction because I didn't like the feeling. When I'd experienced that spontaneous feeling of joy and relief, it was very strong and it lasted for a while, and I loved that feeling. So after that if I would start to go down in my levels of understanding and feel negative again, I wasn't so quick to move there. I had more perspective. And that affected my relationship with Ken, where I didn't take things that he said to me so personally. It affected my relationship with the children, where I didn't think they were doing things *to* me—I just recognized their innocence more. So I guess I was nicer to be around. I wasn't so judgmental. I wasn't so mean. I wasn't so critical, you know? I was gentler with the family, and with myself. And of course from time to time I moved back into the old habits, but they just weren't as strong and wouldn't last as long.

JP: Did anything different start happening since you started catching on to the understanding?

ES: For one thing, physically I saw the world different.

JP: Physically?

ES: Physically I *saw* the world, you know? The reality was brighter, the colors were more vivid, there was more dimension to the trees. I recall that distinctly on a drive through the countryside. It used to be just flat. Everything was flat in my world, and there was color but it was flat color. Truly it was like there was another dimension. The colors were deeper and richer. It was like filters were taken off my eyes. And the colors in the forest, there was another dimension to them. I could see another dimension to the trees. It wasn't just green. There were different kinds of green, and new green, that's the only way I can describe it. There was a different dimension of depth to the world I saw now.

And I saw people differently too. No matter what they were presenting to me. This wasn't all the time, but there were periods of time where I saw beyond what they were presenting to me, and I wouldn't get hooked by it—with my family, my siblings or my parents. Life was not always a good thing for them. Life was not a blessing. Life was a struggle. And I began to see that with compassion. I began to see them with compassion and with more love, so I wouldn't get hooked into their reality, into the way they saw life. Sometimes I still did, but at least this new level of understanding shifted that so it wasn't constant, where I lived there with them. That was kind of the before and after picture. That's what life looked like to me all the time. Now it no longer looked like that to me. Occasionally it still might, but even with those occasional times—and initially, there were longer periods of time where I would get hooked again, and I'd think, "Ain't it awful?" But even with that, this little voice would be saying inside me, "You know that's not so. You know there's something else now." But I may not have enough understanding at that moment to move out of it.

JP: As you began to have your own understanding evolve, do you remember any particular moments along the way when you remember being totally blown away by an insight of yours?

ES: More recently. I can't pin anything down over the years. They've just melded into a general understanding. To me, what was a watershed was moving back toward the Principles after realizing that "the core concepts" were taking us further away from the essence of this understanding. And when we were invited to work as part of the faculty with the Aquanimitas Foundation, there was a shift there—moving back to the Principles for the Foundation's programs—that was a real profound watershed for me, because it gently forced me to go deeper, myself. Although I'd been feeling that we were losing the power of this message by moving into the core concepts, I still didn't have a real deep feeling for the Principles yet. I didn't feel that I could talk about Mind and I would skirt the issue. And Consciousness was kind of a blur to me; it didn't mean much.

But however long ago it was, two or two and a half years, something like that, that was really powerful to me to move into the Principles, and my life has not been the same since then. It moved me more deeply into seeing the simplicity of how the Principles create our experience of reality, and how *we are the Principles in action all the time.* Before, I still was feeling that it was something that we applied—yeah, yeah, we're part of it, but we apply it or we practice it. I didn't have the feeling that we are the Principles in action. I never felt that so clearly as when I moved in that direction to be able to share it with others. And at that time, when I was given the opportunity to do the Foundation's program in Hawaii, and I knew the focus was on the Principles, I had substantial thinking about, "Can I do this? How can we possibly talk two and a half days on the Principles?" But I also welcomed the opportunity. It was a risk, I felt, that I might be left out there with nothing to say, but at the same time, I welcomed the risk. I wanted to go deeper. I just really, intuitively, wanted to go deeper.

JP: Do you know why?

ES: It was just a feeling I had. I felt I'd come to the cusp of what I knew then, and I just had this very strong feeling that I wanted something deeper inside, that there was more, you know? And I didn't know what it was. So it was moving into the unknown, and it was exciting at the same time—it was a little unnerving.

SHARING

And when I actually did the training with Rita [Shuford] and Chris [Heath], it was intoxicating as I heard what came out. New things came out of me—questions that were asked that I'd never answered before. Deep questions that had me reflective in the moment but answers came out and surprised me.

JP: Do you remember any of those?

ES: Well, there was a question that came out about duality.

JP: What was the question?

ES: What is duality? [laughs] Something like that. And Chris said, "You take it." [laughs]. And I thought, "Hmm, that's interesting. What on earth could I say about duality?" And I don't know what I said at that moment, but what pops into my head now was the duality of inside and outside, and at some point you see that duality is really One. And that, to me, was the whole essence of seeing "I am the Principles. We are the Principles." And in that, there is no duality. There's a duality when you "practice the Principles," then there's duality. That never had occurred to me before. I wouldn't even touch that. I would have passed that on to Rita. But I welcomed that question, because it allowed me to go deeper. And since that time I feel like I've been unleashed, so to speak. And I just continue to see the Principles deeper all the time, and I know that it's ongoing, but I see them simpler—the trainings I do are simpler, the feeling is stronger, I find the questions I get from people are deeper, they're a different quality of questions, and there are fewer questions. People are much more comfortable in just enjoying the feeling, where they don't question, "Well, is that all there is?" Because before, I'd say, "It's just the feeling." It's almost like I don't even have to say that, because the feeling is so deep, they go so deep, they intuitively know it. The audience becomes such a part of this connection of the Principles operating amongst everybody, that we enjoy it together instead of any one person being the trainer or facilitator. There's a real connection that happens, I find.

JP: I've noticed that myself. It's incredible.

ES: Isn't that remarkable!

JP: It's funny, I was always trying to teach that way, whereas it seemed most of the teachers were in "speaking" mode. I was always trying to teach by group give-and-take discussion, but I don't think I had the depth, originally, to be able to pull it off as well as I wanted. Now it just kind of flows, and I love that.

ES: What a gift! [whispers] What a gift.

JP: I remember the moment when you realized the connection to soul. We were sitting in an Aequanimitas Foundation faculty meeting, and you came in the next morning, and you talked about what you'd seen. Do you remember that at all?

ES: I do remember. I do remember. I saw more that Soul and Consciousness were the same. Because I'd been seeing Consciousness as something separate, as more of a capacity that allowed us to experience life. But all of a sudden that was more surface. I saw what was underneath that, at a much deeper level, and that was a lovely, lovely thing to see.

JP: When did you start to get the idea that you could actually be of some help to people with this understanding and actually do it for your work?

ES: As I started getting out there more on my own I just knew it was what I wanted to do, and I didn't know how to do it other than to do what I was doing. I'd volunteer my time and attend things. Then somebody might say, "Would you like to do something?" And word just gradually spread. I tried to do something with a colleague in Vancouver to actually get into the colleges and offer programs, like continuing ed', or programs for adults that would come in the evening and wanted to learn something at college—kind of self-awareness programs. And I went to every college in Vancouver and submitted a brief program outline, and I got rejected, rejected, rejected. I did that a lot. I just put it out wherever I could. I would visit the administrator at the hospital and say, "This is something that I think would be of benefit to your staff and to the patients, and would you be interested in the program?" I did an enormous amount of cold calls in those days and got turned down. And then finally, out of the blue, came an opportunity to move to Miami and to do work there with some psychologists, including Roger Mills, who had started a clinic there.

JP: So what year are we talking about here?

ES: That was 1984. So after due consideration and discussion with Ken and the family, we decided to do that. It was an opportunity to do this work in a way that I'd never had the opportunity before. And at the same time, a business client also had been introduced to this understanding and wanted this in his business. And he contacted my business partner and said, "Would you come and do a seminar for our executives?" And they enjoyed it so much that they invited him to move as well with his family. And because we were partners, he and I ended up working in that company together for about five years.

JP: Who was that?

ES: That was Reese Coppage's company, Duval-Bibb. They were our first business client, to that depth. We'd done a couple of other things with some other business clients, but it didn't take. With Reese it took. He had that deep commitment.

JP: Who was your business partner?

ES: Chip Chipman. So he and his family and Ken and our family moved at the same time to Miami. And I ended up working with the institute in Miami part-time and working with Duval-Bibb part-time. It was the first time that I actually got paid for doing that.

JP: So how did that feel?

ES: It felt wonderful. I remember Chip and I doing some work at Orlando for Reese's company, and that was the first company they wanted us to work with. And I remember he and I walking down the hallway almost skipping with delight, like "Here we are! This is our first client of any note, and here we are, going to do interviews and going to do training, *and* we're getting *paid*!" We were pinching ourselves, the two of us, because Chip, at that period of time when I was making all these cold calls to the colleges, he was doing the same thing. He was working and doing his best to implement his understanding in the company he was working for. So for the both of us it was an absolute delight that we could do this above-board, really go for it, that's what they were bringing us in for! It was absolutely intoxicating to do that.

COMMUNITY WORK FROM THE INSIDE-OUT

JP: So when did you have your first opportunity to do community work with this understanding?

ES: When I was in Tampa. We moved to Tampa from Miami about a year-and-a-half later because we were doing more work then with Reese and his company, and other companies in Tampa were coming into the picture. Finally Reese said, "Why don't you just move here? It's cheaper than flying you back and forth and putting you up in lodging." And so we did. We decided that was the way to go. It felt right to us.

We moved to Tampa and ended up joining forces with Sandy Krot, who had a small clinic there. We became the business arm and offered leadership trainings and other programs. I became president of the Florida Center, and out of the blue—I know what it was, Jack—I had heard the Modello residents talk at the annual conference in St. Petersburg: Lloyd [Fields] and Cynthia [Stennis] and several of the other people. I was so taken with them, so struck by what they shared, by their presence, that I thought, "Hmm, I want to know these people." And then shortly after that came an opportunity with the Florida Center, to do some training in a disadvantaged community in Tampa. And, as luck would have it, nobody on our staff had the time to take it, and somebody on the staff, Sandy or Chip, said, "Well, Elsie, you're free right now. Why don't you take it on?" And I thought, "Well, I don't really know anything about communities, but what the hey." And so I went and met this community and put something together, and I picked Roger's brain, and I talked to Lloyd and Cynthia, and I thought, "Hey, this is really neat," and I did some training there, I think a six or eight-week program.

JP: What did you hear from Lloyd and Cynthia, when you were picking their brains, that struck you about the way to go about working in a community?

ES: To listen to the residents. Rapport and listening. That the residents were the experts. And that helped me feel relaxed, because then I knew: Hey, it's not about me. It's about them, and they know what they want. They're the experts in their community. And what I can share is the understanding of creating an internal reality that impacts the outer reality, and there's the partnership. But they know what they want, and if I can listen to them, that's how we can work together—and rapport. Rapport, intuitively, I just knew that was the way to go.

JP: What was the name of this community?

ES: The very first community that I did that brief program for was Tampa Heights. It was six weeks, and then I think I did maybe another six weeks, just strictly training. It was not a comprehensive program where you go into the community and hire staff. That came later.

JP: So you just basically entered the community and did the training, or did you hang out first?

ES: No. I just basically went in and did training.

JP: How did that work?

ES: It worked fine, because the kind of training I did was really group training, drawing out from them, because I've always liked that. That always has been food for me. So I would introduce something, probably in those days more about Thought and Health, that people are innately healthy, and then would draw out of them, like, "How does that sit with you? How do you see that? Have you ever considered that?" So it was a lot of dialogue, and in that dialogue, rapport was being built. So it was that kind of training. In those days

I didn't do much [writing] on the board, and I've almost come full circle, where I don't do much on the board now. It was more dialogue and, "How do you see this? What do you think this might do in your life? If you saw your partner or your children as having Health inside them, what do you think that might do?"

JP: Did ~~you find~~ that they responded to it?

ES: Very much! The person who did not respond was the person who brought me in. [laughs] She got nervous because she saw the residents growing and changing, and she wondered whether she'd have a program left and was most unnerved by it. The residents themselves really took to it and would share great examples, where they would be more thoughtful when they would go back home. I remember one woman in particular, she was really tough, she'd been on drugs and alcohol, had no teeth, but she somehow resonated with the idea that people had a core of Health inside them. She'd knifed her husband at one time and he ended up in the hospital with eighteen stitches—that was the kind of domestic, violent situation between both of them. And when she started to see the Health in him, she came back in and told this story about where he'd come back home drunk, and instead of her taking after him with a frying pan full of hot fat like she had the feeling to, she stopped herself, and she put on her shoes and she went out for a walk. Stories like that would pop up from people. She stopped this thinking where she was getting "het up," and she realized, "Here I go again, I don't want to go there," and she caught herself, and she put on her shoes and walked away.

JP: So she learned that in the training—meeting once a week for a day-and-a half for six weeks. The same group went through the second six weeks?

ES: Pretty much the same group. You know how it is. There'd be some come and go, but there was essentially a core group there.

JP: Was it an African American community?

ES: Primarily.

JP: Did you have any trepidation about being white?

ES: No. I really didn't. I had done some work with Roger as well. He'd invited me in, whether it was before then or around then I'm not sure, where I'd gone to New York with him, to the Bronx, and done some work there. And

I got over the fact that I was white during that time period, and I was just seeing people as people and really grateful for the opportunity. So I didn't feel any qualms about that, just delighted that that was happening—

JP: So when was this?

ES: 1989. Then I think it was 1990 when I got my first opportunity to develop and find funding for a three-year program that was more comprehensive in Riverview Terrace, in Tampa.

JP: So that was where you were pretty much functioning as staff?

ES: I was the project director, and I hired a part-time staff person to actually be in the community, to have an office, so we had visibility in the community. Then within a couple of months we hired some part-time outreach workers and hired a couple of people to work with the youth as well. All of that was resident-driven.

JP: You did that for three years?

ES: Two-and-a-half years. Then I got the opportunity to move to California to start a business with Roger. So I turned the project over to the community and other people, and I would consult with them long distance. I went in at the end of the third year to help them give out certificates and complete the program, but the last six months they really did on their own. We probably started Riverview Terrace in 1992-1993, something like that, and it ended three years later.

JP: What ended up happening in Riverview Terrace?

ES: It ended where half the community was getting torn down, and they were already starting to tear down some of the homes. It was a really old community, and they were going to rip it down and build new units on it. So a lot of the residents got dispersed, and where it is now I don't know. So in terms of community revitalization, I would say really nothing happened because that community is no longer. Again, it was individual changes. There were a number of people who individually changed, moved out of the community—some of them moved out even before the demolition, and others moved out due to that and started new lives. So a couple of them continue to keep in touch with me.

JP: Did you feel that project was a success?

ES: Based on individuals, I would. Based on community revitalization, no. What the resident council brought me in for was leadership empowerment, to get the residents out of apathy so that more people would sit on the board, on the resident council. They also wanted a youth leadership program—which we developed and worked with the youth—that could get the kids off the street. And that also was successful for that period of time. From what I understand, some of the youth that were really impacted continue to have nice lives today. So on an individual basis, that's how I see it. That's why, frankly, I don't know that I would do a community project again in the way that we have done it, where we develop such visibility in the community, hire staff, work with residents to go away on retreats and do action planning meetings and all that.

JP: Why is that?

ES: Because I think you, in essence, can put pressure on people to follow up with the action planning—all the goals and objectives that come out of that action planning. In the spirit of the moment a lot comes out, but the actual fruition of the action plans are few and far between. So I think a lot of money gets spent on areas like that, that don't necessarily come to fruition. I'm leaning more and more toward training, and then getting out of the way. Just train people and turn them loose, and let them do what they see to do in their own time.

JP: You must have had some experience with that. Where was that?

ES: Avalon Gardens. I've seen that in Avalon Gardens in south central Los Angeles. When we moved from Tampa to L.A. Roger asked me to take over that project.

JP: Had he started there already?

ES: Yes. He'd been there for two years, and I came in for the third year to supervise it. Again, that was to be a revitalization of the whole community, and a lot of goals and objectives, a lot of money spent, and I saw individuals change and not the whole community change.

JP: What had happened in the two years before you got there?

ES: A lot of training, and there was action planning that went on with some, frankly, grandiose ideas about what to do in the community that did not pan out. Then when I came on board, there was another action planning where the ideas came down to earth more, and nothing really happened there either.

JP: Interesting. And do you attribute nothing really happening there to the action planning?

ES: No, I attribute it to that people hadn't gone deep enough, so that wasn't what they really wanted to do on their own.

JP: Oh, that's very important!

ES: You know, all of this is in hindsight. In the heat of the moment during those action planning retreats where you'd all go away, where these wonderful brainstorming sessions would take place, these ideas would emerge, committees would be formed, they'd go back home and the ideas would just slowly sit there—where few people, if any, really owned them and said, "This is what we're going to do." It would require, to no avail, frankly, in my experience, calling: "Have you had your committee meeting? What's the outcome? How can I help you? Is there any way I can help you move this along?" Lots of words spoken; bottom line, nothing happened.

JP: You know what's amazing to me? What you're just describing did not happen in Modello. And it sounds to me that what happened in Avalon Gardens was an attempt to take a traditional outside-in approach—an action planning approach—and intermingle it with Health Realization, an inside-out approach. Does that sound right to you?

ES: I think there's a quality of depth where things unfold from, where you can't have the project director saying, "Okay, now it's time—we're looking at our goals and objectives, and within the time frame of the program, now it's time to have our action planning." And it's driven via that, as opposed to the residents coming up with these ideas and driving it themselves.

JP: It sounds like what you're saying is, the idea of traditional action planning is not something that moves this effort along, and it may inhibit it.

ES: Yeah. That's what I'm beginning to feel—because it's not resident-driven.

JP: So it's somebody else's idea to do that, and they don't have the buy-in.

ES: That's right. That's what I'm feeling.

JP: That makes sense to me.

ES: Although, even in the moment, as I say, in the retreat setting where the brainstorming is rich and fertile, it doesn't seem to pan out.

JP: I've noticed that just with traditional action planning. It almost never pans out, but people do get very excited at the time. And I always left those sessions—because I used to do those things—with a feeling that nothing is really going to come of all this. And I also noticed that it was in the people-taking-responsibility-to-follow-through phase where the energy would drop. Vision? Great. Energy's high. Desired results? Energy's high. Goals? Energy drops slightly, but it's still up there. Objectives and what we're going to do. Drops more, but still okay. Then as soon as you get to the, "Okay, now specifically, how are we going to make this happen?" and "Who's going to do what?" Boom. It drops. That's just from my experience.

ES: That's right. Exactly, Jack. And I see that continuing to happen, because that's become the model for community work. I continue to see that happening.

JP: You mean it's become part of the Health Realization model of community work?

ES: Uh huh.

JP: Really? Whose model? Not from what I've seen and done personally. It never would occur to me to do that. That's very interesting to me. Coliseum Gardens, to my knowledge, was another place they did not do action planning—which may be why it was so successful. So after Avalon Gardens, where did you really start feeling like you were having an impact on a community?

ES: I guess it would be in the Bronx and in Visitacion Valley [in San Francisco]. But again, not on the community as a whole, although I suspect in Visitacion Valley there is that ripple effect happening, probably, with some of the drug dealers not being on the streets. But I would say in regard to the training of individuals in both those communities, Visitacion Valley and in the Bronx, the people that we've touched there, many of whom have gone their own way and gone into other organizations in the last five months even, we have seen some wonderful, wonderful changes with individuals, with people there.

JP: When did that project start in Visitacion Valley?

ES: September of, maybe, 1999? I think Roger went in September to start the rapport-building, and January's when we actually hired LaThena [Clay] and Barb [Glaspie] and other staff, and that probably will be two years this January [2002].

JP: What role have you had in that?

ES: I worked with Roger on the actual proposal and developing the model for Visitacion Valley.

JP: How does that model look different than some of the other models?

ES: It's more extensive in terms of time. It's a five-year project rather than a three-year project that we've done before—and there's more action planning in it [laughs]—retreats to do action planning with the residents and service providers to see how to implement and move things along. I think that the grant proposal built on what Roger developed for Avalon Gardens.

JP: What have you learned from this latest project?

ES: I am leaning much more toward just training, and letting people do what they're going to do with their wisdom in their own way and their own time. I think we'd save many dollars that could be used for more training in other communities, rather than hiring staff like we do. It just sets up a lot when you move into a community like that, that already has other programs—even with the rapport, there's always going to be some programs that are already in place that take umbrage at the new folk coming in. And I know that will happen anywhere, but that's why I think the simplest, cleanest way to introduce this in communities, organizations, what have you, is to train people to the best of your ability—as long as it takes to get them to some depth—and turn 'em loose. That's what happened to us.

JP: The only thing I wonder about here is the staff issue, a staff presence. It would seem to me that if you had people as a daily presence in the community—like in Modello as Lloyd and Cynthia did, or in Coliseum like Beverley did—who are just there to help people out in whatever way they can, and just keep a good feeling and do whatever they have to do, it would seem to me that it would have more potential to have impact than just doing the training and letting the chips fall where they may, so to speak.

ES: Yeah. But we are training service providers to do that, who are already in the community. Like in Visitacion Valley we trained residents *and* service providers—service providers that have programs that work, that service youth, that do job training, that work with welfare-to-work recipients, just to a name a few. We're training them, those that have been interested. And that was part of Avalon Gardens as well. To me, the best would be to have those people trained. They're already visible and working in the community. They're already accepted, only now they have this added wisdom and understanding that they contribute. And they're already part of the community, rather than possibly introducing a whole 'nother kind of entity that oftentimes can create some resentment with some of the other providers. In Visitacion Valley there are still a very small group who are saying, "Well, we were already getting some of these results before Health Realization came along." Now, again, I think you're going to have that no matter what. There's always going to be some dissension, but I think that would lessen it.

JP: If you had the opportunity to go into a community now and do it exactly the way that you wanted to set it up, what would it look like from beginning to end?

ES: As much as I can see now, I would do resident training and service provider training. That would be it.

JP: That's all.

ES: Yeah, and I would just see it unfold from there.

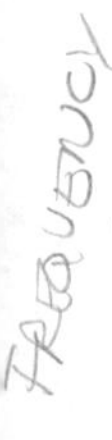

JP: How often would you do the training?

ES: I don't know. I'd have to look at that. It may be that we'd do two days a month, to give them maybe ten to twelve days over the course of seven or eight months or something, and then reassess and see where we go from there: Do we pull back a little bit and let them just try it on and do what they want to do, and see how things work out for them? What ideas occur to them at their own pace? And be on board as a consultant for a period of time. But when people are hired in a community and are employed, that also sets up some resentment with other residents. It sets up, possibly, some prima donnas, you know? It sets up a dependence on the grant. It sets up some things that I think aren't healthy.

JP: What do you think about the training of trainers model like they do in Santa Clara county, where they give a certification—

ES: I do a training of trainers, but I don't give a certification—other than a certificate of completion. And they write a paper or submit an audio or a videotape. I love to see what they've learned. I think it's good for people to actually write down, "What I've learned in this program. How it's changed my life." And I like to do two programs concurrently: A Principles program which is basically an introduction where people don't know anything or very little about this, and a training-of-trainers, so the TOT group helps me train the newcomers, and they make a videotape before the third session of them training before an audience and get feedback.

JP: They still get their certificate, no matter how well they do?

ES: Absolutely, because they've completed the program. Now in Vis' Valley, I went in there a day-and-a-half every month, and out of ten sessions the first three I really work with the group, then I have them train each other. We take a day where I actually assign different topics to the group, in teams, and then for the other half-day they would come back in and present. I had one team present the Principles to the best of their ability, with examples. Then, I would have another team talk about how the Principles relate to rapport. I'd have another team talk about how the Principles relate to listening. I would have another team talk about how understanding the Principles helped them in their work, in the community. So although they wouldn't necessarily say, "These are the Principles and what they mean to me," they always have that as their basis…

JP: When you look back at the community projects you've done and all this kind of stuff, are there a couple of people whose changes stand out in your mind most vividly?

ES: Yeah, I would say Helen [Neale-Pore (Ali)].

JP: I'm interviewing her [Chapter I]. Anybody else—a story or two that comes to your mind?

ES: Well, a woman from Riverview Terrace in Tampa, who, when I first met her, when she just came in to sit in our training program there in the community—a big woman—had three little grandchildren just clustered around her, hanging on and agitated and crying and unhappy. She was wearing a green smock that you get when you're in the hospital as a patient. She looked psychotic to me. She just looked so out to lunch. And I thought, "Hmm. That's interesting. Why is she even here?" And she was even rather disruptive in her care of the children, and noisy and very vocal, and I thought, "Hmm." But we just went along anyways, because you get used to that a lot when you're working in communities. And we just carried on with the dialogue. And over a period of time I found out more and more about her, and she just was drawn to this, with her little grandchildren. I found out later that she had some bookkeeping experience, and the more that she regained her health, the more she was inclined to get out and about in the community, and the more she dressed nicely. Sometimes she had her grandchildren, and sometimes she didn't, but when she did have them it was noticeable that they were also quieting down and were more well-behaved. And she was looking happier. And her daughter started to come in. I don't know exactly the story of her daughter, but her daughter, whose little children these were, started to come in occasionally with her too. And it turned out that she ended up going back to school, night school, and getting her CPA for accounting. She stands out in my mind—and she continues to e-mail me occasionally and is still doing well—because she just looked like she would never make it. And here she is now, a productive member of the community.

Another woman that I remember, again from the same community, when she first came in I thought, "I don't know about her." But there was something about her also that I liked. And when we had to hire someone to work with the children in the youth leadership component, she kept coming to mind. Yet at the same time I saw that when she would get upset and frustrated she would take it out on the kids, and she would threaten them with the belt, because that's just the way she was. And I thought, "I don't know about this." Yet my head said one thing but my heart said, "Hire her." And so I hired her and someone else who I felt would be a really good team with her. And the two of them started to work with the kids. And she was blossoming and growing. Then she was hired to work at the school as a teacher's assistant, and she was really growing. And then I started to hear from some of the staff I had hired in Riverview Terrace that she was threatening the kids in the Health Realization program—that if they misbehaved she'd take the belt to them. She never did, but she would threaten them. And I really felt a little intimidated by her. She had three children, all of whom were in jail, and she had the two grandchildren—she had been appointed the guardian for the children. I was a little intimidated by her, because she was pretty tough. But finally I could no longer ignore it, and I ended up inviting her to lunch to talk to her about what I'd been hearing from the staff, to say, "Could we talk about what's going on?" And I hemmed and hawed and hemmed and hawed and finally just cut to the chase, and we ended up having the most productive, warm-hearted talk that you could imagine. She was in tears, I was in tears. And we left almost holding hands. There was such warmth between us. Because I finally said to her, "You know, you intimidate me. I'm intimidated by you, and if I'm intimated by you, imagine the kids." She didn't realize that! That was such a habit of thought to her to threaten the kids with the belt. She said, "I'd never use that, Elsie, I'd never beat these kids. That's just my way, and I'm doing it because I love them and I want them to behave." Well I never realized that she didn't know how intimidating she was. I didn't realize that she was threatening out of love! So it was a revelation for me. And she didn't realize that I was intimidated, and if I was intimidated, who she respected—and who she felt intimidated by—then what could those kids or other staff members be feeling? So it was a revelation for her. It was a revelation for me, and we became really close in that time. And she became much gentler.

MORE ON LIFE AFTER

JP: What's the most amazing thing to you about the Principles, from your own personal understanding?

ES: That we *are* the Principles.

JP: Can you say more about that?

ES: Because I don't have any place else to look. No matter what is going on in my life, I always come back to me—the big Me and the little me, the universal Me and the personal me. I see that they are in partnership within me. And the more I see that, the personal is getting less and less and the universal is more and more. And what I see, then, is that my life unfolds. I'm so much more comfortable with life unfolding, that life is unfolding for me in a way that, personally, I was never able to experience before. I felt I still had to do much more planning and making things happen than I do now. And it's not like I sit back and don't do anything. I fan the flame. If somebody calls or says something like, “At some point we’d like to have you come,” I will follow up on that. I won’t wait for them to call me twice. I’ll fan that flame, but I don’t go out as such and try to market myself anymore. I just find my life unfolding so much gentler and easier and productively than I ever thought possible. That’s what it means to me. That’s what’s awesome to me.

JP: Beautiful!... Could you say more what you mean by the “universal,” as opposed to the personal?

ES: I see the “universal Me” in terms of being in partnership with this invisible power and wisdom that I’m made up of, that my soul is directly connected to. That’s the “universal Me.” The “personal me” is more the manifestation of my thinking.

JP: That’s great. So one is the very power that you have to think anything—

ES: That’s right.

JP: And the other is the result of the thinking, the manifestation of how we’ve used that power to create what we see of ourselves—

ES: That’s right, yeah.

JP: Is there anything else that you haven’t said that you would really like to say?

ES: I think the blessing of knowing that people are innately healthy, that under all the many disguises we use to hide this core of Health, there is this core of wisdom—that in itself has helped me enormously, you know? Whether people recognize the Principles or not, if they move toward recognizing that people do have wisdom inherent in them, and we don’t have to fix anybody: What a relief! What a gift.

JP: How do you know that? What’s your proof that you have Health and wisdom?

ES: Because when I look to that in people, it comes out. [laughs] That’s the evidence to me! No matter what—no matter what language barriers are in place, no matter what cultures are in place, if you look to that, that’s what comes out.

5. JUDY

Interview with Judith Sedgeman*. When I interviewed Judy, she was director of the Sydney Banks Institute of Innate Health at the Robert C. Byrd Health Sciences Center at West Virginia University (WVU). WVU was the first prestigious institution to adopt Banks's principles as an undergirding foundation for service and education. Previously a successful businessperson and business consultant, after becoming exposed to this understanding Judy worked for nearly a decade with Pransky & Associates in La Conner, Washington and developed into one of the most respected conveyors of this understanding. She has written many insightful essays on subjects related to this Understanding: https://three-principles.com/3p-reflections-essays/. I interviewed Judy at the Institute in Morgantown, WV in April 2001.*

LIFE BEFORE UNDERSTANDING

JP: What were you like before you got exposed to this understanding?

JS: [laughs] Well, you should really ask my daughter this question, because she does this fabulous description, but I was very successful and not very happy. I was a person who had achieved a lot of things—material success and business success and recognition, and it should have been "everything's great." But the more time went by and the harder I worked and the more I accomplished, the more empty I felt, and the less I felt that I was connected in any way to something meaningful. Now, looking back on it, I'd say that I was stressed way beyond anything healthy, and I was also depressed, although I wouldn't have called it depression. I would have called it "responsibility" and the way life is when you're a successful person and have a lot of obligations. I can remember getting up in the morning and standing in the shower crying, morning after morning, just because I had so many things to do, and I was never getting enough sleep, and I was so tired, and I was so conscious of my duties and my obligations and the people counting on me and all of that. I just wanted to crawl under something and stop, but I didn't know how to stop.

JP: When you say you were successful in accomplishments, what are you talking about?

JS: Well, I owned my own business, which was doing very well. I had a medical practice management business in Bradenton, Florida, which is how I stumbled into this, ultimately. I had a lot of clients. We were doing very good work for our clients. I was on a lot of boards. I was active in the symphony. I was on the board of trustees of the Florida State Museum of Art. I was on the Chamber of Commerce Economic Development Committee and on the board of the Chamber. I was on the board of the United Way. I was the first woman to do a lot of things in my community. When I first moved to Bradenton in 1970 there were very few businesswomen. Most women were taking a much more traditional female role, and I was kind of a pioneer in breaking new ground for women to be included in community activities that had been all male. So I took that on as kind of a cause, to open doors to an equal representation from all people. So I worked very hard.

And I had a child. My daughter was just getting into her teenage years, and I was married and had a very active social life. Anyone in the community would have described me as a prominent person and expected me to be deliriously happy. So then I had that expectation to meet, you know? I had to put on my happy face so I wouldn't let them down. I blamed myself entirely. I thought, "You have all this. You should be grateful! Why aren't you happy?" But I wasn't.

JP: So you would stand in your shower crying in the morning because you had an expectation of yourself?

JS: Plus, I didn't know what I was missing. I couldn't figure out what else could I possibly—I would ask myself, "What's left? What could I do? What should I be doing? Why can't I be satisfied? Why aren't I thrilled? Why aren't I happy? Why aren't I at peace? Why am I so driven?" I would look at everything I had and think, "Why can't I just be a happy, contented person? What's wrong with me?"

JP: And so, when you asked yourself that question—

JS: I had no answer. The answer was, "There's something wrong with you."

JP: That's a big answer.

JS: That's a big answer, yeah.

THE INSIGHT

JP: So if you can reflect back to the time you first got exposed to this understanding, what happened, and how did it all come about?

JS: Well, I was in this state of agitation about what to do about my life and how to find some peace, and I decided I had to get out of my business. I was blaming the fact that I had taken on the ownership of a business and borrowed a lot of money and had a financial responsibility for my clients. And so I thought if I just get out of business, start over, maybe—everybody always changes jobs when they're unhappy, right? [laughs] That's, like, your first thought: "I've got to get a different job." And I was sitting in my office, trying to figure out how in the world I could do that, morally—when you had just put a lot of physicians' data on a big computer system in your office and they were counting on you. You just don't say, "Hey, we're not doing next week." It's not like you just shut down a production line. I didn't have the answer to how to wind down something that I had started up in a way that was ethical, responsible and moral and in service to my clients, whom I really cared about. So I was very troubled by that, and I decided, "Well, I'm not going to take any new clients." So of course as soon as I said that, I got a call from a long-time friend of mine, Dick Connor, who was formerly an internal medicine practitioner in our community and he said, "I've got a client for you." And I said, "Dick, I'm not taking any new clients." He said, "No, I really, really, really want you to consider this, because this person really needs business help, and I think that you would really enjoy this person and get a lot out of being in a business relationship with him." I said, "No way. I don't want any new clients." And he said, "Judy, come on now, we've been friends for a long time. I've never led you astray. Trust me on this." I didn't have the courage to tell him I was trying to get out of the business. So finally I agreed to have lunch with him, and that proved to be Bill Pettit.

At that time he had been in Bradenton for a little over a year, I think, in private practice. So I go to this lunch, and I find out en route that I'm going to meet a psychiatrist. And I said to Dick, "You must be kidding me!" So we get to lunch and we had a very pleasant lunch with Bill, and I kept asking him if he was really a psychiatrist, because I'm sitting there with a person who's talking about how much he loves his clients and enjoys the work he's doing, and he's excited about the future of what's possible for people. I was totally baffled by this; it's not what I was used to from psychiatrists. So of course in the state of mind that I was in at that time, I assumed that he probably had a drug—something really good [laughs]. So I'm trying to figure out what he's taking, and what he's giving to them, you know?

So we went back to his office, and I saw that he had a wall of files, which, for a psychiatrist who had been in town for a fairly short time—because psychiatrists usually see the same people for a long time, over and over again—I didn't expect. So I'm looking at these files and I'm thinking, "He mustn't be very good. He must have to keep getting new patients." So I looked at him and said, "Gee, you have an awful lot of files. You're a solo practitioner, aren't you? How do you see all these people?" And he said, "Oh, I don't." And in my mind I go, "Ah ha!" [laughs] And I said, "Where are they?" And he looked at me and said, "Well, I guess they're having a nice life."

I was stunned. I had never heard a psychiatrist ever suggest that a mental patient would leave treatment and have a nice life—I've heard them say things like "back to normal," "as good as they're going to feel," "stabilized," but never "having a nice life!" So I said, "Are you seeing people that are in the DSM description for all these things wrong with people?" And he said, "Oh yes. I'm on the staff of several hospitals, and I see everybody referred to me—the whole gamut of psychiatric illnesses." And I said, "And people get treated here, and then they have a nice life?" And he looked at me like a person would look at a two-year old, and he said, "Isn't that the point?" [laughs] And I said, "Of course it's the point, but nobody does it. What are you doing with these people, what are you giving them?" Then he started laughing, and he looked at Dick and he said, "You didn't tell her that I don't do traditional psychiatry, did you?" And Dick said, "No, I was just going to let her figure it out for herself." So Bill started to explain to me that he teaches people how to be healthy and teaches them how to find the Health that's accessible to all people, and that when they get in touch with that, they're able to have a nice life regardless of how they came into the practice. He said, "The state of mind they were in when I saw them really doesn't matter. It matters that they see it for what it is." Well, his certainty was overwhelming to me. I was blown away by it.

JP: What year was this?

JS: Probably late 1985. I was so suspicious that I said, "I'm just having a hard time grasping this, and I really can't represent a client when I don't understand his work," He said, "I'll tell you what, I do a group for my patients and anybody they want to bring, because frankly their families are often as baffled as you are that the patient goes back home and is in a different state altogether. So I do this public group—anybody can come—and I try to explain to the patients and their friends what this understanding that I've shared with the patients can mean. So you're welcome to come to the group." And I'll never forget this—I was so embarrassed—because I looked at him and, again, this probably tells you more than you ever wanted to know about the way I was living at the time, I said, "Don't you think I'd feel a little strange with all those mental patients?" And he looks at me, and he patted my arm, and he said, "Believe me, you won't be able to tell the difference" [laughs]—which was hilarious.

So I started going to these groups. I just wanted to interview these patients and find out if what he told me was true. I was waiting for the breaks so I could figure out who the patients were and ask them whether they really were having a nice life. Bill was a wonderful speaker and you couldn't help but be engaged, but I wasn't really paying much attention to the details, and then at the break I would start talking to these people. Well, after about three of these meetings it crossed my mind that these so-called mental patients had what I was looking for. They were much happier than I'd ever been. They took it for granted and it was a very ordinary thing, and they had no regrets about the number of years they had spent not happy until they found out how to be happy—they were just grateful for what they had. And they were all so matter-of-fact about it. It wasn't like some epiphany. For them it was like, "I used to think this, and now I see it differently, and I'm fine." And they had this very sweet—but not sticky-sweet or phony or weird sweetness—just a sweetness about them, a lovely human quality.

JP: How did it make you feel to think, "Wow, they have what I want?"

JS: I did want it! I was ready to just call myself a mental patient and go for it [laughs]. But I knew I didn't have to do that. I remember the first thought I had was, "Whatever he's talking about, I need to really pay attention. I need to come here to listen and be a student." So the first thought I had was to stop being so suspicious. When I did that I came with the right feeling, and I started to be touched, by everything—by what he was saying, by what the people were saying, by the questions people were asking. I just became a part of this learning.

And then—I'll never forget—this is like a turning point. One day, just in passing, he said, "You know, a lot of people live their life as though they got up every morning and wrote nasty notes to themselves and left them around the house, and came home at night and started reading them and didn't recognize their own handwriting"—which was kind of silly, but I thought,

"That's what I've done my whole life. That's exactly what I'm doing. I'm setting up all these expectations: You should be this. You should be that. You owe this." And then I'd come home and take inventory at the end of the day, and it was like somebody else was giving me my marching orders. I forget I'm making this up. I don't have to do anything, and I could do anything! And I remember—actually this is almost embarrassing—this place where the meetings were was in this parking lot adjacent to the medical office complex, and I remember running out into the parking lot after that particular evening, and running around the parking lot screaming, "I'm free, I'm free!"—just so happy. I was, like, dancing in the parking lot, and it was so amazing to me to have that insight, which was the first of what I hope will continue to be a lifetime of insights, but that was the first time that I really knew what it was—to see what Bill was talking about: That when people see something inside themselves, and see it for themselves, they change. And everything changes, just like that! So I saw that.

Well then, we did take him on as a client and started working with his practice. So Bill called me one day, and he said, "Remember that book I gave you?"—*Second Chance* was the only book out at the time that Syd [Banks] had written—"Well, the author is going to be in my office next week, and I thought maybe you'd like to come in, since you're working with our practice and you're kind of part of our group. It's just going to be him and the people closest to him, and staff." And so I went and I sat there, and this was the first I'd ever seen Syd Banks, and it was a lovely way to see him. It was a lovely little meeting room that Bill had, and there were seven or eight people there and Syd. And Syd was just chatting, and I didn't really grasp what he was chatting about. I mean, it seemed like he was saying simple, straightforward things that I couldn't remember afterwards, but, you know, I was very drawn to the feeling, and very quiet. I mean, I felt like I was watching sediment settle to the bottom of the glass. I felt myself in those couple of hours that morning kind of settling to the bottom of my life, kind of—not bottom in a bad way, but as kind of "the essence."

And when I walked out of there, without giving it much thought at all, I walked over to the office of one of our troublesome clients—a surgeon who was very rude and mean to my staff—and I just fired him as a client. I was shocked, myself, at the certainty I felt about it, that it was no big deal to me, and I wasn't worried about what was going to happen. What I thought is, "We are indulging this man at his worst. We're not bringing out the best in him, or he in us. I don't understand why he's the way he is, but for us to accept it for money is a disservice to him. That's not right." And that's what I told him. And I then went back to my office and told my staff. Of course, people were a little bit frightened, because he represented a considerable amount of income to us. But at the same time they were grateful because I was standing up for a human value that they shouldn't just have to take any abuse because that's our corporate profit—which was a big lesson for me, how things work out. Because when the word got out that I had done that, I had more business. So that was a big turning point. And I was very touched by Syd. I didn't really know too much about him, but I just thought, "What a lovely man. What a decent, kind, sweet soul I've just been in touch with." And it had a huge effect on me, although I wouldn't be able to say just what.

So then I went to Bill and I said, "I really need to learn this. I realize that in your world this is a therapy, but I'm a businessperson and this just rocked my world. Everything's changing. This is way bigger than therapy. It's way more than that, and I want to learn everything I can." So he made an arrangement with me that I could be, like, an apprentice with him, because there were so few places to go to learn it. I did go to a week-long program put on by the people in Tampa. It was Elsie [Spittle] and Chip [Chipman] and Sandy [Krot]. That's all they did was the week-long things, and infrequently at that, but really I just followed Bill around and listened to him talk—went to all the public things that he did, listening to him talk to other people. And I helped him set up a unit at a hospital for his practice to help him to realize the dreams that he had—

JP: What were you learning?

JS: I just found out that the way to be happy is to stop thinking about yourself and start thinking about other people, and just do what's obvious, and do the best you can, and not start measuring yourself against impossible standards and just, you know, be real. It was so simple, yet it hadn't crossed my mind before. So I got out of a lot of things I was doing without my full heart. I made the engagement of my heart the criterion of what I would commit my time to. And when I did that, it all fell into place, and I was doing everything I loved to do. So it didn't seem like a burden any more, and the things I'd been doing out of obligation or for external reasons just fell by the wayside, and I didn't even miss them. So things started to work out in my life, and from that starting point it was like a magic carpet ride, and the only time it's ever gone wrong is when I've tried to steer the carpet. As long as I just sit on the carpet and go with it, it's been wonderful.

But then, there was the bigger dimension to it, because I'd been working with Bill for about a year, I think, and my daughter had gone off to prep school, and then—you know, this is her story, so I won't go into detail—but she ended up running away from school. And I didn't know where she was for three days, and I went into this tailspin. I was told that she'd seen a psychiatrist at the school, and she needed to be committed. The psychiatrist said that she needed to be in a mental hospital, which I couldn't even relate to. And so in my heart I knew that I had to call Bill—but I didn't want to because he was my client and I was his student, and to be honest with you I realize in retrospect that I didn't want to admit that my family was so screwed up. But in the interest of my daughter I finally did, because I thought, "How crazy! If you do find her, who else would you want but Bill to treat her?"

So I called him up, and by that time I'd talked to all kinds of people, and everybody had an opinion about my parenting and why I was at fault, or why she was at fault, and I was so confused and upset. So I called Bill finally, and I told him what was going on. And he said, "How are you feeling?" I said, "Terrible. I'm a wreck!" He said, "Is it helping you to talk to all these people?" And I said, "No." "Then why are you doing it?" And I said, "Well, I don't know." He said, "Well, I just wondered. Well, when she comes home"—he was the first person that used the word "when"—" don't you think you'd want to be as rested and as calm as possible, to kind of be your best when you see her?" Well, that had never crossed my mind. I said, "Well, yeah." And he said, "Well, I think you should really take care of yourself, because if you can take care of yourself, then you'll have more resources available to you when your daughter comes home, and you can know what to do." And then he said, "Just page me and whenever she comes home, I'll see her. Don't worry about it. I'll be happy to do that." Well, when I got off the phone I was so relieved. It was like somebody had just poured some soothing balm on the turmoil of my life. And I went to bed and slept like a baby. And in the middle of that night I got a call from a friend who Sarah [her daughter] had called, and she was coming home.

Then of course I had this moment of panic. I called Bill the next morning and said, "She's coming, but I don't know what to do! What am I supposed to say?" I started going into trying to think ahead, and there was this long pause, and in one of those beautiful moments, he said, "You know, Judy, you're her mother, so just love her, and you'll know what to say." And that had never occurred to me either. And I remember when she walked in the door, and she was all wrung out and tired, and she'd been through a big ordeal too, and, you know, it was embarrassing for her. It's embarrassing to be fifteen and have to come home after you thought you were going to strike out and go on your own in life. And she started screaming at me, and all this stuff, and I remember looking at her, and I saw her in her crib. I saw—you know how babies start crying and they turn all blue and their little legs and arms are going. I could see that—I just saw her as this innocent little baby doing the best she could, trying to express her grief and sorrow. And I looked at her, and all I could think to say was, "Sarah, I'm really sorry. I'm so sorry it's come to this, and I'm so glad you're home." And she heard me, and she looked at me, and she went, "Mom? Is that you?" "Yeah, it is."

And she did see Bill. Of course I still had thoughts about this guy in Connecticut thinking she should be hospitalized and everything. After she'd been with Bill for about an hour and a half, he comes out to the waiting room and brings me back and says, "You know, she's really fine. Sarah's got a great sense of humor. She's a wonderful kid. She just got caught up in some thoughts that she didn't understand and she didn't know where they were coming from, and she's fine now. You can go home." And I said, "Well, what about the mental hospital?" And I remember he sat there and he looked at me, and he said, "Judy, I'm not going to hospitalize her. She can go home. If you want her hospitalized, you'll have to take her back to Connecticut to the other doctor. She's in my care. I'm telling you, she's fine. Take her home." And I said, "But, but, is she going to be on medication?" He said, "No." And I said, "Well, does she have to see you again?" And he said, "It's up to her." "What?" And he said, "It's entirely up to her. I think she understands what went wrong. I think she's fine, and if she'd like to learn more about it, then I think that's her decision." So Sarah looks up and says, "Yeah, I'd like to see you again. I'm interested in this, curious. I'd be happy to learn more." He said, "Fine. Then we'll make a couple more appointments." He saw her a couple times, and then she started going to the same group that I was going to, just out of interest. But we walked out the door and resumed life, and it's been beautiful ever since. It's the last bad experience I ever had as a mother. Just amazing! And after that happened, Jack, I really was committed beyond belief.

I remember shortly after that, one day I went to lunch with Bill, and I said, "You know, I want you to really tell me, how did you find this? And how did you get over being a psychiatrist in the old school? And who are you? Where is this coming from?" And I remember we had this, maybe, three-hour lunch, and I looked at him, and I saw the soul of all of us. It wasn't a personal thing. I just saw what pure love was, and what faith in people really looked like. And it was the turning point—that was it for me. I went on a whole new path in life, and I committed myself to getting as much understanding as I could get for myself, and helping share it with other people. So that was how I got involved.

JP: What a great story that is!

JS: So as a result of that—and again, it isn't personal—I mean, of course, it's about Bill Pettit because he's the person—but *what I saw in him was the power of the impersonal, the beauty of love unconditionally given, without regard to the person's circumstances, and what this understanding could really mean for the well-being of all people.*

LIFE AFTER

JP. So how did you get to La Conner [Washington]?

JS: Well, Sarah went to college, and I was alone. At that time I was divorced and I had this house, and I wanted to sell my business because I wanted to do this work. I had started doing this with my clients, who liked it, but it wasn't what the company was set up to do and it wasn't what the other people in my company wanted to do. So I ended up selling the company. I was going to go to California for no special reason except, why not? I had met George and Linda [Pransky] through Bill, and they used to have conferences in Florida fairly often. And George called me up one day and said, "Have you ever considered maybe coming out to La Conner? And I said, "No, not really." And he said, "Well, you could if you wanted to." So I did, and that worked out real well for a while.

JP: So, along the way, did you see yourself evolving in the understanding?

JS: It's so much easier to see it in retrospect. It's easier for me to see it in terms of what life looked like to me in 1990, 1991, 1992. When it's happening, it's so natural, you know? You notice it in either what other people say to you, or you find yourself doing things differently. Like the first thing I noticed is that I wasn't reacting to my clients' bad moods any more. I wouldn't do anything with anybody who was all upset and weird. I would look to get to a calmer state, and all of a sudden, it got very easy, because people function better when they're not upset, and so we weren't making so many mistakes and making fools of ourselves. I mean, I could go back to a month ago and say, "Gee, you know, I've seen things and learned things since then," as I think we all do. But at the time it's happening it's so subtle because when you see something different you just see it, and then you're looking out your eyeballs and it doesn't look like it just did. [laughs]

ORGANIZATIONAL CHANGE FROM THE INSIDE-OUT

JP: How did it start here, at West Virginia University?

JS: I met the dean, Bob D'Allesandri, when he was a participant in a Health Care Forum physician leadership group. Although my part in it was fairly brief I was very struck by the depth of his interest, as opposed to everybody else in the room. There were nine physician leaders, and the other eight were filled with intellectual questions, like, "How does this work? How does that work?"-type questions, and he wasn't. He was reflecting. He didn't say very much, and when he did say something, it was different. George [Pransky] and I were just one event within this whole Forum. George did the beginning, and then I did the last part of it, because our schedules didn't work out. So D'Allesandri said that he was going to follow up with this. At that time I was working all over the country doing a lot of public speaking to a lot of health care people, and they give you a card and you never hear from them again. But in this case, he did. He called. He started looking to find ways to get his leadership group exposed. At that time the only way he could really do it was to send them out to workshops, which he did.

JP: This was the leadership group here [at WVU]?

JS: Yes. And Bob came with every group that came out [to LaConner, Washington, Pransky's base of operations]. Then he was trying to find a way to do things on campus, because you can only afford to send so many people across country so often. And Bob would say, "Why don't you join us for dinner?" So I frequently had dinner with the groups, and towards the end of that time one night, Bob said, "I'd love you to think about coming to West Virginia for a visit." I had never been to West Virginia. So I said, "Sure." And I came out, and we talked, and I was here for, like, five days, and at the end of that time he said, "What would it take to get you to move here?" By that time, I'd so fallen in love with this place and him and the people here, that I said, "Just send a truck, and I'll be here."

JP: How much exposure to training in The Three Principles had he had at the time?

JS: Well, maybe four or five workshops of two or three days each, and then whatever else he'd pursued, I don't even know—like reading Syd's books or listening to tapes. But to me, as I reflect back on it, Bob was a person who naturally was drawn to the common sense of bringing out the best in people, and this institution was—before I ever got here—committed to service and love and very respectful interaction with people. So it wasn't, like, shocking that he would be so interested. And when I came here the thing that really got to me was—I went to the new faculty orientation, and he had put me on the program at three different spots so I couldn't leave. I had to stay and listen to everybody else. And I was so moved by the sincerity and the genuineness and the simplicity and the caring of every person that got up to speak—whatever aspect of the university they represented—and I thought, "This place is very lovely. This is not what I thought an academic institution was going to be." So I fell in love with it—I really did—and the people that I met. So then I moved here, without any real understanding what my job was going to be.

JP: So there was no official position that you were coming into?

JS: Not really.

JP: Did he guarantee you a salary?

JS: Yeah. It was a salary of a part-time adjunct assistant professor, which I did get an appointment to be. You have to have a faculty appointment to work here, but an adjunct assistant professor might or might not ever teach, and the suggestion of that position is that you will find a way, if you're responsible, to integrate your service into your department and offer something. So the first thing I did is design this course called "The Resilient Health Professional," which I've only taught once, actually, because then after that they needed somebody to teach the management class, and I was kind of a natural fit because I'd been a management consultant my whole life before I got involved in this and had been the CEO of my own company and obviously knew something about health care. But I didn't even have an office for the first six months. I worked from home or my car or just met in other people's offices. And Bob said, "What I want you to do is spend time with people and see where you can be of service, and if you feel there is something you can offer, then it'll work out." He said, "I trust you to create what needs to be created here to bring this into the culture." Then he set up a certain number of things that he wanted me to do for the leadership group, so I did leadership training. But really, when I think back on that time it was very magical because it's the only time in my life I've ever been in a position where I didn't have to do anything, but I could do anything! So it was totally open.

JP: What year was that?

JS: 1998. And I didn't see that much of Bob, either. I mean, it's like he really just said, "Be who you are and this will work out."

JP: Did he say why he wanted you there?

JS: No, he didn't. I mean, I would never, in a million years—Jack, I have to tell you that when this thing [The Sydney Banks Institute of Innate Health] opened last September, it was as unbelievable to me as it was to everybody else. [laughs] I mean, I couldn't have imagined when I came here that it would come to that. I mean, what I wanted to do was just see how helpful I could be, and because I was still part-time I was still doing other consulting and traveling, and I just created my own life here in a sense. And then I started giving up a lot of my old stuff, and I went through this period of time where I thought, "Financially this isn't such a wise thing." And then I thought, "It will work out," and I stopped thinking about it. And it worked out.

JP: Did you ever have a grand design in your mind about what you would like to see happen?

JS: No, I didn't. What inspired me when I came here was two things: Within the Health Sciences Center I wanted to talk to people about what was underneath their natural goodness and their instinct for service, and underpin this so that it could get communicated to students more effectively. This was a traditional medical school with all the problems of a traditional medical school, in terms of the pressures students are under and the stress they experience. Yet the people here had this desire for things to be different. What I realized was that a lot of people walk around in service to others and in a beautiful, loving state, but it's easily lost and not easily transmitted if they don't have the understanding of the Principles underneath it. So when they lose it, it looks like it was a dream, and then when they get it back, they don't know how it happened and they don't know how to talk about it. So what I saw was kind of a fragile state, uninformed by knowledge. So within the Health Sciences Center I saw the value of the Principles in that regard.

Within the state of West Virginia I saw wonderful people with huge resiliency. This is a very difficult place for people to have a life. I mean, the infrastructure isn't very strong. People live in these rural, remote areas that are almost inaccessible in the winter. People have to get by with very little. There's a lot of poverty. It's just a very poor state. But the people are so nice, and they're so wonderful, yet they have this thinking of resignation and poverty. It's like, "Well, this is West Virginia." They have this kind of overlay of thought that, continually, is like a big, thick coat of dust on their resiliency. If they would just dust it, it would shine, and then it would be something. So the two things that struck me is that this medical school and this Health Sciences Center had all of the goodness and the capacity to bring this beauty out in the people of West Virginia and had everything going for it. And given the knowledge of how to awaken people's Health, this could be a model for what could happen in a whole state. I saw that. So that's what inspired me, but I had no idea how that was all going to work. I just was inspired by that idea.

JP: You know what's interesting to me? In a sense that was your grand design. You wanted people to feel that, to see the underpinnings—

JS: Yeah, and then share it—bring it out in other people.

JP: What didn't matter was *how* it happened, but if you didn't *see* that as your grand design—

JS: It's probably true. And also I had come to a point in my own understanding where I had faith that if you just trust, if you keep yourself in a good state, if you stay rested, stay connected to people and you care, and you stay in love with life, that things will work out however—who knows how? So I just kind of came in every day and hung out with people. But one thing I discovered was that before I got here people had made a big deal about George [Pransky]. They made him into something. And it occurred to me that they may have lost sight of the fact that the idea was that *everybody has Health.* They were thinking, "You have to keep going back to the source, to the well, for the clear water." So my first job when I got here was to put an end to that, and not let that happen to me. So I was really glad I didn't have an office. I just came and went. And if I formed a group for a task and we finished the task, I would disband the group. People would say, "Well, let's continue to meet," and I said, "No, you make up your own group." And it was a tremendous learning experience for me. People do that with Syd sometimes; people do that with Roger. It isn't because these guys are trying to make it happen. But I wanted to be invisible. I didn't want to be "a thing." Even now my office is way far from community medicine, way at the other end of the building. And I would go to faculty meetings, but nobody really knew where I went back to when I left. And I just wanted to listen and learn and share and let people blossom and wonder—I mean, the happiest day of my life would be if they just couldn't imagine how this wonderful thing happened to them, and it would never even occur to them that they might have been to something I did three weeks ago. I really saw that that was important.

JP: So was that what you meant when you said you wanted to "put an end to that?"

JS: Yeah. For one thing I never referred to this as Psychology of Mind. If people brought it up I would, but I just referred to the three Principles. They'd say, "What do you call this?" I'd say, "Well, you don't need a name for it. It's whatever you see. Call it whatever you want to call it for whatever program." And people would name different programs different things that are relevant to the audience, which makes sense to me. I didn't want it to be "a thing," and I didn't want it connected to be "a thing-maker." People would ask me, "Do you think we should organize another trip to LaConner?" I'd say, "Well, there's an awful lot of people here that have their own understanding, why don't you just let people's Health do the work and see what we can do." I never discouraged people—if they wanted to go, they went, fine—but I was always trying to point it back to the person and their own Health, and not let them attribute it to anything else.

JP: At what point did you see that having "a thing" wasn't a good idea?

JS: Originally, I along with everyone else thought the way we were putting it out was a good idea, and I was behind it, and I was trying to help. And then I realized that this conceptual framework [the concepts] and all this intellectualization, people couldn't grasp it. And we're trying to say this is simple, it's in everybody. And people are asking, "Tell me again about the levels. Which levels?" And I'm going, "Something is wrong here." I just kind of got up one morning and I couldn't do it anymore. I didn't want to do that. I wanted to work with something much simpler, just talk about the Principles and just let people find their own voice, and that there wasn't a "right way."

JP: I remember at one point you said it occurred to you that you didn't have to look to somebody else to interpret what Syd Banks was saying. Would you describe that?

JS: Well, at one point I saw that there were people that thought Roger had the answer, and other people thought George had the answer, and I'm, like, "This is crazy!" And that was when it all fell into place for me. I'm thinking, "This is not right. We're all the same here, and we're just trying to do nice things for other people." I just didn't want any part of it. So I just started doing my own thing as a consultant, and I was doing pretty well, so when the offer came to move to West Virginia I was pretty ripe to go. But I realized that when this gets to be about people instead of about *all people*, then it's gone wrong.

JP: Somewhere along the line as this was evolving at WVU, it looked like you wanted to remove all "forms" that this understanding was put out as.

JS: Yeah, I did.

JP: And in a sense, I've always gotten the feeling that if you were going to start something here, it was going to start fresh. Can you say something about what made you come to that?

JS: Well, my biggest concern was that I didn't want to make "a thing." Well it has to be *something* in order to *be*, you know? You can't fund air. So it's still very unclear in my mind in a way. The biggest criticism I get when I'm out trying to help people to see how they could support it is, they say, "I'd love to support you, but I don't exactly know what to tell them they're supporting." Because I don't necessarily know what we're going to do exactly, but I do know what this does. I've seen it with my own eyes, and I've seen it for myself in doing it myself. That is, this understanding—when it's the foundation for education—creates a learning environment instead of a teaching environment. And whatever we do here we infuse a critical mass of people with this reverence for insight learning; for what it means to really *see* something as opposed to just memorize something; for what it means to be a partner in discovery with students rather than being the expert, filling their little heads. And there is no attachment to any particular system of learning implicit in all of that. There are so many dimensions to that experience; that's what we should be doing, creating something deeper than the subject, you know? This is why I love teaching management. They're graduating with competencies in management, but I'm not just teaching management. I'm teaching management in a way that's never been taught before, because no one has thought the students can discover what's good management without reading *The Seven Habits of Highly Effective People* and memorizing it. You know what I'm saying? And the same thing is true if I were teaching genetics or anatomy or biochemistry or whatever—as people begin to understand the mind at a deeper level, their level of respect for learning and the way they see the learning changes. And when that changes it creates a different kind of culture. So that's not a form. That's deeper than a form. So I'm interested in developing for the people who work with us here what Bob did for me—go out and see how you can serve, from what you know to be true about life and the Principles.

Then I wanted to draw influential thinkers to us, because I think the advantage of having a platform, of being part of a university, is that if you hold a conference, people come. It's like it legitimizes things, because when a university is behind something, people assume it has a little more credibility. And we can offer continuing education credits, and these are valuable. I'm not interested in structure, but I don't make fun of the structure I'm in, because that structure is what's provided the vehicle for me to propel this understanding to a new level of respectability.

JP: What made you and Bob [D'Allesandri] get to a point where you saw that this could permeate the institution?

JS: After the first several months that I was here I sat down with Bob, and we had this really nice conversation. He said, "I think this is working out. I think you've sort of become a part of the fabric of our life here." And I did everything I could to bring as many people as I could here—through the Aequanimitas Foundation faculty or whatever—so in the first year that I was here, I brought fifty-two people here over the course of that year, including you, Roger, Kristen, Gloria Newton, Joe and Doris Boyle, the people from California, all kinds of people. Jim Marshall did a wonderful program for the kids. Any way that I could find a way to get people here, I would do that. I wanted people here to get the idea that this was just a regular, ordinary practice that many different people, with different personalities and different constituencies—coming from the same place—were putting out. And that really worked out, because people here were touched by their interactions with all these people. It wasn't just me, and it wasn't some special thing, and it wasn't like there's only one place you can get it, or one person. And I would show that "Applications" video [(2000)] any place I could. This is *before the form*, but work is still conducted *through* the form.

I have so much respect for how beautifully people do the thing they really know how to do well when they do it with a different spirit. And I should have known that from the beginning, because that's exactly what happened to me. It never dawned on me until years later, that I got sucked into this idea that if you had this understanding then that was the be-all and the end-all, and it really isn't. It's the beginning.

JP: Back to this meeting with Bob, how it started to become a vision for the medical school—

JS: Yeah, see, I don't know whether Bob may have had this vision. He might have had a thought about what he wanted to see happen, but he never said anything to me about it. At this particular meeting, Bob said, "What are you going to do with this?" He said, "You know, you're doing great. People really are responding, and a lot of people have been very grateful. You've done a lot of public service. I really appreciate the time you've put into traveling around the state and talking to people, but what do you want to do now?" And I said, "I don't know really."

JP: This was how long after you got here?

JS: Six or seven months, less than a year. So he said, "What do you think would make sense?" I said, "Well, I don't know. I guess it would make sense if it had a sort of a core visibility, but I don't really want a place, I don't want a building—just sort of a focal point. That would make sense." He said, "Well, why don't you think about that?" So what I started thinking about was the number of people over the years who I have met who said, "If there were ever an academic institution that we could provide money to in the future and we knew it was established, we would support it." I thought about all those people, and I thought, "Well, we could set up an endowment that would provide for Syd to be a lecturer, and to provide for a certain identity without too much form attached to it, and we'd provide for the future because if we have an endowment we could endow faculty positions where people would feel secure in undertaking longitudinal research." What occurred to me is that, besides teaching, we needed really good research. So I went back to Bob, and I said, "You know, I honestly believe that we could endow an institute, because I think there are people around the country—I know they're not in West Virginia—that would get behind it, if we do it responsibly, and if we do it without making it a big deal." So he said, "Well, do you want to explore that?" and I said, "Yeah, I think I do."

We had started that research project with the Aequanimitas Foundation, and I knew that people were dying for the results. They're still dying for the results, but we're working on it. But that was part of the reason you need to raise money, so you can process information and get things done. And I saw this big vision for research—I mean, that's really what struck me—that we could become a national data bank. We could give individual practitioners who want to research things that they're doing but who don't know how to set it up and get it published—I just saw a function for an institution to be a service to thousands of people around the country. Bob said, 'Well, if you can raise the money, if you believe in it and you think it's going to work out, let's see what happens."

So I wrote a little statement that became our original document that we sent out to people—and people responded! And the beautiful thing was that when people responded, everybody who gave money initially to start this—without necessarily communicating with each other—did not want to have it named after them. They all said, "We should really just call it what it is: The

Sydney Banks Institute, because that's what we're doing here. So that's what happened. And in terms of the initial sufficient endowment to start, it happened within six months. So it was ready to happen. And then the more I talked to people about it, the more certain this vision became—that it should be education, research, clinical and service, which are the four missions of the medical school; that research should be the defining initial impetus because it will empower everything else. People care about results, and so many people for so many years have seen results but not documented them. And I wanted it to be something really beautiful.

JP: At what point did you talk to Syd about this?

JS: Right when I started to see that, and Bob talked to him too, and then some our donors talked to him. And Syd was delighted. You have to ask him, of course, but for Syd, since I've known him at least, and I think before that, he's always said, "Someday when the time is right, this is going to be picked up by an academic institution, and it will change the world." And so I guess he just decided, "Okay, this must be it; it's happening now." So Syd has had not a very proactive role but a very helpful role in all of this. He's come in contact with a lot of people here, and they really respect him. But I think he doesn't have a big-deal feeling about it. It's like, "Well, now it's time for this, and we'll just see where it goes from here."

JP: So how would you characterize what his role is, in terms of the Sydney Banks Institute for Innate Health?

JS: He's a resource and a teacher.

JP: Did he have any problems with his name being on it?

JS: No. He could have had problems with his name being on it, but it was focused more on the fact of him being a vehicle for the Principles, not anything special about him, so I think he thought it was okay. I mean, he's read our charter and our statement of purpose and all that very closely. Again, you should ask him directly, but I think he felt that it was done in a right spirit, just to be thankful to Syd as the person who articulated something that we are able to use, to take to go way beyond the initial articulation.

JP: So did you ever see what was happening here being a consolidating point for everything happening with this understanding?

JS: No. No. As a matter of fact I think that would be the kiss of death, actually. I think it would be very wrong. I saw it as being, hopefully, the wind beneath the wings of everything that was happening. And I'd like to see it that way, not as a consolidating point but as an uplifting force. Because if I were thinking about going into this field, if I were a young person now, it would be comforting to me to think that academic institutions are taking an interest in this, and that there's going to be a program, and that it will get legitimized, and that research is quoted and published in journals by people who do research and have published before on other subjects. I mean, it would give me the faith to know that it wasn't just some kind of an off-beat thing. And if there's anything I hope that we come to mean to people, it's faith that if it could happen here it could happen anywhere, and it should and can and will. And that the understanding is more powerful than our insecurity about it, you know? And so if it's an inspiration to people, that would be wonderful. As a matter of fact, I would do everything to avoid consolidation here of everything happening, because I think that would be a disservice to the creativity and imagination of so many people that are doing it their own way in different settings, and to the possibility that other institutions will find a whole other way to do this. It could be anywhere.

JP: That raises a really great question. What would you say are the critical elements that would make something like this be able to take hold in other places?

JS: I think faith that the institution will have the wisdom to see how to do it, and see how to work together with others. Faith in not caring about the form but caring about the feeling—deeper than the form. So the first critical element is to know that, no matter what institution you're in or where you are or how dysfunctional it may seem, people want a higher level of functioning. People want stability. People want calm. People want peace of mind. And that the power of Health is phenomenal, and if they get a glimpse of it they'll find their way to it. And you don't have to do anything, except the glimpse. I think to a certain extent you need persistence. Just the ordinary, everyday little things speak more loudly than big things, like showing up where you said you were going to be, and not playing the political games, and apologizing if you're insecure and get off-base with people, and saying, "I'm sorry. I got insecure. It happens, we all get insecure sometimes," and being just a regular person, and living at peace within oneself. I think ultimately, in a big institution, you have to have the commitment of leadership. If Bob didn't want this to happen it wouldn't happen. So if there is one significant person, he is. There is always somebody that can say no, and if that person doesn't want to say yes, it doesn't make any difference how many other people want it.

JP: I heard a couple of other things, too, when you were describing how it all happened. One of them was, at the beginning you just hung out.

JS: Yeah. It was just kind of perseverance.

JP: And you listened, because you wouldn't have known what direction to go in if you hadn't.

JS: Yes. And of course I had to listen because I had never been in an academic institution before as a player—I mean I'd been a student, but that's a difference experience—so I was pretty humbled by ignorance. [laughs] So it was like, when you know you don't know, you just have to "not know" until you see something. And I had a good excuse for not knowing because I really didn't. And honestly, Jack, the other thing I realized is, in an academic institution people love to teach you. I was never thwarted from learning how things worked or from getting the help I needed, or from meeting the person I needed to meet, or from having somebody say, "Here, let me show you what you have to do to get from A to B here." If you asked me, "What's the Sydney Banks Institute going to be doing next year?" I've got a five-year plan, because you have to have a five-year plan, but I wouldn't be sure that I have any idea what we'll be doing next year. I do know that, whatever it is, we're not going to be doing it alone. We're going to be doing it as a part of something greater than we are—the Institute itself—and we're going to be doing it with a shared vision for the well-being of students and people.

JP: Can you recall some real stellar moments, things that have happened here that were really special, like when you saw a spark in people? You have stories?

JS: There are so many of them. One of the first things I did, even before I came here, was that I was invited by Hilda Heddy, who is the head of the Rural Health Education Partnership Program for the State of West Virginia—she works with all the health sciences schools. They have eleven sites around West Virginia where they bring the students to rural areas to work with the rural population and work with rural doctors and learn about rural health. They have site coordinators in each of these sites, and I did a strategic vision retreat with the site coordinators. Hilda and I had talked, but it was one of my very first trips to West Virginia and nobody really knew too much about it [the

Principles]. We got to this cabin out in this wilderness area with these site coordinators who tended to be young, driven, enthusiastic people with a kind of a Peace Corps mentality—in a good sense, that real dedication, and by God, we're going to get out there and help these people and do good things for these poor people. And I remember at that first meeting I started to talk to them about disempowerment versus empowerment. They were so mad at me—

JP: What did you say?

JS: The point was, if you really don't try to do too much *for* people except help them to see how much they can find within themselves, it works out better. But these were crusaders, you know? Their vision was to get out there and get things done for people. So when I started talking with them about it, "Find it in yourself first, and then you can see it in other people, and when you see it in other people, wake it up—and you have to accept the fact that they may know something you don't, and they might have a way of doing it that's better for them than what your best idea is"—well, it completely undercut their whole idea. They'd had a retreat previously where they tried to refine their mission or their vision or whatever, and they had gone through this rather arduous two-day process with a consultant who led them through all these values-clarification exercises. So when I first started talking and saw how angry they were getting, I thought, "Well, they're going to have to experience it. I've got to stop talking about it, and we've just got to live it. They've got to see it happen here." So I said, "Look, I don't want to philosophize anymore. I gave you a little glimpse of just one way to look at working with people, but let's just get down to the task at hand here. We've got something to do." I just saw in that moment—I saw them as deeper than their ideas. I saw that I had to *be* what I was describing. I just stopped *telling* them how to be better at what they did and *let them see* how to be better at what they did. I took a big dose of my own medicine there, and it was a transforming moment for me because I saw the difference between teaching what I knew myself and *bringing it alive*. And we did. In an hour, something happened, and all of a sudden these people were just coming up with these incredible ideas—all of which had to do with releasing other people, setting them free to do more stuff. I mean, the stuff they were coming up with from their own wisdom without realizing it was what I had been describing that they were fighting when we were talking about it in the abstract. And so that was a defining moment for me, because it was a big, humbling learning experience for me. It's just to stop trying to tell people about it and live as though it were true [laughs]. So in a matter of a few hours they had their mission statement, and it was very different from the previous mission. And they were totally baffled and enthralled. And some of these people are now teaching our Stress Cure classes and everything. They have stayed with it. That Rural Health program has really taken on this understanding in a big way. So that was a defining moment.

And then another one was, I really was very anxious to get Bill Pettit here and involved, because I felt that, for doctors, it would be very comforting to meet another doctor. I think I'd been here about a year, and he was able to come, and we did a two-day leadership meeting on values—because I have this philosophical sort of logic that I follow when I work with leadership groups, which is, you start with values. They really have to have an understanding of what's important, what really matters, and that leads to vision: Given what really matters, then what's possible? And then vision leads to mission: Given what's possible, what are we going to do? And mission leads to strategy, which is the final step—which is where most people begin, but it should be the last thing and it should be obvious: Given what we're going to do, how are we going to do it? So we were at the values step in my program, "Bringing Leadership from Within" that I've done with corporations all over the country. This is with the chairs of the various departments of the medical school. The first day they were very grumpy, saying things like, "This is insubstantial!" "Why aren't we talking about strategy?" "We need to accomplish something, where's the agenda?" And Bill has such a deep faith, and we've worked together for a long time, and we just battled it out with them and hung in there. And we had dinner that night, and I remember it just being really pleasant, and then they all went home and came back the next morning. And Bill said to me that morning before they came, "You know, this group is going to be different today. I can feel it." I said, "God, I hope so because yesterday they just didn't want to see their own beauty—how beautiful it could be to really talk about what really matters first."

And they came back, and one of them said, "You know, I think that one of our values should be 'love.'" Now you've got to remember who we're talking to here. So we write "love" on the flip chart, and we talk about love for about an hour. We talked about what it really is, what's unconditional, what it means to express the love you have for people, how love is related to healing, what it would mean in a medical school for people not to be afraid to put that down on a piece of paper as a value—which now it is on our list of values as the first one! And it was such a beautiful discussion, and people were so touched. I mean, people were almost moved to tears, as they were saying things that really, really mattered to them. It really happened, and Bill and I were just there. We were there, but we didn't have to do much, and one of the Chairs, as we were getting ready to break for lunch, said, "You know, this is truth. This is the truth. We're talking truth here. This is wonderful." It was amazing! It was a beautiful thing. I'll never forget that as long as I live. And it's really sweet because we talk about it now, when student admissions people talk to students, they talk about our values, and they talk about love. Other deans from other medical schools are astonished, like, "How did you ever get a group of Chairs to use that word?" In honesty, it's true for everyone. And people start to feel that. And it has changed things here. They do remember that we love our students, and we love each other—not every minute, but a lot. So that was a big deal.

JP: That's beautiful. What about changes within individuals?

JS: Well, a really beautiful thing was that some of the people at student services got the idea that maybe it'd be nice for me to talk to some of the students that are experiencing stress and distress and struggling, rather than them either gutting it out without any assistance whatsoever, or making a big deal of it and ending up on Prozac or something like that. So students get sent to me—and I could tell you a lot of different students' stories, but one that stands out for me is a student who was really in danger of crashing and burning in the second year of medical school. This person was completely floored by the amount you had to learn, how fast you had to learn it, how many tests there were, how competitive it was. And what happened to the person, at one point, was to get sent to a psychiatrist, who then got them involved in a rather intense therapeutic process which involved medication, which made it very difficult to study. So the problem was exacerbating out of control, and the person was warned that they might not make it. So somebody had the idea, maybe the person should talk to me. The thing that had crossed my mind when I first talked to this person is, "It's amazing to me that you've made it through the end of the year, given all that's been going on. Don't you think that says something about the human spirit, and why didn't you quit?" And the person looked at me and said, "I don't know." I said, "Well, I'd look there. I would want to look there and ask myself, given that I was miserable, that I was depressed, that I was hardly able to study, that I was starting to fail, that I'd been seeing a psychiatrist, that I had persuaded myself that I'm a damaged human being inadequate to this task, that I'm on medication—I'm still in school. What the hell's going on there?" And I remember this person's little eyes just lit up, and the person looked at me and said, "That's what I want. I want to be a doctor." I said, "Well, why don't you just forget about the rest of this shit, then, and just be a doctor? The only way to get to be a doctor is to get through medical school." And the person said, "I know, but it's so hard to get through medical school." And I said, "Now, look around you. This building is crawling with doctors. They all went to medical school. What makes them so great that you couldn't be like any of them?" And the person looked at me and went, "Yeah." So I said, "What's really in your way? What do you think the problem is?" And I remember, there was this moment in time, and then this person just brightened up and said, "I guess the problem is that I just think about failure all the time, instead of thinking about just getting it done." And I said, "Hey, makes sense to me!" And within a few months the person was in good standing, had gotten through the crisis, had gotten off medication, still comes to see me occasionally mostly to celebrate good news—but it was one of those moments where you see raw Health, and how hard it is to kill it. I mean, you could look at a person like that—God, it would be so easy to just walk away from it, so easy to go shoot yourself, so easy to just go drink, you know? It would be so easy, but that love of people and desire to be their dream was so strong! And that Health in them was so strong, that despite all that shit happening, this person was still in school, still trying to see how to do it, and when the door opened, man, they went right through it! And I could tell you lots of stories like that.

JP: That's great! I just have two more questions. Aside from the Institute, how would you say that this has permeated the way the WVU medical school does its business?

JS: Well, slowly, in ways that's like water seeping through thick sand. There's still a lot of dry sand out there, but there's plenty of water, too. But I think because people—myself included—whose spirits have been touched serve on committees, go to meetings, lecture in classes, they're different. Jack, you know, every interaction is either a healing interaction or it isn't. So if I was a person who had kind of a dim view of students and didn't have a lot of faith in the learning process, and then I changed my mind and I started to see the thirst for understanding things for themselves and the different ways they find to express that, and I started to look at the learning experience differently, then I have a different kind of class. And if I have a different kind of class, maybe some of the students who might have been discouraged or disheartened in the other class come to life and stay with it. Just little, small things. It doesn't take very much.

JP: What percentage of the faculty has actually been trained in this understanding?

JS: Well, it hasn't been anything that I would call training, because a lot of what I've done is facilitated meetings, but in facilitating meetings I'm cognizant of making the point about why something is working. So I've facilitated a tremendous number of meetings in many different departments. I've since done public talks here, which have been attended by all kinds of faculty, but I have no idea what they took away from it. Thousands of Syd's books have ended up in people's hands, because we buy them and give them away. But there's never been something that I would call "a training." I have a problem with "trainer of trainers" and this kind of stuff; I have a problem with anything that looks like hierarchy. So I look at every opportunity I have to talk to people as an opportunity to touch their spirit in some way, and if it works out that's great.

JP: But it has permeated the philosophy of the way the school does business—

JS: Yeah, I think so. In the values and in the vision and mission, and in the way the Chairs interact with each other. I've lectured and I've facilitated some big committee things here that have to do with the educational process and our educational values and how we deal with students. But it's kind of opportunistic rather than strategic.

JP: Have any other universities or medical schools become interested?

JS: Yes and no. Bob D'Allesandri has been the dean here for more than eleven years. He's got a longer tenure as a dean of a medical school than most other deans in the country. So he's very highly respected among his peers. I believe that he has intrigued others. I think others are watching to see. Bob said, "You know, you've got to remember that we're in this for the long haul. We're not in this for a short term, and you can't push. You just want to keep working and doing the next thing." So people have visited. There's curiosity, but I don't think anyone's ever stepped up to take the obvious next step—yet—but they will.

JP: Is there anything else that you want to convey that I haven't asked?

JS: Well, I could say a few words about prevention, because one of the wonderful reasons that I feel lucky to be here is because the department that I happen to be in, the Department of Community Medicine, is focused on health education and prevention, and I think that we've been operating at the symptom end for the last several years. Most practitioners in this work have not been health educators, not been prevention people, but have been therapists, counselors, social workers—people who work with addictions, treatment—people who are working with the aftereffects. So one of the beautiful things to me—and I applaud you for staying in your field and for writing a book for people in prevention—and one of the things I love about working with my students here in the Master's in Public Health program, because they're interested in social policy, health policy, prevention, education—is that it is a much better place to start the process. Anything that we can do that keeps people from suffering is much better than helping them to stop suffering, because in the meantime they've suffered. So I believe that the future of this work is in prevention. I really do! And I think that prevention education and bringing this understanding alive in people before they have difficulties, will change the world.

6. DESI GRAY WOLF LAUGHING ELK SHEBOBMAN

Interview with Desi Shebobman. *I had the pleasure of meeting and working with Desi at the Hualapai Reservation in Peach Springs, Arizona. At the time Desi had not been exposed to Health Realization for very long, but his understanding was one of the deepest I'd experienced. He "lives the Principles" better than most, because he sees it so spiritually. I interviewed him at the West Virginia University-sponsored conference on The Three Principles in Pittsburgh in June 2001.*

LIFE BEFORE UNDERSTANDING

JP: What were you like before you got involved in this understanding?

DS: [laughs] Oh man! That is a great question! Before I got into this understanding I was quite a lost person. I was an alcoholic. More than an alcoholic, I was a cocaine addict. More than that, I was a crack addict. I thought I was a product of my past. I am 6'1" and I eventually came down to about 115 pounds, if you can imagine that [laughs]. I have this picture that I used to bring to talks that I'd do, because people wouldn't believe it. It's the eyes. If you look at my eyes in this picture, my eyes show someone who is scared and lost and angry and filled with negative emotions and negative feelings, insecure. I was going to be going to jail for an assault charge. By the end of it I had lost my job, lost most of my friends—thought I had friends, but they weren't really my friends, they were just people I could pretend to be friends with or hang out with just so I could get more cocaine. I was very lucky and fortunate because I have an older brother who let me stay at his place, because I was living on his couch [laughs]. Do you want the reason why I felt I was like that?

JP: Yes. Absolutely.

DS: Like I said, I thought I was a product of my past. And being First Nations, my past is that I was taken away from my parents when I was two years old and placed in white foster homes until I was about six. So about four years of that, me and my brother suffered a lot of physical abuse and mental abuse, spiritual, the whole kind of deal, you know? And it didn't matter which foster home we went into—we were in several different foster homes, and in every single foster home we were abused. It was almost an everyday thing.

JP: Every day? Wow!

DS: Every day, yeah. I have certain flashes of other things as well, like being put in a crib on top of a table, and I'm two or three years old, and they are trying to potty-train me, so they want me to go to the bathroom at nighttime. Now, how the heck is a three-year-old supposed to get out of a crib that is on top of a table and get to the bathroom? So of course I'd wet the bed, and then the next day—I just remember this—they would bring in the whole family and friends, and I remember them standing around and laughing and pointing at me and saying, "Ah, this kid wets his bed, and now he's three and he should be potty-trained—

JP: That's incredible.

DS: Things like that, yeah. I always had this nightmare. I remember I would be in this kitchen, kind of, and there would be all these women, all these Native women standing around, and all of a sudden someone from behind me would take my hand and start pulling me away from them, so I would start screaming. And I remember grabbing onto one of those islands in the kitchen, and as I grabbed onto that they actually had me off the floor, so I was being lifted up by my legs, hanging onto this counter. And when I met my family, I realized that this wasn't a dream. It was a memory. Because those ladies that were standing around were my aunts, and that is when the social worker was taking us away from our parents. So that was a bit of the past. And I was pretty much living that when I drank. I would become violent. It was like continuing the cycle. I would just become very violent and very angry, or when I would smoke crack I'd become very mentally abusive, and I would say things and do things to intentionally hurt people, and steal, and the whole thing—

JP: What kind of feeling level were you living in at that time?

DS: Oh man! I had no concept of what a good feeling was. I had no idea. Even when I was adopted there was no trust, absolutely no trust. Because me and my older brother pretty much thought that every big person is out to hurt you. So you just be quiet. You don't do anything. You sit there and just shut up and don't say anything. You don't ask for anything. You just be very quiet and try to be ignored, in a sense. And that kind of feeling kept on with me—except when I'd drink, where all that memory and all those feelings and anger would come out. I was at a very low level, a low state.

JP: What kind of violence are we talking about?

DS: Oh, like beating up people, or just freaking out on friends—family, even. Just going out and smashing cars and stuff like that. Very angry. We used to do things like that.

JP: Were you involved in any Native traditions at that time?

DS: No. And the interesting part about that is, for being Native I was very ashamed. And I think that's another thing the foster homes taught me. I wasn't proud at all of who I was. In fact I was very ashamed, and I wished I wasn't Native. I wished I was a white person. And my thinking in that was that maybe my life would be different, you know?

JP: Just for the record, where were you growing up and what was the tribe?

DS: I am Anishinaabe. That is Ojibwe, from Thunder Bay, Ontario. That is where I was born and spent the first two years of my life. And from there it was all over Ontario, until I was adopted.

JP: So how did your life start turning around?

DS: That is another very beautiful question, because when I was, I think, twenty-one, a friend of mine's mom passed away from cancer, and she asked me to come over there and just be with her and kind of hang out. So I went over there. And she had invited this other friend of hers, Jen Wallace. And when we met it was so funny because it was such a quiet thing. I was so shy and insecure that I didn't really say anything, and she was kind of shy as well so she didn't really say anything. But something kind of happened there, so we started hanging out. And one day her and our friend were in the kitchen, and they were washing dishes, and I was sitting at that kitchen table, and I happened to look over at her. And she had this golden aura around her. It was beautiful! It really blew me away to see that. I had never ever seen that before. And somehow the thought came, "I have to be with this person!" For some reason I felt very compelled to be with this person. So a little while after that I asked her if she would date me, and she said, "No." [laughs] And the funny part about that is that normally when somebody would say no, being the insecure person I was, I would be, like, "Whoa, okay, I'm out of here," and never in contact again. But with her it was so much different. I felt so compelled to be with her that I asked her four different times [laughs]. She said no all four times. Finally she ended up asking me. So next what happened was her parents wanted to meet me, and that scared the heck out of me because I was really insecure—

JP: You were still addicted at this time?

DS: Well, no, actually. I was an alcoholic. I wasn't addicted to cocaine at this time. I just drank a lot. This is very interesting because after that I met her parents and at that time also I was charged with assault. I don't want to get too much into detail about the assault charge. I was kind of wrongly accused. It wasn't me, but I was there. [laughs] But, the reason why I am saying I was going to jail is because I was so insecure that, because of my past I would have just sat there in court and said, "Okay, I did it, yeah, okay."—just so I wouldn't have to talk. Because I knew that I wasn't able to defend myself in any way.

So back to meeting Jen's parents. When I met them I walked up the stairs, and I walked over, and Jen's mom was lying on the couch, and she looks up and smiles at me with this incredible smile. The way she looked at me, I was just kind of taken aback because all of a sudden I felt this feeling inside of me, like a feeling that I could remember wanting back when I was two, like this feeling of non-judgment and love and unconditional love. Right away that is what blew me away. The love in the look she gave me, whoa, just blew me away, because I am used to people seeing the outside and the fear in my eyes, so they react to that. But she didn't do that. And then her dad came home, and the same thing! We just started talking, and that was the first time—because they had this feeling it opened me up, and then I was able to instantly feel comfortable with them, which was something that I never, ever felt before as well. So I ended up really wanting to hang out with them a lot because they had this beautiful feeling, and how do I get that? Or how do I do that? And they started telling me about Sydney Banks, who they were friends with. And eventually they started telling me about Thought. And we had these amazing conversations. And I must have heard something because I got to my court case, and I stood up for myself and I was acquitted. Because really there was no evidence. There was really nothing. It was amazing. I had grown a little bit, enough to hear something, and I was able to stand up for myself in court and not be so insecure. Still, all the while I was still drinking and I was still an alcoholic, so—

JP: Before you go there, what year are we talking about?

DS: Eight years ago, so 1992 or 1993.

JP: And where were you at this point?

DS: I was in Richmond, which is a suburb of Vancouver, in British Columbia, in Canada.

JP: So how did you kick cocaine?

THE INSIGHT

DS: [laughs] That is actually the thing that is going to come up next. What happened next is funny because I realized that this understanding is so much deeper than the words we're using. Even though I thought I had this understanding, and even though I caught a glimmer of something that I've always wanted, I ended up getting addicted to cocaine. I started hanging around the wrong crowd again. And Jen and me, we kind of separated in a sense. Like she was exploring herself in her world, and I kind of went off into this cocaine world. It started off with just snorting coke, and my friend—or who I thought was my friend—showed me how to make crack cocaine. And so I got into that. And, whoa, that was an interesting time. Going over to people's houses, and there's lots of women. It is a whole lifestyle, and it is a very weird sexual kind of lifestyle. Yeah, I got addicted to it, and slowly I started losing weight. I would say I was 130 pounds before I started doing cocaine. If I wasn't smoking crack then I was shooting it in my arms. So I was stuck in that for about two years or so.

JP: So that was after you met Jen?

DS: Yeah, and the funny part about that, too, is that I had also gotten in contact with my family—my biological family—and so actually I went to Thunder Bay. I went back home and I met all my relations. I met all my cousins, my aunts and uncles and stuff. But people would say, "Oh, that is why you quit." No! Because when I was down there I found people that did cocaine, and I was still shooting up cocaine when I was down there, and I was still smoking crack. Really what happened was, I came back and I was talking with my younger brother, and I was telling him about this great understanding that I had [laughs] that I knew. And I go through the whole thing about Thought and everything. And he turns around and looks at me, and he goes, "You know, Des, that sounds really great, but when are you going to start living that?" And I said, "Whoa! Holy, man, he's right!" And that is when I learned that it is more than the words. You can talk this until you are blue in the face, but if you are not living it then it is just words; it is not anything to realize or anything. You've just got this kind of spiel, and you say it, and if you are not living it and you don't understand it, then it's just like any other words out there. That, for me, was very powerful. And right after that there was a Sydney Banks conference, and I went to that one.

JP: You hadn't met him yet?

DS: No. I went to that one, and a little while after that I was still thinking about cocaine. And I remember this one day—it was a beautiful day, and it was sunny, but I didn't have this good feeling inside me. I was thinking thoughts like, "Where am I going to get my next hit?" Or "Who can I pretend to be friends with so I can get more?" And the next morning I woke up, and I remember looking outside and thinking, "It *is* a beautiful day!" And for me that phrase has so much power. Because all of a sudden I was filled up with this incredible feeling of gratefulness to be alive, to look outside and have this beautiful feeling inside me—that it hadn't left me, you know? And that was the beautiful part. It was like all the things that I had talked about, all of a sudden they kind of sunk in. But it wasn't a conscious thing. They [the Principles] just realized all of a sudden. And it was just kind of a flow of insights into my past, and into what the past is, and into what the moment is, and into feeling and into Thought, and all of a sudden that was it! I was cured! And I didn't have any withdrawal. I didn't *want* to drink. I didn't have any thoughts any more about doing crack. In fact, what I did was enroll in school, and I finished off my counseling degree. It was just a complete three-sixty to a higher level. It was amazing. It was amazing! The amazing part was, because I had these insights the feeling stayed. Because these insights helped me and they came from inside me, and I knew that they were real! How could I not believe that! You know what I mean? It was amazing.

JP: Do you remember what some of these insights were?

DS: Well, the biggest one was the past—understanding really deeply where the past is really coming from, and what the past really is. And I realized how the past was affecting me, and I was letting it. I realized that, yeah, the past is sure in my mind, and it's got these feelings and emotions with it, but then I realized what these feelings and memories were.

JP: Which is?

DS: Which is thoughts. I realized that they were just my thinking. And when I realized that, it was, "Whoa, it's not real any more! *These people aren't hurting me any more! In fact I'm hurting myself in memory of that!*" I thought, "Whoa, what the heck have I been doing all this time?" It is such a beautiful thing. I realized living in the moment. I realized what the past is, and the past isn't real. I have heard so many times before that the past makes you realize who you are, but I realized that's not true. Because if only the moment exists—is real in this reality—and only in this moment, we actually have a choice. Then I can choose how I want to feel. I can choose not to take that path, not to take those thoughts, and just let them go. Because that is all they are, is just thoughts.

I also realized innocence, I realized forgiveness, forgiving. I realized here I was living in this low level of consciousness, unaware of the fact that it was my thinking, unaware that I had a choice, and I didn't have to go there. *I had the power and the gift inside of me to create a beautiful world, to create my reality, to create how I want to experience life.* I didn't know that. So I realized innocence. I realized that those people in the past that abused me are in the same state of mind I was in when I was drinking and a crack addict. *They're in the same low level of consciousness, unaware of the fact that it is their own thinking creating it.* When I realized that, I realized compassion, I realized innocence. And when I got that feeling it just empowered me so much more. These were the big ones that really helped me. And I realized the power of Thought, and I also realized the powerlessness of thought. I realized the neutrality of Thought.

JP: What do you mean when you say that?

DS: What I mean is that thinking, or thoughts, are neutral—*until* we give them action, *until* we give them power and take those thoughts into reality and put energy into them and make those thoughts real. So, the way I saw it was, a thought could be very powerful, or it can be powerless—depending on our choice of how we want to live. A thought is neutral, but it is powerful or powerless, and that is something that I realized, too.

JP: That's like a thought about a thought, right?

DS: Yeah! [laughs] And like I said before, the phrase came to me that it *is* a beautiful day. And that was the biggie for some reason—the biggest insight that I ever had. Because when I looked outside, that is what I saw. From then on, that is how I see life now. It is a beautiful day out—

JP: No matter what the weather is.

DS: No matter what the weather is! No matter what's going on around me. I realized that our gifts, the gift that we have inside of ourselves, is the power of creation. It doesn't matter what is going around outside of us. All that matters is our inside, is how are we going to react to these things, and we have a choice in it. Whoa, yeah!

JP: What year was this insight of yours?

DS: That was probably about five years ago.

JP: So that was 1997 or something like that?

LIFE AFTER

DS: Yeah. And another thing that happened after that was I started realizing a lot about culture. I started meeting other Anishinaabe people—and again, life is set up for us to grow. It is set up for us to gain a higher level of consciousness, a higher level of awareness. There are things out there that happen to us, opportunities that come, and if we take these opportunities then they will help us because that is what they are there for. I've met a few Anishinaabe people, and they started teaching me things about the culture. It was funny because it seems to go up in levels as well. I met this other guy first and he gave me this gift of an abalone shell and an eagle feather, and that is what we use in our smudge ceremony. And that is a cleansing ceremony, a cleansing of the spirit and the mind of negative energies with medicines, and we burn the medicines and we take the smoke and wash it over ourselves and cleanse ourselves. So I learned that, and when I learned that I realized the truth behind that, and how doing that smudge ceremony actually is putting us in a quiet mind, because it is a preparation for prayer ceremony, because it is putting us in touch with The Creator, and ourselves, and opening that up into prayer. And prayer for me is just a silent mind, thinking really good thoughts about other people and wishing and hoping and praying for good things to happen for other people. And that is a quiet mind, for me.

And then from there I met this other guy who is still my teacher now, and he has been teaching me so much about the culture. And a lot of the stuff he is telling me I'm realizing is very beautiful because if you are listening for his words, for what he is teaching, then you miss it. But if you get what he is really saying underneath, you go, "Whoa," and you just grow.

I have been hearing a lot of teachings and realizing the truth in our culture, there's truth in it. This whole understanding, of prevention—of the whole thing—is in there. Our elders talk it. It's been our ancestors' teachings. It is amazing! And now I have such appreciation, and I am very proud to be Anishinaabe. I am very proud to be who I am. I am very proud to be Native. I look around and I see other Native people walking down the streets, and a lot of them have their heads down. And I remember walking around like that; maybe I was walking around in shame. Now I walk with my head up and look up, and I feel like saying, "Be proud of who you are," and just sharing that. [long pause]

JP: When you are saying that the teachings that you are learning and this understanding are connected—can you say something about the connection?

DS: Yeah. Well, I realized the connection when I started attending ceremonies. And what I realized was that when we go to our ceremonies—just like in any other culture when you go to the church or something—when we go to ceremonies we gather together and we laugh and we get a great feeling. And we share and communicate and we dance and really celebrate and just have a great time. But when we leave the ceremony, it's like we go right back to our thinking again, right back to our habitual thinking. And I realized that these ceremonies, like the smudge ceremony and the sweat lodge and the Pow Wows and all these things are reminders for us. They were given to us to remind us to keep that feeling. When we go to these ceremonies it is a reminder for us to keep that feeling going, but we have lost that, we have forgotten that, but this is what the elders have been talking about. They have such beautiful words. Really, what they say is, look for the teachings. Elders, they *know*—just like this understanding—if you get a teaching from something, that teaching is coming from inside you, and it is a hundred times more powerful than if they were to tell you. Because they can't really tell you what the teaching is. Because it comes from inside, and they knew that, so they couldn't give you a teaching but they could say look for it. Again, they can guide you with words but that's all. Because the power of the gift is inside of us. So that is something else that I realized, too, is that there are many teachings out there, and what they are saying is that there are many, many insights out there for growth.

In our culture, in the wintertime was our time of gathering together the small families and separating and going off, but every family would have a group of elders, within their grandparents, and the wintertime was our time of learning and growth and sharing the culture. It was a time of storytelling. So every night they would gather together after dinner and the elders would start telling stories. But the neat thing about it was that they would tell the same stories that they told the year before, and the same stories that they told the year before that. But the interesting part about that is that the generations, the young children who hear the story, they hear something out of it, they get something from it, maybe something very simple and small, but they get something from it. The people who heard it last year, the older ones like the teenagers, they hear it again, but they catch something else from it this time, and go, "Ohhh," and get more from the story. The adults who hear the story go, "Whoa," because they get something different from the year before too, and it's a continual growth. They get the teachings from these stories that we tell, and it is a beautiful way to pass it on without giving a teaching, yet the teaching is in there. The teaching is beyond the words, and again that's exactly like this understanding.

There is a very beautiful teaching that for me really relates with this understanding, and that is the teaching of our wingashk, what we call sweet grass. The teaching is in the braid of it, because it is a braided piece of sweet grass. It's like a long kind of grass and we braid it together, and it's a very sacred medicine. We use it in our smudge ceremonies. And the truth is in the braid, because what it is is three different strands to make one braid. So one strand represents mind, one represents spirit, and one represents body, and when these are braided together they form one, and they all become the same. And that is the same with this understanding, is Mind, Thought and Consciousness—three seemingly different elements but all the same, all talking about the same thing. So for me, that was very powerful.

JP: What do you see is the connection between The Three Principles themselves and the Native teachings? Like, Mind is comparable to—

DS: Oh, yeah. Okay. [pause] You know, I don't think that I can explain that. That is a really deep question. [laughs] For some reason it is like the Principles are working within the culture. The Principles are the basis of our culture, and we have built this culture around The Three Principles, coming from it. This was our way of describing the Truth. That is the only way I could describe that, but that is a very deep question. [laughs]

JP: So what is your inner life like now?

DS: It is beautiful. Every time I share this understanding I just grow more and more. Because every time I share it I look around and look in people's eyes, and I see the Truth inside them, and I see they are seeing the Truth inside them as well—even if it is only a glimmer. And for me, that makes it so much more a fact. So when I know that it's a fact, I grow more. And I *am* living it now. I live this good feeling, and I realize that there is no reason not to [laughs]. It's like a lot of people in this understanding say that it's okay to wait in the stillness, and the feeling or the thought will pass and they will come into a good feeling again. But for me it is like, "Well that's just a thought"—that's *all*, and that is the *only* thing that is stopping me from being in my good feeling. And I know that. I truly know now what a good feeling is. I know this sounds really simple, but it is beyond the words, it is coming from a deeper understanding, a deeper level. So when I know that, I recognize a negative thought now coming, and I go, "Whoa, I don't have to go there. I am going to stay right in my good feeling." And it is having faith in that. And that is kind of where I am at today is living that good feeling and trying to more and more live in that good feeling all the time. And for now, that is my goal, to achieve that. And it's a very realistic goal, because it truly is a Thought-created world, and it's our gift to do that. We have that power inside of us to do that. That is kind of where I am at now. My life is beautiful. People in my life are beautiful. Everybody I meet—and the elders tell us this, too—people are put in your path in life because you are to learn something from them, and they are to learn something from you. And then when you have learned that, you kind of go on. It's like I see that, and I do that. So I'm constantly growing and learning and really living this understanding and hearing a lot of Truth and getting insights and sharing it.

This understanding is true prevention. Because this client asked me this question one time. He couldn't get his head around how I quit drinking and crack in just one day. He couldn't understand that. So he goes, "Okay, okay, let's take alcohol. I don't understand how you cannot say that you are not an alcoholic anymore." Because in Alcoholics Anonymous they are constantly told that they are alcoholic, so they start believing that. He is kind of coming from that way. So he goes, "Okay, okay, what if you were to walk into a bar, order yourself a drink, now could you have that one alcohol drink and not have anymore?" And so I thought about the question, and I thought about it some more, and I realized I couldn't answer it. And I said, "I'm sorry but I can't answer your question." And he thought he had me there, right? But then I said, "And the reason is because I've never had the thought. *I've never had the thought of drinking again." And that is true prevention!* Because his question was coming from where I use to be at, and I'm at a different level now, it is impossible for me to think that way. I don't even have those thoughts any more—I can't. It is impossible. With this understanding it is true prevention because you don't even think the thoughts any more. It is amazing! [laughs].

SHARING WITH OTHERS

JP: So once you had this understanding, you started using it as a counselor?

DS: Yeah, what I did was I went back to school when I got the understanding. I realized, "I've got to make changes. I've got to make some dreams come true." So I went in and I finished off my counseling degree. I am a Family Community Counselor now. I had this understanding while I was in school. And it was an incredible experience in school, because my professors were just blown away by me. Like, at the end of the year the program coordinator—she was also one of our professors as well—she was taking the students into her office and kind of interviewing them, and giving them last minute advice before we graduated. And my turn came up and I walked into her office, and I sat down on the couch and she sat down on a chair next to me, and she looked at me and she said, "You know, I have no idea what to say to you. The stuff you've written has completely altered my thinking." She was blown away. Like, she actually asked me, she says to me, "Are you Jesus?"

JP: You're kidding, right?

DS: No. She said, "Are you Jesus?" And I said, "No!" But I said, "That's what I have been trying to say, what we're talking about is Christ Consciousness, and it's something available to you, and it's something available to everybody." So I was really lucky because I had this understanding so I survived this school experience. A lot of my classmates didn't. We had a large class of about thirty or so students, and in the end I think fifteen or sixteen graduated. Unfortunately it was because of the psychology—the traditional psychology. With a lot of Native people, it is definitely our past, our immediate past, even our ancestor's past, that we've let affect us. So without this understanding, without this shield in a sense, without this prevention, they became victims of their own thinking. And unfortunately they couldn't handle it and ended up dropping out. Or other things happened in their family or something like that.

JP: And when did you start talking with other people as a group? Was it the first time that we—

DS: Yeah, the first time—okay, I did my practicum with the Selah group, and the Selah group is in West Vancouver in British Columbia—very sweet ladies. And every last Thursday of the month we do a talk. So I would do talks every now and then with them. But the best experience I had was when you asked me to come and do that talk with you guys. I mean, that was, for me—whoa! Here I am, this counselor, and these psychologists are asking me to come and present with them! It was such a beautiful experience. I was so grateful for you guys to—[emotional pause; tears came to eyes]—it really started me. Yeah, it was our talk when you had invited me to come and share with you guys with the Hualapai in Arizona, and I was so honored to do that. Wow! [emotional pause] And for me that was my first real teaching or sharing this. And it was such a great experience working with you guys that I just realized, "I've got to do this!" This is what I've got to do! I've got to continue doing this." So that's what I am doing, and I know that this is the way to do it. This is my path.

There's a lot of things in my life that, before even, like when I was eighteen years old, I was working in this warehouse, and I was with my co-worker and we were putting stuff up on the shelf. And all of a sudden he stops, and he kind of points with his head behind me. So I turn around, and there is this girl standing behind me. And the first thing she said, she goes, "Are you Ojibwe?" This is before I knew Jen. And I said, "Yeah." And she goes, "Wow! I felt so compelled to come in here. I was just passing by, and I felt really compelled to come in here, and now that I see your face I know why. I have something to tell you." And I said, "Well, I'm kind of working right now and I've got to get stuff done." So I got her number, and I phoned her that night. And she goes, "My father is a medicine man, and in our culture it's passed down through family, that is how our medicine people keep passing it on, because it's our clan totem." That is how they work. So she was gaining the knowledge from her father, and she said, "I have this dream. And in this dream, you were in it. But your hair was braided, and you looked a little bit different. You are supposed to lead people." And then she goes, "What do you want me to do? Can you lead me?" And I was, like, "Whoa! I mean, I'm drinking all the time. I'm hardly taking care of myself. How can I lead people?" So I hung up and never talked to her again.

And when I got my name, Gray Wolf, I got it in a dream, and I went to the elder and asked him to interpret the dream for me. And what he came out with is, "It is the ancestors giving you the name Gray Wolf." And he says, "That is a very powerful name. Because gray means wise. And the wolf is a leader. So your name means 'wise leader.'" So again, my life is showing me something. All my experiences have been preparing me for this. And here I am today, and I know how to braid my hair, and I do look completely different. It is because I have this understanding. I have this great feeling inside of me. And that's what we're all after. Everybody! Everything. Psychology. Mental health. Psychiatry. Culture. Religion. Every human being is after this one thing, and this one thing is a good feeling. That's our connection, and I think that thought is the connector between everything.

JP: You know what feeling I just got?

DS: What?

JP: There is no stopping you now!

DS: [laughs] There isn't.

7. BARBARA

Interview with Barbara Glaspie*. I end this book with another miracle. We see homeless crack addicts on the street and think there is no hope. But that is only a thought! Barbara is living proof of innate health in action. As with all the people I interviewed for this book, and so many others touched by this understanding, I feel so privileged and grateful to know her. I interviewed her at the Visitacion Valley housing project in San Francisco, California in May 2001.*

LIFE BEFORE UNDERSTANDING

JP: What were you like before you got this understanding?

BG: Depressed. Drama mama. Empty. I was a little empty person. I had a really, really long, dragged-out kind of past. I was addicted to crack cocaine for many years, I had been through CPS [Child Protective Services], turned in by them because I could no longer take care of my children, and I didn't have the courage to tell someone I needed help. I had been homeless. I was homeless for three or four years. I start there because in this understanding that I know now, I heard so many times that this is already in you, and the Principles are always in action, you just know it, and that kind of thing. And I just get really tickled inside because I know that it's true. It's true because for many years most of the thoughts that I hung onto were negative thoughts. Like, "I was the most terrible parent in the world," "I was a dope fiend," "I was homeless." "I was a disgrace to the population"—let alone being an African American woman, feeling like it was expected of me to fail. And I fed into that, and that all looked real to me. So for many years that's where I lived. I lived in depression, I lived in agony, I lived in pain. And that seemed like my place—that felt comfortable for me.

And I was a drama person, I liked to fight. I liked to get drunk and challenge men. I had this thing with men because they were, I felt, like, the source of what had happened to me. They took advantage of me. I was addicted to dope and I needed your money, and so you knew, in order for me to get your money you'd want to trade for sex. I had this thing with men, and I felt like I was powerful when I drank, so I would just challenge them, you know? I was challenging them, like "You're weak. You're really a weak man for taking advantage of someone when they're in such a vulnerable state." So I had all kinds of crazy stuff going on, and all in between time, I was having children. And all of this sick and insanity type of behavior that I was in—and it all just made sense to me—I thought I was in love, so if you're in love, you have a baby, or whatever.

I look at all that and I remember one time laying down in the middle of the street, Van Ness and San Francisco or something—I really wasn't familiar with my surroundings for about four years. So I laid down in the middle of the street, and I remember saying out loud, "I want to die! Just kill me!" But something inside of me really didn't want to die. And I couldn't figure out how could I think something so sane when I was feeling so insane. And that was another time when I realized the buoyancy in all of this, and how these good feelings and all this natural ability kept trying to surface. And I kept submerging it with drugs and alcohol and my behavior that I was on.

And as we talk about the Principles always being in action, and we are the Principles in action, it's true! Because I didn't know Health Realization when, for some miraculous reason, I came out of all of this stuff. I don't even really know when. I just remember I would always have thoughts of, "Oh, what if I really could be a good mother? What if there's a possibility that I am somebody?" and naturally, unfortunately, I would always not believe that part. So I'd stay in the addiction and stay in homelessness, not even make an attempt to try to find a place to live, let alone, hey, check out where are my kids. None of that ever occurred to me.

JP: When you were homeless, where were you?

BG: I was in San Francisco. I was right here.

JP: Just walking on the streets?

BG: Yeah, I just pushed a cart, like everybody else, and I'd collect the cans and whatever I could. And I stole a lot. And to me, people who steal from their family and stuff like that, I think they're sick, but I also think there's a part of them that really doesn't want to do that. Because I felt like if I stole from a family member, then that would lessen the chances of someone killing me or really causing me some bodily harm. So my family members naturally I knew loved me—didn't like what I had become but they loved me—so I would see my family here and there, and they'd be so glad to see me because

I'd disappear for months at a time—any opportunity I got I'd steal something from them and sell it. Or I'd do whatever I could do—whatever made sense to me at the time to get the drug, I'd do it. So even though insane as that seems, it really makes sense to me now because I was still thinking of my safety. Even in all that behavior that I was doing in the stealing, I never stole from a store, I would never steal from other people's houses, I would always go take from my family. Because people will hurt you for taking their things, especially when you're taking things that are valuable to them, because I would get caught, and I would make up excuses to my family as to, you know, "If you just give me money I wouldn't have to steal from you," and all these things. So at some point, I really, really, really felt like I wanted to change.

JP: Do you remember what the circumstances were around that?

BG: Yeah. All my kids had been taken from me. At that time I had two children, and actually I got kicked out of a homeless hotel. I was living in a homeless hotel, and I began my drug activity there. I would sell drugs and smoke and do all that stuff. I couldn't keep appointments naturally because I was on drugs, so finally they stopped sending me my welfare check. And I would go down in an outrage to the welfare office and say, "*I need money to pay my rent*!" and all kinds of stuff and be truly upset with the social workers because I felt like they had taken ownership of my money that they were supposed to give for me and my kids—which I never used for the kids. So people get smart to what you're up to, so they cut me off. And they kicked me out of the homeless hotel. And with me not having somewhere to stay—naturally I shouldn't have had my kids anyway because I was totally gone on drugs—they allowed me to make a decision to where I could give my kids to my mother and she would take care of them temporarily. She was really sick. That didn't matter to me at the time. I felt like anybody in the world had to be stronger than me, so even if she was sick she had to be strong enough to take care of my kids, because I couldn't do it.

So I kind of just wandered around the streets of San Francisco for the next two years, in and out of drug hotels and wherever somebody would let me lay down for the night—or in the corners of the stores, I would lay there also. And it occurred to me one day that I wanted to be—not even happy; happy was too big for me at that time—I just wanted to be content. And I wasn't even content, because I maybe wore size three and I was just fading away. I was just fading away. And when you use crack cocaine a lot of people say you have illusions and all this stuff, which could be possibly true, but for me I had been up four or five days on one of my drug runs, and I went in the bathroom to my sister's house—this was when Geneva Towers was up—and I was actually staying pillar to post there, anywhere in the building that I could stay. And once I was down there and I was getting high, and I couldn't get high for some reason this day. It just wouldn't happen. I kept thinking, "Oh, I don't have enough money," and I was making all these excuses why I wasn't getting high this day, because I was always able to get high before. So I looked at myself in the mirror—and I saw something other than myself. It wasn't me! It could not have been me. I didn't recognize who the person was. And it was really scary! It was really, really scary. It scared me to death. And I couldn't tell people, because they already gave me names, like I was a dope fiend and I was crazy—all kind of things wrong with me—so people made fun of me all the time. So this was not something I was going to go run and tell people who were in the other room getting high, is that I just saw somebody else in the mirror. So I kind of sat with that and I didn't get high the rest of that day, because I was really scared. So I said, "Maybe this is a sign from God. What's going on?"

Even at night I was so tired. I had been so tired from the streets, from the drugs, from the abuse, from everything. I was tired! So it occurred to me that maybe I can get clean, maybe I can give it a try, maybe I'll try it. So what happened is, I went and tried to check myself into a residential place, and they said I had to be clean three days. To me that was impossible. I had been getting high for years every single day, every moment I was awake I was getting high. How in the heck could I stay clean for three days? But somehow I did. I don't even know how I did that. I stayed clean three days! And I went back down and I told them. And she said, "We have no space." And I just broke down. I said, "You know, if you don't take me today—if you don't see me today then I may be dead tomorrow!" And something that I said, the lady that was there felt and resonated with that. And I think that's that universal connection that we talk about, when people are not necessarily listening softly but *feeling* where somebody is coming from. And I said, "It's only by the grace of God that I have made it through your door today, and if you turn me away, I may be dead tomorrow." And she went and talked to some people, and she said, "We can get you in, but we don't have any room in our inpatient." And I'm thinking, "I'm homeless, so some of the reason for me to even try to get in here is so I could have somewhere to sleep, stay, and try to get clean. And she said, "Well, we only have outpatient." So that was scary. I was just scared. I'm thinking, "Outpatient? So that means I go home every day where there's dysfunction and people use drugs and come back here and be clean the next day?"

But, see, something was already happening inside of me at that point, because I had never made it to a drug rehabilitation place. I couldn't keep thirty-five cents to get on the bus, you know? I'd spend thirty-five cents, or put thirty-five cents with other people to make a dollar trying to get high, so what really registered for me is that it was a miracle. I got thirty-five cents, and I made it downtown to the women's alcoholism center—I made it there! And I told her how I got there. I didn't know how to keep money and I got there. And I said, "Something's going on. I can do it! I must be able to do this if I can get thirty-five cents." I'd been trying to get bus fare. This is going to sound really crazy. I had been trying to keep thirty-five cents for bus fare for over a year, saying I was going to go to the drug rehabilitation place—and I couldn't make it! I kept saying, "Tomorrow's the big day! I'll do it. This could be the first day of the rest of my life"—all these things, where my normal thinking would have been, you know, like, "Just fuck it, because I can't do it!" Somebody will have to help me up and walk me through it, or it won't get done. But I had did it myself, and that was big steps for me: Keeping the bus fare to get down there, begging for her to take me until she said, "Yes." So that's the beginning for me.

So I come back to this place, which is Geneva Towers, where drugs were in abundance all around the whole vicinity, right here where we're sitting today. This is where Geneva Towers was. So the first three days I think I was on this natural high thing. Then I started to feel myself breaking down and getting weak. But the difference this time was when I had what they call an urge—which to me now is what I understand to be the thought about using—instead of succumbing to that thinking that I could get high one time and they wouldn't know it, I didn't do it. I said, "I can't do it! If I do, then I'm doomed." So that worked. And before I knew it I was just walking through it. It had been three months and I was still going in and out of this drug-infested place, and they don't have a clue today how I was getting back and forth there, and where I was coming to when I left them every day. And before I knew it years had passed by.

JP: Years?

BG: Years! Years had passed by. But in the time when this was happening, I'm constantly moving and going forward. But I don't see it, though. I don't see myself going forward. I don't see that I'm making steps to prepare to welcome my children back into my life.

JP: Did you have a home at that point?

BG: Well, no. I was still staying with different people. My sister lived on 9, my mother lived on 12, and I had friends that lived throughout the building.

I couldn't stay with them because all my friends were dope users or drug addicts.

JP: How many years are we talking about?

BG: Well, my drug abuse started in 1985. So I'm in Texas doing drugs, and I'm graduating to California. Then in 1989 I come here and actually go on a worse kind of binge thing, so 1989 was my worst, worst year of using. And 1990 was just kind of like where I was getting kind of tired, but I just kept going because I felt worthless and that was my space. My space was to be a drug addict, a dope fiend, homeless, and that just felt like what I should be doing.

JP: So what year did you enter the program?

BG: At the end of 1990.

JP: And then when you said, "It went for years—"

BG: You mean not using? Clean?

JP: Yeah. But the point where you said for years that you weren't feeling like you were getting anywhere.

BG: Right, two years, because 1992 was the last time I did drugs. In that time, I was moving forward but I still couldn't feel myself. I couldn't see that I was moving. I had already taken steps. I had made arrangements with the CPS worker so that I could have visits with my children, because I was told not to go near my children—who lived with my mother. And so I had started making arrangements to do that. I went downtown and got on the list for public housing and made arrangements. And I had put my kids on there, although I didn't have my kids. My thinking was that I would have them back someday, and so when I got my house I would have to have enough room for them.

JP: So at what point did you bump into Health Realization?

BG: Oh, man! See, let me just tell you, I was clean all those years, just think about it, from 1992. But I was still miserable—until I learned about Health Realization two years ago. So what I'm telling you is that even with me being clean and getting my kids back, I still was not complete. Because I was doing it the hard way. I was hustling and bustling and punishing myself and trying to show myself that I got to create a challenge and solve it to show people that I'm strong now, that I'm not the same dope fiend they used to know, that I'm a good mother now. And yet I didn't really know how to be a mother. I didn't know how to even nurture my children, let alone myself. So even being clean all those years, I still didn't realize where all this pain was still coming from.

JP: It still felt like you were in pain?

BG: I still felt like I was in pain. I was clean. I didn't say my life had changed; I said I had stopped using drugs! I had stopped using drugs and alcohol, but I did not know myself, and I did not know how to take care of myself still. I was in the hustle and bustle and the struggle of showing other people that I'm doing it.

INSIGHT

JP: So bring me to that moment where you first bumped into Health Realization. What happened to you?

BG: Okay. How that occurred was, at this point in time like I said, I'm still going through the motions, I'm not really happy still, I still have a lot of pain going on even after all these years. And what I learned later was that I was still living through my past. And one day I was really actively involved, because remember I'm still trying to prove to people that even after seven years I'm clean and I'm a good parent and an active member of society—so I joined the Parent Advisory Committee at the Boys and Girls Club, which is here located in Visitacion Valley. I was the chairperson. So the guy that was over the Boys and Girls Club said one day, "Some people are coming to do a presentation." In fact, it was like a joke to people. They said it was something like "Health Revitalization" or something, and I'm thinking, "Why do you guys always want me to be the guinea pig for stuff? Why do you want me to be the one that goes?" And he's like, "Well, you have rapport with people, and we just kind of want you to sit in and bring information back to us. None of us really want to be involved, but we just want to be nice and a Dr. Mills or something is coming." And I thought, "Okay,"—because remember I'm still in this state of trying to prove myself, so I'll do this if that's what it takes.

And I went that night, and it was Roger [Mills] and Beverley [Wilson] and Barbara Bailey. I remember being there that first day and just kind of looking at them and having my own ways. Like, I thought I could only hear messages from people of color, and if they weren't of color then they didn't know my struggles, so they couldn't relate to anything that I needed. And so he came in, and "Oh God," Roger was Caucasian. And I thought, "Okay, now I'm really not going to listen because he came to brainwash us, and they want me to bring this message back to my people." And what happened during that whole time, with me sitting there doing all this thinking about these people that I had never met and never talked to—and Beverley was there, but I thought, "Okay, he has her under lock and key, too; that doesn't make any difference." So he kept talking, and he started talking about *Thought*. They started talking about Thought, and while I was sitting there listening to them I realized that the thinking I was doing was preventing me from hearing what they were saying. Because I had sat in that room at least thirty minutes and didn't hear a word they were saying. But I heard "Thought,"—that our Thought create our experience, and that made it so real for me. Not because they said it—because I didn't believe nothing they said that day—but I was experiencing it. I was sitting in that room, thinking, "Oh, I'll be glad when they're done. What's taking so long?" and every time, the more I had all this habitual thinking about why they were there, and I didn't realize that I was almost laying down in the chair. And I thought, "How did I get here?" The more I was sitting I was thinking, and the more I thought about it, the weaker I got.

And then it occurred to me and I just leaned up in my chair, and I remember saying something to them like, "Oh, yeah, that's right, because I remember when I used drugs in the Tower, and I used to go in the garbage room and I used to think—" And it hit me, just like that! It hit me. I truly understood what they were saying about thought, and from that moment they had my attention. They had my attention and I won't say that I was all in, but I knew that there was some truth to what they had came and said. And so for the next two times, I forced myself to sit in on the training. And after that, it was like I couldn't miss one. I had to be there because something was happening to me.

JP: Now before you go there, when you said it hit you, can you describe what you felt at that—

BG: I felt a tremendous amount of energy.

JP: Really?

BG: Yeah. It hit me through my body. It went through my body. And I remember grabbing my shoulders and pushing them together because it was just feeling overwhelming. It was an overwhelming feeling like *I* was doing something. I had never, ever felt in my life that I was causing or creating *anything* that had happened to me. And I realized that I was creating some misery for myself, and I just like hugged myself, grabbed myself and squeezed really tight. And Beverley looked at me and said, "Mm, mm, mm!" And she said, "Just hold onto your seat, girl!" And I said, "No, you just don't understand what a feeling I just had." I said [emotional now], "I've been causing myself so much misery for years." Because I seen, literally, just then—even though, remember I had been clean for years—I had *seen* at that moment how much misery that I had caused my own self. *How could I do that to myself?* And then I had to go through a process of forgiving myself, and that was really hard, because I couldn't figure out what had I been instilling in my kids—if I'm making myself so miserable, what kind of message was I giving to them? But then I learned about psychological innocence. And boy, let me tell you, when I did that, I didn't even relive all those things but I recognized that they happened, and it was a beautiful thing for me to know that when I was doing those things to myself, that *I didn't know that I was*. But it was even more powerful for me to know that *I created my own experience*. I never in my life knew anything that had happened to me—from the scums of sleeping on the floor to drug abuse—that I had nothing to do with that. And it took me to a plateau I had never been to. It took me to a place like, "*Now I know!*" and all I could do was cry. I cried and I cried. I cried a lot. I cried for, like, two months. And it wasn't a painful cry. It was almost like a release, like I was releasing and forgiving. But I had released myself, and I had never in my life felt that type of freedom before. I had never felt free. Even after I got clean I had never been free. And I thought, "*Oh, my God, I can free myself! I can free myself from this!*" And that was the part that kept me crying for months, because I was truly, truly free! You know?

SHARING WITH OTHERS AND LIFE AFTER

And then in deepening my understanding, it kept going to a different level for me. I always felt like I was stupid, and can you imagine, like Three Principles—I'd hear people say, Three Principles—and I said, "Oh my God, it's so much bigger than that. How do I tell my people?" Here I have to explain to them how I came to understand this understanding, so I can't do that without talking about The Three Principles. You can't make up something that's not true. How do I tell my people that you are free? *You are free!*" And I hear people sometimes, getting caught up in this thing blaming people for these conditions—and that looked real to me. It was real! "If they would just do this for us." "They held us back. It took too long to learn, now some of us are really slow, and we can't understand things." And just telling people, "*Everything you need, you have.*" I could never tell somebody that before. I could never have imagined how to fix my mouth to tell somebody that everything you need, you have—to be whole, to be complete, to be happy, to whatever you want. And the thing is with this, that this is so life-altering, to me it's not even about, "You can change your life forever; let me tell you about The Three Principles." It's more to me like to explain it to people that "*This is something that you were given—the gift of life!* This is something that you had when you was born."

And I remember trying to tell this lady something. I was talking to a lady over here who was still actually addicted to crack cocaine. And I remember going to her one day, and I still have moments like an overwhelming feeling of love and joy that I have—it's not the pain anymore, because I used to sit on the stairs and cry in pain. And now if I do cry, it's just like the freedom that I feel I can't explain to them. So this lady, she said, "Oh, my God, you look so well." She said, "You been clean for a long time?" I said, "Yeah, but I haven't been free." I said, "I'm free." And she was looking at me like—she knows me very well, and she also knew me when I was drama mama. And she looked at me and she said, "Please tell me how. Please tell me how!" And she's somebody that's still using that lives in this complex right now, and I went on and I started talking to her about the Principles. But I couldn't, my throat started cracking up. And that's what happens to me sometimes—and I think that's the part where I have to slow down and relax—because when I talk about this, not only do I get excited, I get emotional. Because I think of the agony and pain that I was in for so many years, and I understand that *I'm not a prisoner of that anymore!* But the beautiful part to that is, sometimes I have to cry—I caused a lot of that myself and I caused it out of psychological innocence. And I couldn't even tell her anything because I just started to break down. I was telling her about the Principles and I was trying to tell her how they all work together, and you *are* the Principles, and she was just kind of looking confused. And I understood her confusion, because I remember that same confusion when they were telling me about these Principles. I couldn't see how they would ever change my life, and they have changed my life forever.

And the beautiful part to this, I always went places to give something, to be better, to do better, to be right, and I would only remember that technique for a short time, of how to do it, when to do it when you're feeling down and out, or pick up this when you're feeling like that. And now, I tell you, this understanding is just like—I can't explain it to you—I remember what a struggle I had, even when I was becoming clean. Because they said, "You do it one day at a time"—where you're talking to somebody who loved to use drugs—and a day, twenty-four hours, is a lifetime. And I can remember that whole struggle with that. And knowing now when I go to drug and rehabilitation places, I talk to the people in charge first, and I say, "Look, I'm going to say something and I don't know if it'll be okay with you or your staff, but if I can't say it, I can't talk. I have to tell these people that they can do this moment to moment. They don't have to be strong for a day." That was one of my weakest, weakest points in recovery, remembering one day at a time. And see, knowing this understanding and what I know now, I know my experiences are created moment to moment.

JP: It's like one moment at a time.

BG: One *moment* at a time! And if I'm getting through moments, then I'm going to make it. But you're talking about a day. And I'm not saying it's wrong, because I believed the Twelve Steps would work for me, and they did. So I don't have anything against that. I just can't tell people one day at a time, especially someone who is in any kind of addiction.

JP: When you said that the Twelve Steps worked—they got you off the drugs but it didn't sound like it stopped the pain.

BG: They didn't. That's what I'm saying, *it didn't stop the pain!* I was still in pain four or five years after that, still in pain. So that's where it takes me back to my thinking. When people want to be clean, that's where it comes from—the *thought* that you want it. It's not necessarily the people or the Twelve Steps, because for me the Twelve Steps were really humiliating. But I had to be strong, and that was my whole thing, my whole persona. So I can do the Twelve Steps—I can go back and tell people I stole this, or "When you went out of your kitchen I took a piece of chicken, and I'm sorry for that." That was humiliating! You know what I mean? And to me there's a more loving, compassionate way to do that. And I'm not saying, "People, convert to Health Realization." It's not about a conversion. These are things we're born with. They belong to you. Use them! And I don't even know how to exercise the Principles—I think I get caught up sometimes still, but the thing is that I don't stay there long, because that's not where my happiness is, it's not where my peace is, and I used to believe that it was. And that's the sick, insane part. I can't say that because I would be hurting my neck, my back, my throat—everything inside of me would lock up because I know the pain that it is when you're going through something like that. But if I had ever, ever in my life known that my life experiences were created moment to moment, how I could relax, how I could just be myself, how I could just know that I could just *be*, and not have to try to be something that I thought people needed me to be, that I could just be Barbara—and who Barbara was was very beautiful. And I'm not an ugly person. That's what I created. And that is the beautiful thing about thought, the ability to create! And *I could create any future I wanted for myself.* Anything I wanted, I could create it, and I knew that, and the freedom, freedom, freedom, freedom, *freedom*!

And I hear the Martin Luther King speech, and people don't know the meaning that it has for me now. And I believe in heritage and all that. With my people, I'm down! I'm down with humanity now, though. Can you imagine how much bigger that is than "my people?" So my life and my possibilities and the realm I'm in is just beyond the outer limits! And it's, like, crazy for me. But that speech has something different for me now. I tell people, and I talk to teenagers sometimes, and the first thing I ask them is, "When you hear that Martin Luther King speech that he did, what do you feel?" They say, "Strong." And even though he says, "Thank God Almighty, I'm free at last!" none of them ever say that part of it. And to me that was a very intricate part of that speech. But when I used to hear it, I just used to think of a very strong, powerful black man that had knowledge. Honestly. But when I hear that now, I hear, "Free at last! Thank whoever your creator is, almighty whoever, free at last, and I'd just like to tell you, brothers and sisters, today that *you can be free, and the choice is yours*. And I'd like to help point you to where that is!"

And my God, I'm just astounded by presentations. I don't know why they want me to do something like that, I cry too much. And my tears are always of joy and happiness, but it's just so overwhelming to me how much love and compassion that I feel for myself and other people. I was always a person who was down for myself, "What I can get, what I can do, what can you give me, what I need." Always, always, always, always, always. And I just feel so real. I feel like I'm not a fake any more. I've tried to fake to people like I was this cool person, or I was an outstanding person. I didn't believe shit of it, though, that's the cold part. But the difference today is that I know it's true, and that comes across to people when I speak to them. I don't need to be a speaker or a presenter. I don't need to be anything. I do need to be myself, because when I'm myself something shines through me that's like—Whooo, I don't know, something just shines through me, and it goes through my body and I feel it, and it's almost like other people just magnetize to it. And I think that's what they talk about, when you come in this understanding, and you are content and you are all these things, and the difference is you still have things go on in your life, you still have those same things that you had before that go on in your life, but they definitely don't hold onto you and grip you like they used to.

I used to be incapacitated, couldn't move. I'd be in the bed for five days, 'cause I'd be mentally sick like, "Oh my God, what am I gonna do? I don't make enough money, I have all these kids, how will I provide? What will I do? Well, how will I do it in the bed? So who was I lying through that [laughs]. I will laugh at myself sometimes and say, "Well, how would you do it in the bed?" And I'll get up, and I may not go to do anything but cut my lawn. I'll do something like that, and believe me, unbelievable, I will forget that I even had the thought of not surviving—forget all about I had that thought. It will be gone and dismissed and out of there. But yet, a few moments ago, this is the same thing that used to hold me down for weeks, just physically incapacitated 'cause I don't know what to do, I don't know which way to turn, I don't know to do, my life is in shambles, and the same thoughts will come back and they occur and they happen, but they never in life could ever grip me the way they did before. I know what they are: I see you passing, and I'll see you later. Because you'll be back, and I'll be here. But the difference is, it will never be the same. It can never be the same once you understand how we operate. And I think that is so important.

And I remember how to see, I see all kinds of people who really look important, and now I look at them differently. I used to look at people—I'd sit in the doctor's office and just have all this thinking about, oh, what kind of house people have, and what their life must be like, and, oh, I bet you I'm the only one in this room using low-income housing. I mean, I was at this feeling, and now it's just like so far from me now. Now it doesn't matter to me what walk or phase of life that you come through. I know that I don't need to be judgmental about that, or of anything or anybody.

COMMUNITY WORK FROM THE INSIDE-OUT

JP: How did you get this Health Realization job at Visitacion Valley?

BG: Well, that's special. That is so special for me. The funny thing is, I was feeling so good about this Health Realization stuff, I had no credentials—only the fact that I had been before in the community with the people. They needed a project director and an executive assistant, where I didn't know how to type and I had minimal skills about computers. And it was amazing. I'm telling you, this understanding will blow you out of the water. I had this notion one night when I woke up—see, I wasn't going to apply for neither one of those jobs because I wasn't qualified to do either one. But somehow I had to be involved with this stuff, I couldn't let this get away from me because it had already started to change my life in a week or two. So I thought, "Oh God, I don't have these skills, I don't have anything. All I have is that I had been in this community as a homeless person, as a drug abuser, and now I'm here and I don't do anything." So I figured the only thing they can say is yes or no, we can use you or not, so I applied for the project director [laughs]. I applied for the project director, and I'm telling you, I had no thinking about it because if I'd had a thought about it there's no way I would have took my butt out there applying for a project director's job which I had no clue [laughs]. So they set up this interview. They wanted to hire people within the community, which I thought was really beautiful. So in that short period of time I told you, "Thought" was the thing that first hit me—the fact that our thoughts create our experience. So I go out there, really nervous, and I thought, "Oh, my God, I know they don't want me. They can see that I'm uneducated—they can see all these things." I didn't do any of that thinking until I got there, but seeing Elsie and Roger sitting there—now, remember, I'm still seeing things like I'm the ant and everybody else is a big giant. So I went in there and, God, they looked so professional. And I thought I'd dressed up that day. But I didn't feel really dressed when I got there and seeing them.

So I did the interview, and I got a call like two or three days later from Roger, and he said I didn't get the job. Well, oh my God, I couldn't even talk—and not that I even expected to get the job, but hearing it was something different. I kind of just wanted them not to call or not to say anything and let me come to my own conclusions [laughs] about not getting the job. So it was so funny. What I did was, I went earlier that morning, and I said "Beverley, can you please meet me there?" I said, "I'm really going through a lot of things. I don't really understand what this stuff is, but this stuff is really doing something to me. It's moving me in my life like nothing's ever moved me before. Can I just talk to you for a minute in confidence?" I said, "I have no credentials. I have none of this stuff. I have nothing that I think they're looking for," but see, Beverley understood about Health Realization, and she knew it was something more than what I did. But she said, "This understanding—they need you!" I could not understand her saying that for the life of me. I thought she was so full of shit, that she was saying something to make me feel good. Who would need me? I mean the way she said it was like, "They *need you*," in a like almost made me believe it, you know? So I said, "Okay." And I went and I didn't get it, and Roger called and said, "Ann Shine got the job as project director." Well, I was going to hang up on him—not be mad at him but I needed to hang up right then because I was having a lot of feelings about that at that particular time. He said, "Oh, but we're creating a job for you." And I dropped the phone. He'll remember this very well. I dropped the phone, couldn't pick it up, all I heard was, "We're creating for you." And that's all I could keep saying in my head, and I was like, "Oh, God, this stuff is so real!" And I couldn't pick the phone up. I just looked at the phone. And after a minute I was out of shock, but no one had ever like offered something that was just for me. And then it started playing in my head what Beverley said, "Oh, they need you." I had been coming to every training, but I was coming for me, because I needed to, because whatever was happening was really, really changing my life. So I finally picked up the phone. And he said, "Hello. Are you there?" I said, "Yes. You're doing what?" "We're creating a position." I said, "Well, you know I have too many children, and I really can't take a part-time job." He said, "It is full-time." And I just started screaming, just screaming and yelling and screaming and screaming, "Oh, thank you very much, thank you very much," and I hung up on him. I guess he kind of knew my excitement and didn't worry about it, and that's how I ultimately came here.

But the beautiful part is that I was feeling like whether I got the job or not, I had to be a part of this whole thing. And I really just said, "If this thing does anything for anybody else like it does for me—see, at the time I'm still thinking of it as a concept. I haven't grasped on to what it really is yet. All I know is that it's doing something to me and now I'm recognizing my thoughts, which is saving me, because I'm having some stinkin' thinkin', don't even know about it. And it was happening so much that I didn't realize them, and I was playing them out. So that's how I got it, and it was like amazing. I could not believe it. And just like, oh God, I can't even tell you—I don't even know where I'm going, but I'm not afraid. See, I'm just not afraid.

MORE ON LIFE AFTER

JP: How long from the time that you first got exposed to Health Realization did the job happen?

BG: Maybe two weeks, three weeks—not a month.

JP: Oh, that blows me away. You really must have caught something.

BG: I did, I must have caught *something!* And I'm so happy for it.

JP: And when you were talking about stuff shining through you, it's been happening right here, right now!

BG: [Screams] *Ooh, God*! [laughs] Okay, good, I'm telling you! And you know what? With my kids, I said, "If I'm blessed, if I just know, I know they'll be okay." And I don't try to push it on them, but I'm the Principles in action in my house, and I can't stop doing that. And if that catches on to my kids, I'd be like, "Yes!" But it's my little kids, like seven and eight, who say stuff that would blow me out of the water. My daughter told me the other day that her quality of thinking was very mellow. And I asked her, "Well, why do you think that is?" She said, "Because I was thinking that I wish I didn't have a brother because we fight all the time, but now I'm thinking, if he wasn't here, I'd just die." I have four kids of my own, two kids are kids from drug abuse, people that I knew and went on the same path that I did, and it almost felt like my fate to take on their kids. They had no family, and I was there. So two more kids I picked up, and now they've been with me so long it's like they're my children. People say, "Are those your six kids?" The difference is the struggle is not the same. I used to feel like a housemaid. I wore different clothing. I wore different perfume. And people would walk by and say, "You smell like old women perfume or something." But unconsciously I was doing that. And I would dress different because, like, I had a certain persona that I needed to put up so that people wouldn't bother me. I can take care of my four kids and two more, but what they don't know, see, is I have a secret. It's that I live my life through the Principles—the Principles are in me, and it just takes away a lot of the extra excess baggage that I was carrying. There's six kids in a three-bedroom house, but they feel my spirit in that house, and they know that I'm only there to love and nurture you, and I want you to be happy. I don't care what anyone else is thinking about that. Go ahead, do your thing, because I'm doing mine, and it's not worrying about what you're thinking, because I know I have no control over that.

PART II.

COMMUNITY AND ORGANIZATIONAL CHANGE

1. A GUIDE FOR REALIZING COMMUNITY AND ORGANIZATIONAL CHANGE FROM THE INSIDE-OUT[10]

The goal of working with communities and organizations from the inside-out is to help people gain access to their own internal Health and well-being, then ripple out to create healthy communities.

The question is often asked, "How does one do it?" or "How can this best occur?"

An answer emerges from how we see the causes of people's problems. If we see the cause of people's problems residing in the outside world, we will naturally look to change those external conditions, provide information, teach skills, build supports, etc.

What happens when we do not look to the external world for the cause of behavior? What does it look like when viewed from the inside-out? Sydney Banks (1998)[11] offers an answer:

> Cut off from innate wisdom a lost thinker experiences isolation, fear and confusion… The misled thoughts of humanity, alienated from their inner wisdom, cause all violence, cruelty and savagery in this world (p.83).

If we see the cause of people's problems as being severed innocently from their inner Health and wisdom by their own thinking, *our solution would be simply to help people connect with their innate wisdom and see how their thinking inadvertently obscures it, which then raises their level of consciousness.*

---

[10] This chapter was originally titled "Applying the Three Principles (a.k.a. Health Realization) as an Inside-Out Approach in Communities and for Organizational Change" in *Prevention from the Inside-Out*; it has been revised and brought up to date.

[11] Banks, S. (1998). *The Missing Link.* Renton, WA: IHRC/Lone Pine Publishing

The word "simply," of course, is both accurate and tongue-in-cheek. The simplicity is what I pointed to earlier: 1) people aligned with their wisdom do not create problems for themselves and others, and only their thinking can obscure (or at least give the illusion of obscuring) innate wisdom; 2) only if people's thinking changes will their behaviors change. Thus, if we help people realize their innate Health and wisdom or resilience, and that what they are seeing is not really *reality* but only "a reality" created from their own thinking, out of which they feel compelled to act, problems are thus prevented. On the other hand, there is no simple, sure way to help people find their wisdom and see the inseparable connection between thought and "reality."

What we do know is this: People who *realize* the source of *all* their experience is Thought combining with Consciousness, emanating from the infinite power and possibilities of Universal Mind, tend to become more hopeful. They see a possible way out for themselves. This combination of realization and seeing new hope seems to be enough to right people, as a tipping-over boat suddenly finds its equilibrium. Such is realizing the Three Principles of Universal Mind, Consciousness and Thought.

Prevention from the inside-out is, first, a recognition that true change can only come from within *through a shift in perspective, a new insight, that leads to a change in consciousness.*

So many people *think* there is no way out of their lot in life, that they are stuck with their hopelessness. So many people *think* they have to continue to be beaten because they can't imagine how it could change. So many people *think* they need to harm others or be violent. So many people *think* they are damaged goods for the rest of their lives because they were sexually abused. So many people *think* they have to drink or do drugs to have a good time or survive. So many people *think* they can't get a job because they will fail, because they have always failed. So many young people *think* they need to join a gang to be safe and survive. So many young people *think* their parents will never understand them. So many parents *think* they will never understand their kids; that their kids are "good-for-nothing." Could anything be more empowering than for any of these people to *see* the thought-reality connection from a higher level of perspective and consciousness? This is what the inside-out/Three Principles approach to prevention attempts to help people see.

How do we best help people see this? Practitioners have pondered this question and often struggled with it since they first tried to understand what Sydney Banks *saw* from his direct experience. What did he *see* that the rest of us didn't?

An answer lies in these questions: What do we understand for ourselves beyond any doubt about how our thinking creates our experience of life and/or how wisdom will always guide us if we deeply listen to it? How can what we understand then be best communicated to others? Fascinating questions.

The reason there are no easy or set answers is because, were we to look inside ourselves to the times we had the greatest leaps of understanding or when our lives underwent major change, if we asked ourselves how we learned what we did at those times and looked closely, we would see that we changed when we had a major new *insight*. Always! It may appear on the surface that something outside ourselves caused us to have this insight, but it is never true. That same outside event could have happened in the lives of thousands of others, and they would not have had the same insight. Further, we may not have had the insight if that exact event had happened at a different time in our own lives. Thus, massive change in anyone's life—a shift in the very way one sees life—*must* arise as a shift from *within*.

The difficulty in working with people is we are outside their heads. We are attempting from the outside to somehow convey knowledge or truth about the way we function so it is experienced on the inside. How can we teach something from the outside that makes change occur within? We can't! This is another paradox. We can only point people in the right direction. If we can get people to look in the right direction, they have a chance of finding it. If they are looking in the wrong direction they won't find it, except by accident. Therefore, all of our "teaching"—and by this I mean attempting to draw out an understanding that is already inside but presently obscured—is geared to pointing people in the right direction: within themselves. As George Pransky says, we can get people to the bus stop, but we can't make them get on the bus. If people are not at the bus stop, the odds of getting on the bus are mighty slim. We can lead a horse to water, we can't make it drink, but if the horse is not at the trough or other water source, odds are against it finding a drink.

With this backdrop we set about our task: to point people within themselves and attempt to find some spark that will ignite an insight. It is an attempt to get under the radar of people's current thought-mindsets keeping them stuck. To do this we sometimes have to talk around the point—tell stories, use metaphors, use other examples—do anything that might strike a chord in people, because we cannot simply tell people what we know and expect it to have any impact. But we can't even lay that on people out of nowhere. A process can help people's minds be ready to hear the new.

The Inside-Out Community/Organizational Empowerment Process

I can't state this enough: The first and most important intent of the inside-out community/organizational empowerment process is to help people have their own personal insights about how their (and everyone's) experience of life is created moment to moment, and how they have all the Health and wisdom or resilience within them they will ever need to navigate well through life.

If they truly *see* it and understand, if their insight is of enough magnitude, their perspective will likely shift to Health and well-being.

Once people catch on to this and see their lives improve, they naturally want to give it away to others, such as their families and friends. The change within themselves tends to have a calming effect on their neighbors and acquaintances. When a critical mass of people catches on they naturally want to create constructive community or organizational change to improve where they live and work.

Hence, prevention or community work from the inside-out.

The Logic

To get a sense of how Three Principles practitioners attempt to bring this about, we can look to logic. The "logic model" has become popular in prevention, and without adhering to a specific "logic model" design, we do apply a certain logic to create our community prevention strategy.

Most everyone would agree: Fewer problems exist in a healthy community. So we begin with that assumption. If community conditions are currently unhealthy and we want healthy, constructive community change that will decrease problems, here is my take on the logic behind inside-out prevention. Working backwards:

- Constructive community [and organizational] change likely will not occur unless people work together to make it happen.
- People will not work to make it happen unless they want to and can see the possibility of change.
- Given where many community people currently are at, without a shift in perspective they will likely not want to try or will not see the possibility of making any change happen.
- People have a shift in perspective only if they have new insight.
- People either have insights spontaneously (unpredictable at best) or they can be positioned to have best chance of gaining insights.
- People will be in the best position to have new insights about themselves and their relationship to their lives when they see how they truly function from within (by seeing the Three Principles in action in their own lives).
- People will best take in this new understanding if conveyed in a way they can *hear* it, meets them where they're at, and it feels relevant to them.
- It will be conveyed in a way most relevant and likely to be heard if people are deeply listened to; in other words, the more deeply we listen to people, the more we know what to say and how to say it so they will hear it.
- We can only deeply listen to people if they let us get close enough and if they are open enough to say what is on their minds.
- People will be most open if their minds are relaxed.
- People's minds become most relaxed when having fun, when it feels good or when they feel rapport and closeness, so they want to open up.

- To best create a good feeling we ourselves must generally live in a healthy feeling and be in that good feeling in the moment when working with others.

If we begin at the end of this logic—with the last item listed above and work our way backwards—it would reveal an inside-out prevention "process" or "system." Were we to proceed through this process, logic dictates how we would have the best chance of achieving our ends.

The Process of Applying The Three Principles (a.k.a. Health Realization) to Prevention[12]

Following the logic above, four "components" appear necessary to successfully apply an inside-out/Three Principles approach to prevention programming and community development. While the four components generally flow from one to another in sequence, much overlap occurs, so there is much back-and-forth movement. The sole purpose of the four components is to move people to a fifth—a shift in perspective through new insight—which no one can make happen but is really the desired result. When people have an insight of enough magnitude it changes their lives so they function at a higher level, they naturally want to reach out to touch others' lives, and community change ripples out accordingly.

This same inside-out approach, process or system—whatever anyone wants to call it—holds true whether one is assisting a

[12] This inside-out prevention "process" came to me when Bill Lofquist, author of *Discovering the Meaning of Prevention* [Lofquist, W. (1983). Tucson, AZ: Associates for Youth Development (Development Associates)] asked me if I would write a chapter on "Health Realization as a prevention system" for a book on prevention systems he was authoring. So I had to ask myself, "What exactly is the 'system' for prevention from the inside-out?" With a fine-tooth comb I went back through *Modello* [Pransky, J. (2011). *Modello: A story of hope for the inner-city and beyond.* British Columbia, Canada: CCB Publishing] to discover the application process Dr. Roger Mills had applied there—Mills had referred to what he did there as "flying by the seat of his pants," which was true at the time but not particularly helpful for others—and at one point the entire system came together for me. I submitted it to Bill Lofquist, who rejected it for his book because he couldn't see how it fit with the other prevention systems in his book. Hilarious! But I had found something big, and the same "system" or "application process" has held up over all these years. Thank you, Bill.

community, an organization, conducting a training or even individual counseling or coaching.

What can be said in this book about each of these components or "steps" only scratches the surface. Deep understanding means experiencing each and having one's own continuously growing level of understanding deepen within each area.

It is difficult to find the right words; these are not "steps" or even "components" so much as bases to be covered. As I said, there is much overlap. This sequence follows from the above logic:

I. Living in a Feeling of Well-being/Living the Understanding
II. Creating the Best Feeling for Minds to Relax and Loosen Their Grip
III. Deep Listening
IV. Conveying or Drawing Out the Understanding (Teaching)

V. Insight: A Shift in Perspective
VI. The Ripple Effect

This is the simplicity. Yet its practice contains a lot of depth and must be truly understood to have the desired effect. There is no set way to bring about each of these "components." Each practitioner must find her or his own way that naturally feels right. In so doing the practitioner must pay close attention to (deeply listen to) its effects, knowing humbly that something more can always be done that has not yet been seen. Experience suggests certain ways of proceeding are more effective than others. The ingenuity of the worker in the moment is the only limitation, and this ingenuity can be hindered by the community/organization worker's own limited thinking.

I. Living in a Feeling of Well-being/Living the Understanding

It would be wise for the Three Principles practitioner to be the model of the Health s/he is attempting to bring forth in others. Thus, the *health of the helper* becomes the first focus. This is quite practical, for if the worker does not walk her/his talk or speaks not from personal experience but from the intellect, then whatever s/he tries to convey will be heard merely as words or beliefs or an intellectual theory and will fall on deaf ears.

The first "step," then, is for the practitioner to be "well grounded" in The Three Principles. To me, this means:

1. having a solid understanding of the practical meaning of *The Three Principles*
2. generally living one's own life in well-being, and knowing the "mechanism" at play when one slips out of well-being
3. responding to adversity and to others without getting reactive or being "brought down"

All of us lose our bearings in moments. But if we notice, if we wait a while, we somehow manage to regain our bearings on our own. This better feeling comes about naturally, so long as we don't allow our beliefs, fear or our personal egos to get in the way.

If we see ourselves *in a state of service* to others, our well-being is less likely attached to any thoughts other than how well we are serving others. Any thoughts about ourselves or how well we are doing are irrelevant and can only interfere.

In essence, we want to *be in and emanate a good feeling*, know where it comes from and how we lose it. When hiring a worker for an inside-out community or organizational project, we first look for this "good feeling" within the person, regardless of his/her experience. Some have this feeling naturally. Others can be helped to find it within themselves through training and immersion in understanding the Three Principles, for it always exists deep within everyone. Prospective effective inside-out workers reach the point where they see in most moments how the Principles are playing out in their own and others' lives.

Again, living it is the only thing that makes it real; otherwise it is only theory and has a hollow ring. Others can feel it and will not listen. And why should they?

How do we know we are well grounded enough?

Effective Three Principles practitioners are those who generally live in a state of Health and well-being themselves and who can draw the Health out of others. Their own lives are a testament to the Principles working well within them, because after being exposed to this understanding their own lives became generally less stressed, more calm and lighthearted, with better relationships. They came to realize that no matter how bad things look at the time they have essentially made up with their own thinking how they see and experience it and the meaning they give it. No matter what happens, no matter what problems they encounter, most times they know it is a thought-created illusion—even if they miss this in any moment it is still a backdrop in their minds, so to speak, and they eventually recover when they see it. In addition, no matter how terrible things seem they know their thinking can and will change, and with it their experience. They realize no matter what horrible things are happening, they are protected and guided by wisdom and their innate Health.

II. Creating the Best Feeling for Minds to Relax and Loosen Their Grip

Once we are well-grounded in the Three Principles *and* once we emanate a healthy feeling, we are now ready to interact with others.

As I see it, this stage has a few different purposes: to create a good feeling around us; to see people in their Health and innocence; to open people up so they can hear the new; to give hope that there is something worthwhile here, which stimulates curiosity and interest; to build rapport and connection within a group or community so people are more willing to share what is on their minds; to draw out people's innate health. All this allows people's current thinking to slow or shut down so they become open to the new.

All these purposes are directly connected; to accomplish one is to accomplish all. If we live the understanding and have the feeling in our hearts we naturally emanate healthy energy, which creates a healthy climate around us, which is an environment or atmosphere that radiates a good feeling. This feeling is no mystery. It is a feeling we all like to be around: lighthearted, fun, warm, supportive, respectful. We need not make it any more complicated than that.

It seems to me there are four main facets to creating a fully healthy climate or creating a good feeling:

1) *Seeing people's Health and how it gets obscured*
2) *Having fun with people*
3) *Building rapport*
4) *Building hope*

These obviously overlap with what was stated earlier, but here we are interested in how a good feeling is created when we walk into a community or organization. Let's consider each one at a time.

1) Seeing people from a perspective of Health

No matter how badly people act, we want to see them as the innate Health they really are deep inside. We *know* and see in the moment that everyone deep inside *is* this Health, because it is embedded within everyone's spiritual essence, so to speak.

Suppose we don't believe in a "spiritual essence?" That's okay. In that case, could we see people's unlimited, infinite capacity to rise above their presenting behaviors or above their circumstances and to see new? Can we see either that when people's minds calm down or clear they have innate qualities of natural mental health, natural self-esteem, wisdom and common sense no matter how poorly they usually behave, or that they have the capacity to achieve these at any moment? As inside-out workers we see this potential in each person. We see hope. We see them as having within themselves all the answers they will ever need. We know they have the capability to tap into this inner, healthy state for themselves, *because it is who they Really are*, and this can happen at any time, no matter how bad things look in the moment. If we see beyond people's presenting behavior, no matter how troubled or troubling it appears, and truly see this innate Health in people, they *feel* it. Or even if we do not believe people have innate health in them, if we treat people as if they do, they generally respond better.

Another aspect of this is to see people's innocence; in other words, seeing people as always doing their best, given their current thinking. If they saw it differently, they would do it differently. Everyone is an innately healthy Self that from time to time innocently gets lost. We *know* the only reason people are not in touch with their Health is because their thinking has obscured it, diverted them from seeing it.

When people break the law, are violent, abuse their kids or partners, abuse drugs, are depressed, give us a hard time, it is only because their thinking is "off" and they aren't aware of it. They have no choice but to act on what their thinking tells them is "real." They have no idea their thinking is off-kilter, skewed; they are only following the "reality" they see. In that sense, people are innocent because they can't see anything else at the time.

If they're innocent, it is not difficult to see them with compassion, for it must be hard to live life the way they see it.

We can see them with humility, because we ourselves have done things in our lives that, looking back, we wish we hadn't but didn't know any better at the time. We all get lost sometimes. They're no different than we are. It just comes out differently because of different thinking, and some thinking is more extreme than others.

We can see them with forgiveness, "for they know not what they do." Thus, we do not have to take personally how they act toward us because it is just mixed-up thinking talking. This insulates us. When Roger Mills first started teaching his classes in the Modello housing project (Pransky, 2011)[13] the residents treated him with anything but kindness and caring. They wanted him out of there, and they treated him accordingly. Yet, in Dr. Mills's mind, he thought something like, "Of course they're going to treat me this way, given the way they see things now." That was his protection, the reason he didn't get brought down or get his feathers ruffled. He had complete faith that once they began to see their Health they would eventually come around. And they did. The initial meetings were chaos. Yet it was Roger's own Health that insulated him from both the chaos and however the residents treated him.

One reason people lose touch with their Health is they don't realize everyone sees the world differently; they don't realize everyone sees and lives in a "separate reality." Everyone has had different experiences through their own thinking and has been taught to see the world in different ways. This forms a perspective—a lens through which they see the world—that makes perfect sense to each individual, given the way s/he sees things, just as our perspective makes perfect sense to us.

---

[13] Pransky, J. (2011). *Modello: A Story of Hope for the Inner City and Beyond.* British Columbia, Canada: CCB Publishing

When people's perspective takes them away from their Health, wisdom and common sense, their own constructed "reality" has given them a distorted view. They are simply swimming in their own thought systems, which they have created without knowing it. Within their worlds they can justify anything they think and do. When people act disruptively or destructively, they are simply unable to see beyond their own creations of illusion that to them are "real" right now. But we know their creations are not real, and that is what protects us.

Seeing innocence does not mean denying someone is causing harm to another or displaying a lack of conscience by their actions. It has nothing to do with appropriate consequences. If they did harm, if they broke laws, they may have to pay, but that has nothing to do with the way we see them. If we hold grudges it only harms us, for those grudges are only within us. Forgiving and forgetting is letting go. It is our release. It frees our minds, so we can regain our clarity, regain our perspective and move forward with impunity. People are innocent because they aren't aware they've lost their perspective. We can see that people's worlds make perfect sense to them—as much sense to them as our world makes to us. When we see this, we take what others do and say less personally and our egos are less likely to bring us down when people aren't responding.

To see people this way gives us a certain perspective and feeling that helps to naturally guide us in our interactions. With that feeling in our hearts we approach others.

2) Having fun with people

Nothing draws people out of their conditioned thinking more than being relaxed, lighthearted, having fun, and feeling supported, cared about and respected. At those times people seem to forget the way they normally think. Practitioners who go out of their way to create this atmosphere around them in whatever they do find people drawn to them, because it feels good.

Having fun with people makes them want to come around. Simply hanging out with them and being lighthearted vibrates at a level that allows people's thinking to more easily feel good, which makes their defenses start to break down.

We also can create opportunities for fun. In the Modello housing project Mills and staff began to celebrate people's birthdays. They then went on picnics together, then to the beach, then on larger outings. Staff and residents were equal participants—no barriers. Lo and behold, the residents responded and began to open up.

What could be a better job than this!

The idea is to create a relaxed, light, positive environment where people will be most open to new learning, to have a good time with people so their barriers will naturally drop away. People's defenses and belief systems begin to break apart a bit. If people become immersed in good feelings they may inadvertently leave their entrenched thought systems behind. This is why this and the next related point are essential.

3) Building rapport

With a relaxed, positive environment and good feelings comes the building of rapport, which is our primary concern when dealing with anyone at first. In its simplest form, especially in the beginning, rapport is simply getting to know people, becoming friends. Lloyd Fields tells the story of when Roger Mills first hired him to work in Modello. Lloyd asked what he wanted him to do. Mills said, "Just go and be with the people, make friends with them." Lloyd asked, "And then what?" Mills said, "All I want you to do is go and be with the people." "I know I'm supposed to do that at first, but what do I do next?" "*Just go and be with the people!*" In other words, don't even think about doing anything else until you have hung out with them to the point where you have developed rapport. Unless that exists, there is no sense doing anything else with them or saying anything because they won't be able to hear it.

When working with anyone, one-on-one or as a group, a certain feeling exists within the relationship, a certain closeness or distance, a certain warmth or coldness. Without a reasonable feeling of closeness people's walls are often up. They are on guard. We would like people to see their lives with more perspective and understanding, but if they don't let us in, no learning can take place. Rapport breaks down the barriers so we can get in.

When working from the inside-out, practitioners who see rapport as their *primary task* tend to get further with others than those who do not. Even when confronted or challenged people respond better if rapport is high. Without it, people get defensive. We can see this in our own kids. Teachers can see it in their students. If we want people to learn from us, rapport must be at a high level. We can *feel* the rapport or lack of it. If we don't feel rapport, or if we had it but feel it slipping, we need to stop what we're doing and rebuild it.

For example, if I'm talking with my child about a concern and I can see he's not paying attention or is in a bad mood, I realize I'm not going to get anywhere with him at that time no matter how hard I try. I either have to wait it out until he recovers on his own or go out of my way to reestablish a warm, caring feeling before bringing up the concern again later when we are both more open. For the most part rapport comes from the respect we feel for the other person and having a warm feeling which comes from seeing the person's Health. We can be dedicated to staying in rapport and enjoying our time with people because it leads to trust and mutual respect.

Rapport is easiest when we are in a positive state of mind. If someone is in a low state, we do what we can to help their mood level rise before dealing with them.

If we want to be effective with anyone, people need to know we are there for them and they can count on us. Rapport comes naturally when people are grounded in their own Health and see the Health in others.

4) Building hope

Again, everything the Three Principles practitioner attempts to do initially is to open people to the fact that no matter what their lives have been to date there are always new possibilities. We can create the kind of climate where people begin to feel the Health within them. Some haven't felt this for a very long time. For a seed to fulfill its potential as a healthy plant it really helps to be in an environment that helps draw out or doesn't impede what is inside. When people begin to feel this Health, the thinking that has held them in place begins to break up and have less hold over them. When we see people as healthy, they begin to feel healthier. It gives them hope. When they see hope, a world of possibilities opens before them.

It is curious why some people see hope and others don't, even in the same situation. For example, most prevention practitioners see hope and possibilities, while many of the people they work with do not. Why? Are the hope and possibilities not there? Of course they are! They are only obscured from view. Why? Conditioned thinking is in the way—maybe it was their parents telling them they were no good or would never amount to anything; maybe it was having all kinds of terrible things happen to them. Whatever it *was,* it is *now* incorporated into their thinking, blocking them from seeing hope and possibilities for their lives. It's like a wall stands between them and the hope that exists. The way out of this, or the way one can be helped to see beyond it, is to see this barrier for what it is: only one's own thinking and nothing else. Their own thinking is the *only* thing blocking hope and possibilities. So people begin to see they are constructing their own barriers, and when they see this, the barriers begin to break up. Once the barrier disintegrates, what is left? The hope and possibilities that were always there in the first place!

Without hope, people have no reason to do anything. With hope, possibilities abound that we can't even imagine.

How do we give people hope? It is hopeful for people to know they are never stuck with the experience they are having because thoughts change, and they change on their own. The greatest hope, however, is the hope that comes from *knowing* that all people, no matter what their lives look like at the moment, have Health and wisdom inside them that can spring forth at any moment. It is *knowing*, as Syd Banks says, that people are always only one thought away from that Health. We just don't know when that thought will come. But it could happen in the next moment, because it has happened for many people. People's thinking has been known to change at the drop of a hat, and when it does their experience changes and with it sometimes their entire lives. Any of us who have seen this happen have a story to tell, and often those stories can give hope to others. We can tell those stories when the time feels just right. We can suggest to people that the way it looks right now isn't necessarily the way it *is*. We do have to be careful—the rapport and the feeling and the moment have to be right—but when it happens it can be very special.

Here is a little story of the power of hope:

The daughter of two close friends of mine, Walter and Valerie Crockett, gradually began to lose her coordination. She was diagnosed with an inoperable brain tumor, or so said a couple of brain surgeons. After Walter and Valerie recovered enough from the shock so they could function, they held out hope and kept exploring until they found a top surgeon who thought there was a chance of helping her. He operated with his "magic hands," as Valerie sings, and was able to get out most of the tumor. All were overjoyed, but the long-term prognosis was not good. The doctors said it would likely grow back; it was only a matter of time. Emily showed tremendous bravery going through radiation or chemotherapy treatments, where her head swelled up to twice its size. She was in tremendous pain.

Valerie and Walter Crockett are excellent musicians and gifted singer-songwriters, and they had cut a couple of CDs, but because they had to stay home and care for Emmy they couldn't tour to promote them. Because they are such wonderful parents and their kids always come first it never occurred to them to do anything else. Meanwhile Emmy began to listen to country music, especially to her favorite singer, Garth Brooks, on whom she had a pre-teen crush. She dreamt about him and was convinced she'd meet him. Her parents didn't see much chance of that.

One day when her condition began to look extremely bleak, with Emmy in tremendous pain, looking like she was losing all hope, it occurred to Val and Walt to contact the *Make a Wish Foundation* and *Dreams Can Come True* and *Why Me, Inc.* to see if they could arrange for Em to meet Garth Brooks. The Foundation said he was just coming off a long world tour and would be playing his last concert in New York City, and there was a slight chance they could meet then. A limousine arrived at their doorstep in Worcester, Massachusetts to bring them to New York City. They sat in a room waiting. The Foundation could not guarantee he would show up at all, and if he did they said he would likely be able to visit for only a few minutes.

Suddenly, Garth Brooks bounded into the room. He became so taken with Emmy that he stayed with her for over a half-hour. Emmy beamed. As he was ready to leave he said, “So you’re coming to the concert tomorrow night, right?” Walter said, “Gee, we weren’t really planning on it. We’re not even prepared to stay. We didn’t bring any extra clothes with us. We just thought we were coming down and going right back.” Garth said something like, “Of course you’ll stay,” and pulled out a roll of bills. He said, “You’ll stay on me. Buy yourself some clothes. I won’t hear of anything else.” They were floored! Keep in mind, at this time Garth Brooks was *huge*—so huge that, worldwide, only the Beatles and Elvis had sold more records. And this exceptionally popular man put them up in a hotel at his own expense and arranged for them to be at the concert in the set of box seats with his own family. At the end of the concert, on his own, he visited with Emmy again, and they spent more quality time together. And as they were leaving, he gave Emmy his guitar, the one he’d had with him on this worldwide tour, and he signed it personally to her. [Aside: I was not a Garth Brooks fan, music-wise, although I definitely admired his performing ability, but now he’ll always hold a very special spot in my heart.]

The family went back to Worcester to resume their lives, but a miraculous thing began to happen. Emmy’s spirits had lifted so much that she began to get better—not completely better (she became legally blind), but enough to resume fairly normal activities. For years afterwards, Emmy gained new hope for herself and began to thrive. She got accepted at Harvard University. Valerie and Walter Crockett put out a CD called *Emily’s Angel*, after Valerie wrote an extremely moving song by that title about their experience meeting Garth Brooks. Emmy even wrote a moving song herself about her meeting with Garth called, “One Special Day,” which she performed on that very CD.[14] Emmy lived far longer than anyone expected, even outliving her mother, Valerie who, extremely sadly, died of cancer some years later. For Emmy’s funeral, Garth Brooks sent an enormous and beautiful bouquet of flowers.

---

[14] Valerie and Walter Crockett, *Emily’s Angel*, Big Bark (783707292625), available from CD Baby https://store.cdbaby.com/cd/crockett1. There’s some great stuff on this CD, if I do say so myself.

But hope had given Emmy a very fulfilled life.

I don't even know how Walter made it after losing both his wife and daughter. Things looked bleak for a while. This man, whom I believe is arguably the best unknown songwriter in the U.S., somehow managed to channel his sorrow and energy to write more great songs about all that went down.

And now Walter Crockett is happily married again. There is always hope!

Hope is the most powerful thing in the world. Without it, people give up.

III. Deep Listening

If we want to affect people from the inside out, we must be able to see what is within them (figuratively speaking). The best way I know to see or hear this is through what I call "deep listening." Other terms I have heard to describe it are "soft listening," "quiet listening," "passive listening," or when working with little kids "magical listening"[15] or with teenagers "extreme listening." It doesn't matter what one calls it; it matters whether we engage it.

As I see it, deep listening has a number of related purposes. Each could perhaps represent a deeper level of listening. Some of these are: to feel a close connection to the person; to not be distracted by one's own thinking when listening; to understand how the person sees his or her world; to hear the grain of truth in the other person's point of view; to hear what the person does not see about his or her own thinking, to realize the best place to potentially have impact; to hear the answers embedded within spiritual energy about the situation or problem or the person.

In a workshop in Tucson, Arizona, when going around the room during the initial introductions, I watched one woman become so interested in what others were saying that at the break I approached her and said, "I couldn't believe how much you were listening to others when we were going around. I was impressed!" Matter-of-factly, she

---

[15] This term was coined by Debra Crosby of Swampscott, Massachusetts

replied, "Oh I'm just really fascinated with what other people have to say." That is deep listening! That's the idea, *to be fascinated* by others.

When people feel deeply listened to, rapport improves even more, so this also helps with the second "step" in the Three Principles Application Process.

Let's be very clear, many prevention and human services professionals have been taught "Active Listening" or "Reflective Listening" or "Empathic Understanding"—all different terms for essentially the same thing. *Deep listening is none of these*; in fact, it may be its opposite. In Active Listening the listener concentrates on the content of the communication so s/he can repeat back or clarify what the other person is saying. In deep listening we do not really pay attention to the content, we do not really listen to the words, we do not listen for the facts or details, we do not pay attention to body language or anything else. In deep listening we have *nothing on our minds*. In Active Listening we fill our heads with what the talker says; in deep listening we want our minds as empty as possible; we are *empty vessels*. In deep listening we are simply taking in the other person, almost as if listening to music. Most of us when listening to music do not analyze it, we simply let it wash over us and if powerful enough move us. In short, most of us *don't think about it*. This is what we are after in deep listening. Even the implication of "doing" is misleading. Deep listening is more a "nondoing." It is completely natural. It is the way we were meant to listen to others without our own thinking interfering.

Listening to be touched by a Feeling

Many of us in the fields of prevention and human services believe we are good listeners. I no longer think so. I used to think I was a great listener. Once I learned deep listening I could not believe what a poor listener I was. It wasn't my fault. I never knew there could be a deeper way to listen.[16] I used to think listening was about what people were saying; I never realized I could listen way beneath the words, even beyond what the person is trying to communicate, even beyond what

[16] I thank George and Linda Pransky for teaching me originally; then one day it just clicked in.

they are aware they even know. I had no idea we could actually listen to the spiritual energy that knows All. This is certainly not the kind of listening we are used to.

We can listen with soft ears the way a baseball player learns to have soft hands when fielding a ball. When a hard baseball is hit hard at a fielder, the hands must give with the force of the ball; otherwise the ball bounces off the hands like off a wall. In deep listening, we want to take in what the other person is trying to say without it bouncing off our thick skulls.

We could listen to be touched by what the person is saying.

First, we want to clear the decks of our minds. Take everything off it. To repeat, we become an empty vessel. Nothing in it. Nothing!

The first thing that helped me grasp deep listening is I discovered that when listening to others I never realized that while they were talking I would have thoughts. I might have thoughts about what they were saying, or what they were saying would remind me of my own issues or something else, or I might drift off, or any of a million things. Then without realizing it I would follow my own thoughts while the other person was still talking away; sometimes I would lose the talker completely. I have run enough workshops in the Three Principles and deep listening to know I am not alone. We all have this tendency. This is the opposite of having nothing on our minds.

Later I realized there are four main culprits that cause our minds to leave the listener a lot more than we would like:

1) Distractions (such as noise in the room or what I need to do later)
2) Ego (making it about me, such as how well am I doing with her, when my ego has no business even being in the room with us),
3) What I know (holding beliefs on our minds that we think we know, such as a psychological or spiritual theory or the way people should act or our values, and inadvertently filtering what they say through it)
4) Solutions (what they should do, or advice).

There are others, of course, but I've found these are the main types of thoughts that inadvertently take us off deeply listening.

What, then, are we to "do?" Again, it is not really doing, it is more of a *noticing*. No matter how hard we try we can't shut off our thinking. When listening to someone else we are guaranteed to have such extraneous thoughts. All we have to "do" is notice our thinking has left the other person and is now off in our own heads. As soon as we notice our thinking has "gone off," our mind automatically jumps back to the moment, like letting go of a taut rubber band.

From running many workshops and trainings I've observed that when most people experience deep listening for the first time it feels wonderful to them. Simply by deeply listening to another human being they feel such closeness to the person who is often a complete stranger. At the same time they are amazed at how often their own thinking leaves the other person and travels off into their own heads.

While a number of people pick this up easily because, really, it is our natural way to listen (even though we sometimes as easily slide back into our old listening habits), some others run into difficulties because they think they need to "do" something. They try to concentrate on it, so they find it hard. There is nothing hard about it, nothing to concentrate on. It is simply *being with* the person in a state of caring, fascination or love. The only thing that makes it hard is we get in our own way. With our own thinking we interfere with our natural way of being with others.

A Deep Listening story:

In a workshop in Western Australia, Danesh caught the importance of deep listening until he realized that his mother-in-law, who drove him crazy, was coming over that evening. I had the audacity to suggest he might want to try deep listening to her. He put his arms straight out and shook his head vigorously. "No way!" Apparently, his mother-in-law told the same stories again and again, and it drove him mad. I said, "Look, you're already having a lousy experience with her, what have you got to lose?" Danesh shook his head some more. Everyone laughed.

The next morning he came in beaming. He said, "I decided to try it, and it worked!" He said he heard things in what she said that he had never heard before—even in the same old stories—and it was really interesting. He felt a lot closer to her.

This is the power of deep listening.

Even with the most boring or repetitious person, wouldn't it be interesting to listen for what would make a person feel he had to do and say those things? This raises another point: Deep listening can occur at various levels.

Remember, deep listening is simply feeling a close connection with another human being. Because we are all part of the same formless energy, we would naturally feel this connection if we weren't thinking extraneous thoughts. If we didn't have the thought, "This person is boring!" we would not be bored; we would be naturally interested in whatever the person has to say. A close connection automatically has a nice feeling attached. When we feel it, we are listening in a deep, connected way. We feel an ease float over us. If it is effortful we are off the mark. The feeling is in the connection.

This would not be difficult at all if we realized we're about to sit with someone in a *sacred connection.* This human being is about to tell us something important about her or his life! S/he is entrusting us with it. We can feel *love* for the essence of who that person is.

Listening to Understand Another's World

The feeling remains, but at a slightly deeper level we also pick up an understanding of how the person sees her world. We see why she sees things as she does, what makes sense to her and why. From her viewpoint, what she sees makes perfect sense. We may not see it the same way ourselves, we may not agree with it (later), we may question it (later), but we come to understand why she would see it that way; her reasoning makes sense to us. It's like, "Oh, I understand how she could see that!" At this level we can pick up how the person may be trapping himself—not by analyzing it, not by trying to figure it out, not by fitting it into anything we know, but simply by what we pick up in the moment from what we hear. With a clear mind, intuition speaks.

An example: A woman in an inner-city housing project, was being bruised and battered by her live-in boyfriend. Asked why she stayed with him, she said, "It means at least I know he loves me." The Health Realization worker was taken aback; he had difficulty comprehending this connection, but he kept quiet and listened more deeply. Suddenly when his head cleared the idea popped into his head that she was insecure about being alone; that all she really wanted was someone to love and care for her. She didn't say this, but he heard it. Yet something didn't compute. No matter what? A question came to him: "You mean he shows you how much he loves you and cares for you by beating you up?" She seemed almost startled by the way he put it. It occurred to him to then offer, "That's not how I show my wife I love and care for her. I think she's worth a lot more than that. I think you are too." Within two months she booted the man out of the house and found a new boyfriend. It all started from the power of deep listening.

In deep listening, we are in "I don't know" mode; we don't know where we're going. We may well ask probing questions that occur to us in the moment or throw out various things to see if anything takes hold, but the only purpose is to then listen even more deeply to the answers. Then we might ask more questions that arise. In deep listening we never analyze or "figure out." Our questions may surprise us as much as they surprise the other person. We don't want to be thinking up questions; they simply arise. It is far better to ask nothing and simply listen than to try to think up a question. Making comments is even worse. The comment in the above example came out of listening in the moment. It felt right to say it then, which is the only reason it had impact.

Listening for the Grain of Truth

Our listening can easily get off track. Fortunately, we can realize it and get back on. Here is an example: On the first day of a Health Realization Applications training, a man objected when I made the statement that everything is an inside-out affair; no matter what experience we have it is always the result of our own thinking. Khalil said something like, "Now wait a minute! I can't buy that. Some experiences are absolutely determined by the outside." He raised the example of as a large black man walking into an elevator and coming upon a white woman. He said, "I know damn well she is afraid because I can see it in her eyes." Very forcefully he said, "Cultural and racial issues determine this reaction because of where we are in this society today, and neither that woman or me is making it up."

I asked whether this always happens with every white woman he encounters in this situation. He said, “Always!” His answer surprised me. I can’t remember exactly how I responded, but I remember feeling very solid and confident in what I said—something like, “That is certainly the way it looks on the surface. Clearly some people learn things like that as they go through life, but that doesn’t mean the outside world determines how we think and that we’re stuck with it.”

I remember leaning back in my chair feeling very relaxed, even while he was still objecting forcefully—until the thought popped into my head, “I can’t believe I’m sitting here discussing this emotionally-charged racial issue with an African American man, when I’ve never had the experience myself and it has obviously affected him big-time.” A killer thought! I believed it. I took the thought seriously. Big mistake! Suddenly I no longer felt on solid ground. He said I was polarizing the issue; that it is both the inside and the outside that makes a difference. He said with force, “It is *never* good to polarize and dichotomize!” The conversation became tense. All eyes were upon me to see how I would handle it. The feeling in the room dropped. In one respect I was kind of amused. This man was extremely intelligent, sharp as a whip, very tall, well-built, strong; I knew he had spent time in prison and I had the thought that if he ever wanted to wipe me out it would be like flicking a fly off his arm. Fortunately, I then had the thought that this conversation was no longer productive for the group, offered some feeble closing comment, and we took a break.

During the break I pulled Khalil aside. Before all this we’d felt a good connection; I thought we’d had good rapport and he really liked what he’d been hearing. So I said, “I hope you didn’t think I was putting down what you were saying or giving you a hard time or anything.” Before I could even finish he cut me off and said, “Oh, no, not at all! I really got a lot out of that conversation. I could tell you were really listening to me, and I appreciated that.” I was a bit surprised, but we talked some more in a good feeling. After the break, to be certain no uncomfortable feelings lingered, I announced to the group that Khalil and I were cool. The feeling in the group rose again, and we proceeded on from there.

In the middle of the night I woke up realizing that as soon as I started to run scared in that discussion I had stopped listening to him.

My listening had been pathetic. Taking a step back, I realized I had been too caught up in my "position" to hear the grain of truth in his side.

I realized his view contained two grains of truth: 1) Dichotomies are dangerous because they polarize, and it is best to find common ground; 2) Social and cultural forces tend to affect people's thinking. Both points are absolutely true. Had I been listening deeply enough at the time I would have picked those up, and we would have had common ground from which to proceed. On top of that, I had a grain of truth of my own: It is always and only our own thinking that ultimately determines our experience, no matter what social and cultural forces we are subjected to.

The next morning I explained to the training group what I had realized: how I had lost deep listening, and last night when I found it again I had seen the grains of truth in both our views. It elevated the entire conversation and feeling.

One of the morals of this story is that there is *always* a grain of truth in the other side, and if we listen deeply enough we can hear it. I could now see Khalil's world—at least as much as I could as a white man regarding this issue—and after I explained the "truth" I saw, he could see mine. We then had common ground from which to proceed. Both our worlds were elevated. The point, again, is when we listen at an even deeper level we can hear the grain of truth in the other side, and this comes directly from seeing how the other person sees his world.

This is the realm of curiosity. We are curious about what the other person is saying.

Listening for What the Talker is Not Seeing about How His Experience of Life is Created

At a still deeper level, our listening can pick up what the other person is not seeing about how her own thinking creates her experience. To hear this, our minds really must be free and clear. We are still feeling the feeling, still curiously picking up the other person's world; now we are adding a new dimension: *puzzlement*. At this level of listening we are puzzled by what the person is saying: "Wait a minute. This person says he understands his experience is created from his own thinking, yet he is still upset about what is happening in the outside world. This doesn't compute. I'd like to see more about what he's missing."

Here, other types of questions might occur to us. Again, we do not try to *think up* questions, for this will only get in our way. If a question does occur to us, by asking it out of our puzzlement we may help the talker enter a state of deeper reflection. This is because *we* want to better understand. However, the questions we ask are not the kind that keep the person going further down the same road with what she already knows, such as "What did you do about that?" or "How did that make you feel?" or "What were you thinking?" The talker already knows the answers to those questions because the answers are in the past. Nor are questions about the future helpful here, such as "What are you going to do?" or "What do you think will happen?" because the talker will base his answer on his current view.

Instead, we want a question that helps the person see more deeply, such as "What do you make of that?" or "Is that really true?" [Note: It is tough to come up with sample questions of this kind because there are no standard questions; they occur to the listener in the moment.] Questions such as these force the listener out of what he knows and plunges him into unknown territory, so he becomes surprised. He never considered that before. At an even deeper level of impact, the talker has new insights simply from our listening and questioning.

An example: Barbara rattled on in great detail about being frustrated by someone she felt was not being respectful to a group of teenagers because he appeared to be pushing his own political agenda on them. The listener asked, "What did he say?" "What did you do?" This caused Barbara to go into even more detail. I happened to be eavesdropping because this occurred during a listening exercise in my training, and a thought of curiosity and puzzlement came to me. I wondered what was behind her reaction. So I asked, "What makes you bothered by that?" It stopped her dead in her tracks. She had to go into reflection and consider it. She began to see it had something to do with her own expectations for the meeting and for kids' needs not getting fulfilled. Then she wondered, "So what?" Why was that important to her? Then she realized she carried some beliefs about how kids should be treated and how bad it was for anyone to thrust political agendas onto others. Suddenly she had an insight that not only were her own expectations a killer (that is, they gave her a bad experience of that meeting), but *any* expectations are deadly. She then had an "ah ha!" moment, as she realized that expectations always come from beliefs. Her own beliefs, her own thinking, had gotten in the way of an experience that would likely have been a good one otherwise. Furthermore, she realized she did that to herself a lot! It was a huge insight for her. All this came from deep listening, puzzlement, and a question that arose from that puzzlement. [Note: One can still point out in a caring way where someone else is off the mark, but this comes well after listening deeply.]

Questions such as "What did you say?" and "What did you do?" are horizontal questions. They yield more detail about what the person already knows, keeping the person at the same level of understanding. Such questions take people further along the horizontal road. Conversely, questions such as "What makes you bothered by that?" are vertical questions; they come out of our own puzzlement and draw the listener into a zone of deeper reflection. They are vertical because they take the person deeper.

When we listen with an empty mind we are able to see how people have innocently become lost in their own habitual thinking. The listener hears what to zero in on to help the talker gain deeper understanding. How would we know specifically what to teach people—how unbeknownst to them their thinking creates an insecure or fearful or angry or blaming or judging or anxious or stressed feeling in life—if it is also unbeknownst to us? The only way to discover what is going on inside them is through listening. Otherwise we're shooting in the dark, teaching about Health and thinking in general, in a vacuum, and expecting it to strike a chord or take hold.

Most of us have a tendency—I know I used to—to be too quick to try to teach. Deep listening slows us down.

Our own views can be one of the biggest drawbacks to deep listening. For instance, if we see a "client" or a housing project resident or anyone we're working with as a victim or a survivor or a perpetrator or an addict or a delinquent or whatever, we're listening through that image. If we have a tendency to agree or disagree with people based on our own views, we are listening only to our own views. If we see ourselves as having the answers (and they don't) that is what we are listening to. In any of those cases what we need to hear is blocked by the film of what we're holding onto. Our minds must be completely clear to hear what we need to hear.

What we're listening for is the fundamental assumption that keeps them stuck or in bad habits. With a clear mind we might realize, "Oh, I see what they don't understand." "I see what they're missing." On the surface this may sound like a contradiction, "Aren't you holding something on your mind by trying to find the assumption?" But it is not. All we're doing is setting an intention to see it, then taking it off our minds and forgetting about it. Seeing it does not arise through analysis, but from insight. We can tell the difference. What pops into our heads from analytical thinking sounds like old news. What comes from clear-minded insight surprises us. And with that surprise comes an appropriate response. If compassion is in order, it automatically arises. If we see they're getting too serious we automatically attempt to lighten things up.

Okay, in my attempts to be thorough, here, I probably made Deep Listening far more complicated than it need be. All we need to "do" is *be with* the person in a state of fascination or love, as an empty vessel with nothing on our minds. When extraneous thoughts do pop in, simply notice we've gone "off," which makes us snap back to the moment. When our minds are empty of all else, we have the best chance of picking up answers from spiritual energy that knows All. That's all we really need to know.

IV. Conveying or Drawing Out the Understanding

Once we have listened deeply to people (not that this should ever stop), when the moment feels right, which means when we get a hit about something, we are ready to help people understand where their experience really comes from. This is not teaching in the traditional sense; this is *knowing* everyone already has within him or herself the understanding of how our thinking creates our experience and how everyone is perfectly Heathy and whole within. Our job is to help draw it out of them, to bring it into the light. After all, this *is* everyone's essence, this is who we all really are deep inside; we can't teach that! We can, however, help people see who they really are, and how it is only obscured from view. Most people don't realize this, as we once didn't.

The information imparted through the Three Principles is a description of how the mind works to give us experience of life, moment to moment. It is about what makes people tick as human beings. It is about what allows people to live in well-being. It is about how people create illusions that look like reality. It is about how everyone has something inside themselves so beautiful and so perfect that they are already everything they are looking for, and how they can be guided by their own wisdom. If people hear this, it gives them the key that unlocks new worlds and new possibilities for their lives.

Because they already really know this deep inside, our job is to help them realize they know it. When people *do* see it, it comes in the form of an insight. Remember, an insight most often comes when the mind is relaxed—and people's minds are most often relaxed when they are in a good feeling. So when teaching, if people experience a good feeling we know we are headed in the right direction.

To help create real transformative change, a change in consciousness, we can help people see the Three Principles in action in their own lives. In inside-out prevention this understanding is the foundation for change.

As inside-out practitioners we each have one thing that cannot be refuted: our own personal experience and understanding. This is the only thing we can convey with certainty. However, if what we are doing is drawing out what others already know deep in their souls, somehow there must be a convergence. What, then, do we teach? In this sense the word, "teaching" is really a misnomer. It is more of a "drawing out" or "unveiling." I use the word "teaching" only because it is easiest.

Ultimately, Three Principles understanding attempts to help people realize the power they have to see differently and therefore to create their lives differently. Could anything be more empowering than to see that they are not really stuck in their hopelessness? Could anything be more empowering for people than to see their lives anew, to see that such views are only thought-created illusions of the mind? That people don't have to freak themselves out by what they've made up? To realize they are already what they seek? To see any of this could set them free.

Teaching from the Heart

How do inside-out practitioners draw out what lies hidden inside? Unlike outside-in prevention, there are no "how to's." In outside-in prevention, especially in these days of set "evidence-based" programs and curricula, many would have us believe we can almost follow a script: Here is the information and the skills that must be taught, and here is how to do it; here are the risks that must be reduced and the assets that must be increased. If we do these, we have been led to believe, we will produce fewer problems. As we have learned, however, it is not that simple. In inside-out prevention we approach teaching in a completely different way.

How we approach inside-out teaching is akin to someone asking, "How do you create a love relationship? How do you make it happen?" Can we really give an answer? We could say things like, "Well, you want to be interested in your prospective lover, you want to be yourself, be supportive of them, treat them kindly, be lighthearted," etc. You can do all those things perfectly but a love relationship still may not occur. It's a mystery. All we know is, if we have this as an intention and are pointed in that direction, we may have a better chance of achieving a love relationship than if we did the opposite, but even this is not a guarantee. This is similar to inside-out teaching. If we point our minds in the direction of drawing out people's Health and helping them see how their experience of life is created and changes, we might have a better chance of helping them see it, but *we cannot make it happen.*

Therefore, it is wise not to take responsibility for it one way or the other. Everybody has the answer already within them—they just don't know it *yet*. The emphasis is on the "yet." As a conveyor of this understanding all I can take responsibility for is my own life and my own intention and to give it my all. Anything else is ego-involvement, which does not serve anyone well.

Again—I keep repeating this because it is so critical—the entire idea of this teaching is to point people in the direction of realizing that at every moment they create their own experience of life, which up to now they have been calling "reality" but is really their own self-created version of reality, out of which they then think, feel and act; and how they are beautiful, wise beings inside. By realizing this, their experience of life is created anew; it becomes healthier and they experience more well-being. If this were so easy, of course, merely telling people how it all works would be enough to change their perspective, feelings and behavior. But the understanding is elusive—until people see it for themselves. God knows why, but our own little minds or egos often seem to try to protect what we've constructed for ourselves and block us from seeing the Three Principles in action.

Unfortunately, all we have at our disposal to convey this understanding are words (and pictures), and they have no power. Words need life behind them, a feeling behind them, to have a chance of affecting others. If we have felt the power of this experience ourselves, that is what we convey, because it is part of us. Only then will others be able to feel it, yet only if we feel it in the moment we're conveying it. Otherwise even our own experience has no power behind it.

Entry Points

Needless to say, in many communities it would not work at first to go in talking "Mind, Consciousness and Thought." We could use that language, but few would listen. More likely, they would think us crazy or from outer space. How can we best help people hear the message of the Principles, then, without (at first, anyway) using that language? Well, what will people be open to hearing? What will be our entry so ultimately they see Mind, Consciousness and Thought in action?

For the first year or two, perhaps more, residents of the Modello Housing Project neither heard nor saw the language of "Mind, Consciousness and Thought," yet their lives changed dramatically. If they didn't see the Three Principles, what did they see?

Let's look at how the understanding of the Principles was conveyed in Modello. What did the residents pick up and how? Dr. Mills and his workers first followed the "steps" of the inside-out process: 1) They emanated a feeling of Health themselves; 2) They went out of their way to create a healthy environment and gain rapport; 3) They listened very deeply. From these alone, the residents began to see that they were cared about no matter what, that there is hope and that they were listened to. It felt good to be around the staff—they had fun around them—no matter what the staff were talking about.

On top of that, through what the staff conveyed, the residents saw-

- their own Health
- how their thinking took them away from this Health, mostly through:
  - low moods
  - separate realities (everyone sees the world differently)
  - taking things personally
- that in a calm state they had access to their Health
- that their feelings came from their own thinking, not from what happened to them

When people saw their internal resource of health and wisdom, it enhanced their hope. When they saw they were not at the mercy of their circumstances, they found even more hope. Though they did not hear much about "Mind" and "Consciousness" at first, they certainly began to see "Thought" in their lives. The residents didn't have to learn the Three Principles, per se, but they experienced their essence. What they found was enough to raise their consciousness and lift themselves into a new life.

What, then, might be the "*entry points*" to learning about The Three Principles? An entry point, as I envision it, opens the doors to hearing. What points of learning might be heard fairly early on? To answer this, it seems important to ask ourselves a few questions:

1) What do people see when they do not see the Three Principles operating in their lives?

It seems to me people who do not see Mind, Consciousness and Thought in their lives see reality (the way things are); circumstances (that the outside world does things to them and affects them); feelings have a life of their own; what they think is right, etc.

That's pretty much what I saw before I had this understanding. So this is what we are up against. People do not easily let go of these. After all, it is life as they know it. It is their world. It makes sense that people would resist these new (for them) ideas. As soon as they see something new within, resistance begins to subside.

2) What specifically do we want people to see and realize?

While it may make little sense to talk to community residents about Mind, Consciousness and Thought, at least at first, it makes a lot of sense to teach or draw out that everyone has Health and common sense inside them that will arise when their minds clear. It makes sense to teach that their minds are not clear in low moods or when they're angry or running scared, so it would be sensible to step back and calm down before acting. It makes sense to help people understand how everyone sees things differently, how people act based on the way things look to them, and how it doesn't help to take personally what other people do or say to us because that's just the way they see it. While it may make little sense to teach about "levels of consciousness," it makes a lot of sense to help people see that there are many different ways to see the same situation, and the way they're seeing it now will change when their thoughts change, and whatever they see causes them to feel whatever they're feeling, and sometimes what they see brings them closer to their Health than other ways.

The key is always to help people look to the inside-out nature of their experience, to Mind, Consciousness and Thought in action. If we can point people in this direction, the life they experience can and often will change.

When people are exposed to such understandings our hope is it resonates with something deep inside them, leading to new insights that allow their innate health and wisdom to guide them in healthier ways. They must see it operating in their own lives. This is its only relevance. Once they see the Three Principles in action in a way that makes sense to them, life never looks the same. We all get off track and lose sight of it at times, but once we *see* it, in the back of our minds it is always there. Everything we do as practitioners is to help people see how the answer lies inside them. As people quiet their minds and clear their heads, they are better able to hear and tune into their own wisdom; then they will have even more insights.

3) How do we help them see these?

How do we know what specific points to try to convey at any given moment? This can only come from deep listening with a clear mind. What we teach comes out of the present moment as things naturally arise. This keeps our teaching fresh and relevant.

Remember, it is important for the hearer to be in a receptive state. If the person we are working with is in a low mood, forget about teaching. Instead, do whatever we have to do (without being obnoxious) to *elevate their mood level.* This isn't being "touchy-feely"; this is what works!

Still before attempting to convey anything, especially if people are riled up about something, we want to help them disengage from the situation and quiet their minds. We want to *help their minds calm down.* Then we can help them see the difference in their thinking, feelings, actions and results when they're calm compared with when they're not.

Now we are ready to teach. Now we can take any opportunity to help them look in this inside direction. This can happen in a nearly infinite variety of creative ways, limited only by our own imaginations (thoughts) as practitioners.

Mills, for example, used community conflicts to point people in the direction of Thought. As he described it, "When meetings would start to get negative or conflicted we could point back to how people were thinking about things at that moment," and how different the thinking was on each side. This was not a set, canned approach. It occurred to Mills in the moment—not by listening to the different sides of the conflict but by *listening deeply to what was behind the conflict*; that is, to the differing thoughts each side believed were real.

A little story may help here.

I once taught a course at the New England School of Addictions Studies called "Deep Listening, Conflict Elimination and Peace." In the middle of the session, out of nowhere, a Puerto Rican student pulled out a camera and snapped a picture of another Puerto Rican student across the room. The second student flipped out and started yelling at the first student. A heated argument erupted. I and the other students were taken aback. Then I remembered the title of the workshop. I realized, "What a gift! Here we have a conflict right in front of our eyes!" Clearly, these two fellows were not listening to each other. So I calmed everyone down and said, "This is great! Let's turn this into a learning experience." I talked a little about how sometimes we all get so caught up in the way we see things that we can't see the other side.

So I asked the fellow who'd flipped out, "What made you get so upset? What was behind that?" He said where he grew up in Puerto Rico he was brought up to believe that if someone took a picture of you, they were taking away part of your soul—so he expected his permission asked before anyone took a picture of him. The group was stunned, including the Puerto Rican photographer. So I turned to him: "What made you want to take his picture? What was behind that?" He said, "Hey, I just wanted to take a picture of mi hermano, my Puerto Rican brother, you know?" He said he just appreciated having him there and wanted a record of it to take home. Again, everyone was surprised.

Just by listening deeply to the other side the conflict disappeared. They could appreciate and respect each other's sides, and their own views became elevated. It was a tremendous learning experience for everyone. The teaching came from the listening; I hardly had to say a word. (My other option was to run scared and try to stop the conflict.)

Deep within ourselves as workers we have answers for how to help any individual, organization or community, *if* we quiet our own minds and stop trying to figure out what to do or say.

Vehicles Through Which the Understanding Can Be Conveyed

Since we can't often go up to people and out of the blue start talking about any of those points above, we usually need some *vehicle through which to legitimately convey this understanding*.

Obviously, if we are engaged in a counseling or training session, or if someone comes to us for assistance, those are legitimate vehicles automatically. But what if working in a community?

In Modello (Pransky, 1998), at first Mills attempted to establish a Leadership Training course as a vehicle. This gave him legitimacy to talk about Thought and common sense within the context of leadership. While it served the purpose of a legitimate vehicle, it did not work well. In my view, this was because the people did not ask for it. A few months later, through a survey questionnaire, he and staff did ask the residents what they wanted and what their hopes and concerns were. This requires listening, so we are able to see the places we might best have impact. What are people interested in? What do they care most about? Through what venues would they most likely show up to hear something new?

Okay, first they fed them. When they offered free food, people showed up.

Modello survey results indicated residents were concerned about their kids' behavior, so Dr. Mills and staff set up an informal parenting class. They did not use a traditional parenting curriculum but instead used the class as an opportunity to talk about their kids in relation to Thought and common sense and moods and separate realities and taking things personally. It took hold. It began to make a difference in people's lives because it hit home. But the residents still did not show up in droves; they were still skeptical, still angry about other times when other service providers and politicians had come in and let them down, still fearful. So it didn't happen all at once.

But having only a few people show up was enough for Mills and staff, for they knew once people had a good experience there and their lives with their kids (and their own lives) began to improve, word would get out. Once word got out they knew other people would come. "If you build it [right], they will come."

Other vehicles also were developed from questionnaire results. It showed residents concerned about the way school treated their kids, so the staff helped them set up a Parent-Teachers Association (PTA). They were concerned about the Housing Authority not fixing the problems in their apartments, so the staff helped them set up a Residents' Association. It didn't matter that most of the same people were involved in each, each vehicle served the purpose of meeting people where their interests lay, and all those vehicles became the venues through which most teaching occurred. For example, the staff helped the residents to see that the nasty woman behind the desk may have had a bad day, perhaps a difficult life. This enabled them to see her with new eyes, so they became less confrontive. It is hard to fight with someone for whom you feel compassion.

At the same time, Mills and staff would hang out around the projects, and when residents began to feel comfortable enough with them, they began to share their problems. Thus, informal, friendly counseling or coaching became still another vehicle to help residents see their problems in relation to the Principles. Further, the staff played the role of social workers, their first intent being to help people with whatever they wanted or needed. When those residents felt comfortable enough, as issues arose they would use this connection as another vehicle to draw out this understanding.

The proper vehicle for teaching is whatever the community process yields or whatever the prevention program is. People learn in different ways; some are more open to particular things than others, so each vehicle provides a different opportunity to convey the understanding in ways connected to day-to-day life. We can use educational settings, cultural settings, religious settings, parent-child settings, youth programs, community prevention partnerships, etc., as opportunities to provide information to their participants that might bring about insights about how one's experience of life is created.

Teaching from the Impersonal

When talking with folks it is important to remember *we are not dealing with their personal issues so much as with how everyone gets caught up in the same ways yet has access to the same Health and wisdom to rise above any circumstances. We are after the universal connection, not the personal.* We can use the personal as examples of what we *all* do.

Sometimes, ironically, when we hit too close to home people's walls go up, and they will not hear what we have to say. When Three Principles practitioners counsel alcoholics, for example, they may avoid examples that pertain directly to drinking, at least at first. It is too close to home. Defenses are summoned to protect. On the other hand, they may be able to hear something about people who, for example, have gotten caught up in other addictions such as food or heroin. In other words, because we don't want them listening through their defenses, we may not want to use examples about their specific problem. For example, in speaking with a problem drinker, we might talk about how some people's thinking tends to get them to see food or their bodies in a skewed way so that their food intake gets messed up, and the way they eat makes sense to them but to no one else. [Note: I do not like giving such examples because people may think this is *the* example one should use with someone who has a drinking problem. It is not; it is just something that came to me. All I'm suggesting is that people can sometimes see things better when their defenses and denial are not directly attached.] If they see it, it may strike something in them about their own lives, but it happens inside their own heads. They make their own connections.

When people experience a problem, they can be helped to realize the relationship between the problem and their own thinking. One can see where this might be a touchy subject. When people have a problem they don't often want to look at themselves; they don't want to see their own thinking as the culprit. People tend to see the causes of their problems residing in the outside world. When faced with the possibility that their problems may emanate from within, defenses abound. It may sound at first as if we're saying what happened to them is their fault, or they attracted the problem to themselves somehow, but that is not at all what we are saying. We *are* saying what they are now seeing as a problem might be seen by others—or by themselves at some time in the future—as, for example, an opportunity. If so, they wouldn't be seeing a problem. They're the ones who decide, with their own thinking whether something is a problem or not.

Again, we're not talking about what happens to them—what happens in the outside world is what's real; but from then on it's all interpretation and the meaning they make of it. This is via Thought. We are talking about *how they experience* what happens to them. This does underscore the care we might take to teach this understanding as impersonally as possible, because it can be heard wrong.

Besides, we are not so much interested in helping them solve one particular problem as we are in helping them see how they get themselves into these types of problems in general; in fact, how people in general tend to get themselves into such problems. And getting out starts with the opportunity to see it differently. A bigger picture exists than their individual problems. The larger the perspective, the better. On their own they will make the connection to their own problems.

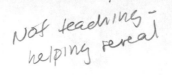

A Spiritual Connection

Remember, we don't want to lose sight of the fact that no matter how it is conveyed our intent is to touch people on a deep, heart level, to help people transcend their analytical thinking and jump directly into that deeper knowing or deeper intuition that holds the answers. We want to help people see how they have a built-in, natural tendency to move toward their Health without needing to rely on anything external; they need only get out of their own way (just like us). In certain states of mind we have thoughts that interfere with our natural healthy state, but we can discount such thoughts. We don't have to listen to those thoughts; we don't have to believe them as truth, thus, we don't have to follow them. In so doing we strengthen our psychological immune system—our natural, internal resilience. As Mills said on the Today show in 1990, "People's lives become what they think is possible. Take the blinders off and their own natural wisdom and common sense will rise to the surface."

Our job is to help bring what they know deep inside into the light.

Why don't we simply come right out and describe the Three Principles and how they work? Sometimes we can; sometimes we do, but many people won't hear it. To try to describe the formless is a contradiction in terms because we only have words (form) to describe it, so it can never be truly accurate. If words are inadequate, pictures or diagrams aren't much better, for people have their own interpretations (thoughts) of what the pictures or diagrams mean. With some people they resonate, and with others they won't. The idea is not to rely on other people's diagrams or the way they say things (unless it particularly resonates) but to use illustrations that arise from one's own insights.

Metaphors can help bring our points to life by stimulating visual images not easily forgotten. George Pransky is king of the metaphor. For example, when describing how we give thoughts power, he likened a thought to a seed that blows in on the wind. Without nourishment, he said, that seed would simply blow away with the wind. A seed's nourishment is water. Give that seed water, and it begins to take root. A thought's nourishment, he said, is attention. Give that thought attention—take it seriously—and it begins to take root in your head.

Otherwise it is just a harmless thought that blows out of your mind; it blows in, it blows out. That image has never left me and is now part of me.

Metaphors can be used to convey meaning. For instance, a metaphor came to me about how our habits of thinking begin to look normal to us and becomes our "reality." I realized when we put on a strangely colored pair of sunglasses like yellow, at first everything looks weird, but if we leave them on for a while everything begins to look normal. That's how our belief systems work. When we look out at the world, without realizing it, we are filtering whatever we see through our own self-generated belief systems, and whatever we see looks real.

Another image I got was picturing an anorexic person looking in the mirror thinking she is fat when everyone else considers her bone-skinny. This illustrates how the world we see with our eyes combines with our thinking, regardless of whether it has any basis in so-called reality or not, and the reality we see with Thought determines how we think, feel and act. But that person can't see it! We can see it with an anorexic, but we can't see what we have made up about ourselves any more than an anorexic can about herself.

When people are attuned to pick up metaphors they begin to see them everywhere. The metaphors we ourselves see are the most powerful when talking with others.

Stories can also be useful—if they are relevant to the point and help illustrate it. Particularly our own stories.

Here's one of mine: One day I realized that with our thinking we make up what is important to us at any given time, and later it changes. One slippery winter's day in a town near Boston, with snow falling, I had driven down from Vermont for one of the very early "Psychology of Mind" New England gatherings. The driving had become intense, so I was glad I made it. I carefully parallel-parked my car on a street with a slight hill. As I picked up my notebook and papers for the meeting and half-opened the door to get out I put my left foot on the ground and happened to glance behind me for a split second. I saw a car sliding toward me down the little hill, out of control, wheels locked, on the slippery snow and ice. Thank God I still had reflexes then, because instantly I leaped back into my car—I have no idea how—just before the other car slammed into my half-opened door, smashed and bent it nearly off its hinges, clipped my left elbow in the process and propelled my notebook and papers out into the street. As the car skidded by, miraculously missing the main body of my car by less than an inch, I somehow rebounded back toward the door and ended up hanging upside-down with my head nearly on the ground. My arm was slightly cut and bleeding, but that's all! It had all happened so fast I was stunned. When I recovered I realized I could easily really have been killed, and only by the grace of God was I not. At that moment, suddenly life looked different to me. All the difficulties I'd been holding onto, thinking one moment before that they were all-important I suddenly saw as the trivial, petty things they were. I had been talking with people for at least five years about how Thought creates our experience, but until that moment I never realized how much Thought really, truly did. Life suddenly seemed very, very precious, and I no longer felt like wasting my time or energy on trivial garbage. This thought, of course, is not unique to me. I originally wrote this shortly after 9/11 when the World Trade Center was wiped out by terrorists and many people lost their lives. Many who made it out and who witnessed it suddenly realized what was important in their lives, and it didn't have much to do with what they considered important moments before. More fascinating to me was the fact that, over time, I found myself sliding right back into my old routine, getting caught up in the usual pettiness—because it was such a habit! This blew me away. A month later it was like my nearly getting killed had never happened. Same with many witnesses to terrorist attacks as it began to fade from immediate memory. Yet, what we glimpsed then, even though it faded not too long afterwards, was a lot closer to the truth of our inner selves. And when we do remember, it comes back. More important, that truth of what's really important can be accessed at any moment because it *is* who we *really* are!

Telling other people's stories can be powerful as well, but only if we are feeling the power of it in the moment. This is why in this book I included other people's stories in their own words through interviews. It makes this understanding come alive.

Some people, of course, can tell stories and use metaphors and give talks as if it is second nature. This is George Pransky's gift and Michael Neill's. Syd Banks spoke at such a deep level in such a quiet way that people listening to him were usually on the edge of their seats. Because Banks and Pransky could do it so well, somewhere along the way "giving talks" became *the* way to deliver the message, and this proved to be as much of an "activity trap" as anything else. Some of us aren't silver-tongued devils. But nearly everyone can speak from the heart. Still, practitioners must use whatever means of communication resonates with them most.

This brings us to the use of ***experiential activities***, highly regarded in the field of prevention. In the past, they had not been so highly regarded in the Three Principles world, but I, for one, like using them. For example, I went through a stage in my teaching development when at times I asked people to pair up with someone to reflect on and talk about what they picked up from their parents that may have developed into their own thinking habits today. Such activities helped people see vividly how they had inadvertently taken on their parents' thinking. Yet this, too, can be a trap. The more "canned" approaches we bring in, the less in the moment we are. Something that worked once won't necessarily work again if it doesn't have the same energy behind it. I found myself not using that question anymore. Besides, when working in a community it is very unlikely we would use experiential activities, except possibly as part of a formal training.

Interestingly, metaphors and stories and examples and activities are only relevant when we know our ***point***. A clear, succinct one-sentence point guides us. What point are we really trying to make? Do we even know? If we don't, it would be wise to go into reflection about what it is. Going too far into illustration or examples may obscure the point. On the other hand, if we simply state the point, people will likely not get what we're talking about. They will hear the words but will not connect in any meaningful way. It is wise, then, to strike a balance between the point and the illustrations. The best point I ever realized is "All we are is peace, love and wisdom, and the power to create the illusion that we're not." Our job then becomes to help people grasp what it really means for them and their lives, by any means necessary. This is where metaphors, stories and experiential activities come in—to help them grasp it.

One of the trickiest yet potentially most impactful ways of teaching is through participant ***questions***. Here is where the presenter, trainer or practitioner must have a truly solid grounding in the understanding. Some people's questions can be downright challenging. Personally, I teach best through having people ask me questions, because it keeps me fresh. I love it! It takes me out of myself and requires being in the moment.

I remember an incident when I was running a training at the Red Lake Reservation in Minnesota. I was talking about how we create our reality with our own thinking. One Native man, Duck Soup, who apparently had always dreamed of becoming a professional baseball player, raised his hand and with kind of a smirk on his face asked, "So, are you saying that if I think I'm a great baseball player, then I will be?" The question took me by surprise. It was a brilliant question I had never considered. I paced around for almost 15 seconds in deep reflection. It came to me! I said (something like), "What I'm saying is this: If you go to a baseball tryout thinking you're a great baseball player, and you're in the field and make brilliant plays, you'll walk away confirming the fact that you're a great baseball player. If you go to that same tryout and make a bunch of errors, you'll walk away thinking you had an off day. Either way you still think you're a great baseball player. But this has nothing to do with whether you are or not. Our thinking determines what we see about ourselves. The notions about ourselves that we carry with us are self-validating and self-consistent. In other words, no matter what happens, either way we make it fit our view. Either way, we validate what we believe to be true and it keeps our view consistent. It's just another way our thinking tricks us. But the way we see it doesn't necessarily make it true or 'the way it is.' It's only true for us, according to the way we see it."

On the other hand, I remember hearing George say (something like), "People who have heart attacks and religious experiences change their world view." World views can change with a large enough insight. If that fellow went to ten major league baseball tryouts and kept making errors and being rejected, at some point it may sink in that he might not be as good as he thinks he is. That would be an incredible shift in thinking for him. When I first realized this, I remember thinking, "Wow, we're never really stuck with what we see. It could change any time! We just don't know when." I remember thinking of the many people with whom I had worked over the years who believed they were stuck where they were, and it was *not true!* It could change at any moment. And people don't need huge epiphanies or religious experiences to do it. Any change of thought of enough magnitude accomplishes the same thing, because it is the same thing. In Modello, for example, many of the teen drug dealers suddenly realized (something like), "Hey wait! This is a dead end. I could be somebody!" Suddenly they saw no matter how much illegal money they gained, it never seemed like enough because they would go through it like water, but if they worked for it legitimately they would appreciate it more. Partly because they made far less money legitimately they would spend far less, and they realized they actually ended up with more in the long run. Plus, it felt better. This change could not have come about if their world view had not changed. One moment they're drug dealers, and the next moment they're kicking the rest of the dealers out of the neighborhood and keeping it safe. Why? They had a new thought, a big new thought about their lives, a new thought about who they were, a new thought about what should be. *Only one new thought* and the world one sees changes. Only a thought! That's all! That's the amazing thing about it.

They are the ones with the answers, not us.

Again, once people begin to see it is not the circumstances of their lives that cause their problems but the way they *think about* the circumstances of their lives, life can't look the same. It simply can't! Even abusers and victimizers can begin to see what has seemed so real and compelling maybe isn't so real and compelling and can be questioned.

In my observation it often takes a couple or few days of training for most people to truly see the Principles in action in their lives and to understand how the Three Principles can be used to help others. Or it takes hanging out with people in a community or organization over the long haul. Some see it right away; some never see it. It cannot be found through the intellect, only by being struck by the feeling of it, so one knows it in his or her heart. None of this can happen, none of it means anything, without the next "step" in the process.

V. The Ultimate: A Shift in Perspective

As I have said repeatedly, intellectual beliefs about the Three Principles mean nothing; it only matters whether people discover these for themselves. This can happen only through *insight.*

Again, we cannot make an insight happen in anyone else, yet it is *the critical point of change*. An insight is a sight from within, a moment of understanding, a vertical jump in one's "level of understanding" that lifts people into a new "reality" where they see more of the big picture and see things less personally. *Understanding* here refers to the degree to which Thought is recognized as the source of one's experience.

Very little can be said about how to help spawn insight, except it happens in a moment when the mind clears. Sometimes this happens when the mind quiets down, sometimes when one forgets what one knows; sometimes it comes from dropping into a feeling of momentary Health from out of the blue, sometimes from having one's world shaken up when the mind is so scrambled that it goes "tilt" as in an old pin-ball machine and the world one saw no longer makes sense. Again, we can get people to the portal, but we can't make them go through it. We can't take responsibility for whether someone has an insight. No one can change anyone's thinking except the person herself, and most often it doesn't happen on purpose.

People either connect with this or they don't. We may never be able to reach everyone. But anyone can be reached! If we see people are not connecting, not having insights, there is not much we can do—except ***make adjustments*** to what we are doing. We might go back through all the steps or components above to see if we are on track. We might ask ourselves, for example: Am I in a good feeling? Am I creating a lighthearted feeling around me? Am I seeing the person's Health? Do I have still have rapport? Is my mood right? Has the other person slipped into a reactive or negative state of mind? Am I listening deeply enough? [That might be the most important one.] Am I being judgmental, or am I running scared for some reason? Am I really heart connected to what I am conveying? Am I being creative enough in how I'm attempting to help them see it? I don't mean this as analysis but as reflection. Impatience won't help. People have insights in their own

time. If they experience a good feeling they are on the right track; that is all we need to know.

If the people we're working with are not "getting it," if no matter how hard we try we still have not been able to help spawn insight, we may have to become even more creative in helping them see it. The most important adjustment we can make is to go into even deeper listening.

Once while conducting "an intensive" weekend counseling session, my client, a member of a fairly popular rock band, spent the entire first day getting nowhere. He was scared to death of getting married to a woman he'd been living with for a long time who, by all appearances, was perfect for him. He was even more afraid of having kids because he didn't want to mess them up like he felt he'd been messed up by his father. He couldn't commit. He didn't want to chance tampering with his life-style (which included a lot of women falling all over him). That night, reflecting on it, listening deeper, I realized, great guy that he was, he didn't really want to change; he wanted life to change around him. I realized I needed to shock him out of it. An amazing thought came to me out of the blue: "Kick him out! Give him his money back and show him the door." The thought really unnerved me. I said, "I can't do that!" I didn't know if I had the nerve. But the thought kept coming back. It felt right. Besides, we had good rapport.

So next morning that's exactly what I did. After explaining that we weren't getting anywhere and how I felt, I said, "There's the door" He was stunned—shaken. "Or," I said, "you could really commit to opening your heart to change. Take your money and run, or commit for the rest of our time together and pay the full amount. It's up to you." Freaked out at the prospect that he'd be leaving in the same condition as he'd arrived, he broke down. Something shifted in him, he decided to stay, and we got further in the next hour that we had the entire first day. I wouldn't recommend this. I never have done that again; I never had that thought again, thank God! Scary! Sometimes wisdom we can't even believe and seems totally off the wall is the best—for that particular moment. But it must feel absolutely right. Wisdom knows more than we do.

If someone is stuck, and we don't know how to reach him or her, we could say to ourselves, "I don't have a clue how to reach this person, but I know the answer is there." Then take it off our minds, put it on the back burner, and wait for something to occur. If it doesn't, it may simply mean the person is not ready to see it yet (or we aren't), and that's okay.

Insights happen more when typical thinking disengages. The mind disengages more in a good feeling.

People, of course, can have insights anywhere. Most prevention programs, however, leave this to chance. The Three Principles appears to move more people more closely to having big insights about how their experience is created, because it is intentional.

VI. The Ripple Effect

When people see the Three Principles play out to the point their lives improve, they feel so good they automatically want to give away what they learned to others. The contrast with their former lives means they have some real live experiences to offer. Their own lives reflect more well-being and they are so excited by it that they want to give it away to others.

Once their own lives improve, a natural process seems to unfold. First, they act differently in their relationships at home, so their family relationships improve. They begin to emanate a better feeling. Others like being around them more. They begin to see value in applying this in their work, so their work relationships improve. They begin to listen more deeply to others. They may then try to teach this understanding to others. Sometimes they find this is not so easy because they cannot find adequate words, but by simply living the feeling and talking about their own experience they begin to impact others. Note, these are the very same steps in the process as outlined above, yet they have begun to occur naturally—living the feeling, creating a good feeling around them, listening, and passing along what they know.

When they do have an impact on others, the improvements become exponential, like ripples in a pond. If a critical mass of people in a community or organization whose lives have been affected then begin to meet together as a group, they have a natural inclination to use their understanding to improve their community or organization.

To sum up this rippling process, first their own lives improve, then they reach out to others, then they improve the relationships around them and change their immediate conditions. When a critical mass of people with this new perspective come together, they naturally work to create community change by changing community conditions. Given their newfound health, they no longer want to live in unhealthy conditions and work together to change them. Hence, prevention from the inside-out.

Teaching Maintenance

Once people learn this understanding—just when they think they've got it nailed—almost inevitably at some point they bump into their old habits and lose their good feeling.

As I've said, habits are often hard to break. Though people may see something new, they sometimes slide back into their old habits of thinking. That's what we're used to. It's ingrained. The deeper the insight the less likely this is to occur, but it still can. This is where it can be helpful to teach maintenance to build sustainable change.

By this I mean people might have to be reminded that their old habits of thinking will likely return, and the lower their mood the more "real" this thinking will seem. They can be helped to be aware that such thoughts are just trying to trick them at these times, so it would be unwise to be fooled by them. If fooled by old habits, if people also realize that *their thinking combined with consciousness is only making it look like reality,* they will less likely fall for it. It may be helpful to see when thinking is riled up it is also giving them faulty messages, and their uncomfortable feeling could be seen instead that their thinking it is not reality and can't be trusted at that time. It is a signal to get calm, to clear the mind or if they can't clear their heads at the time, don't believe the reality of their thinking. The job of Consciousness is to send it through the senses and make it look and feel very real and feel exactly like truth, but it isn't.

Of course, it is helpful as a reminder to have other people around who also have this understanding. It is nice to be reminded that our minds are too busy, or we're caught up without realizing it. But it is not necessary. Sometimes it seems we are alone and isolated, because to date still comparatively few people have this understanding. But really we are never alone because we have the power of Mind behind us. It is always present for us, though we sometimes forget. Once we have glimpsed this at a deep enough level, our forgetting is usually temporary. Even when we forget, something in the back of our minds is saying, "This too shall pass," or "I know my thinking is off right now and I can't help it, but I know somewhere down the line my thinking will change and I'll be back on track." Comforting.

At least part of our mind might be saying, "You have to solve this—now! You need to bear down and get to it!" The lower the mood the more immediate it looks. Setting our intention to see it and taking it off our mind and wait for an insight to come can seem too passive. This is another of those paradoxes. Yet, to find it we have to forget it because it clears the mind and an insight from wisdom only comes when the mind clears. Knowing this is part of maintenance.

Even the most practiced Three Principles professionals at times forget what we know and disconnect from our Health. Then we think we should know better and can get down on ourselves even more. But God knows we're only human like everyone else. Yet if we set our intention to see our Health, keep it in view and act out of it, we would be more likely to do just that. We would be able to help each other with gentle, loving reminders when any of us slips away from that state. So I invite us all to use our creative power of Thought to see anew, and to start afresh with anyone we may need to, and work in harmony for the common good.

After all, only three things really count in the work we do: 1) the feeling we have in our hearts; 2) understanding how things work (the Three Principles); 3) the results we achieve with others and with ourselves. Everything else is an illusion. (This, too, may be an illusion, but at least it's a healthy one.)

2. FOUR OPTIONS FOR INSIDE-OUT COMMUNITY APPLICATIONS

Communities or community-based organizations considering a full-blown inside-out change effort might consider different options. Four are presented below. Remember, any application of the formless Three Principles in a community or an organization is form, and as form it is not perfect. Each has advantages and disadvantages. It would be wise for the option selected to best meet the needs of the community and best fit the community or organization.

I have seen each of these four applications in action. Combinations also have been applied. There may be others as well. The titles below are used only for convenience. These are in no particular order.

Option # 1.: The Bemidji model: One or two trainings for many different groups

Brief Description: A 2 or 2½-day Three Principles training is provided to a small group of 10 to 30 people, possibly followed by another 2-days of an Inside-Out Applications training. This training (or set of trainings) is then repeated periodically over the next year for two to ten other groups of community or organization members. The trainers then leave and allow whatever happens to occur on its own.

Rationale: People who catch on will work on their own to create whatever can be created for that community. If they think it appropriate, on their own they will arrange more trainings or create a community process to yield community change.

Resources Needed: One or two trainers for each group trained.

Advantages: In this option many people receive training over time. Because of this the odds are high someone will catch the feeling enough to take the responsibility of creating a constructive community response. This option allows for the most natural propagation because it evolves completely on its own. It is probably the least costly.

Disadvantages: This option relies on at least one and preferably a few people being affected strongly enough and on their own, without much training and only because of their goodwill, taking the responsibility to make something happen, and it may not.

Option # 2.: The Long-Term Training model: Six to twelve trainings for one group

Brief Description*:* One group of 8 to 30 people meets for 2 days once a month for 6 to 12 months. This training is designed to deepen understanding and personal grounding in the Three Principles to the extent that participants "live it," and to learn and practice how to apply it with others and in communities. The trainers then leave and allow whatever happens to occur on its own.

Rationale*:* Same as above, except it intends to provide much more intensive training over a longer period of time to fewer people, in hopes people will be affected so deeply they will have no choice but to create community or organizational change.

Resources Needed*:* Two trainers are preferable for a long-term training. Therefore, it may cost a little more than Option 1, depending on the number of training sessions.

Advantages*:* This training goes much deeper for fewer participants, increasing the likelihood that someone will create, or work with others to create, community or organizational change. This model still allows for natural propagation.

Disadvantages*:* Comparatively few people attend the training, thus lowering the odds that someone will pick up the ball on their own. It still relies on people taking the responsibility on their own to make something happen, which may lower the odds of it actually happening.

Option # 3. The Training of Trainers model (used in Santa Clara County, California):

Brief Description: This is an extensive, on-going training system where Three Principles trainers train others who then become qualified to train others, who then train others, etc.

Rationale: Community or organizational change most likely will occur if a self-perpetuating, ever-expanding system is established that continually brings in new blood and ensures ongoing training of new people.

Resources Needed: High cost, because many trainers keep needing to be paid, *unless* they are able to do trainings as part of their existing job descriptions.

Advantages: This model keeps an ongoing cadre of trainers continuously trained and improving their grounding and skills, which allows for an ongoing community presence. New people are continually being trained, which spreads the understanding. This is the most systematized of the models. It possibly turns out the most "well-schooled" trainers.

Disadvantages: This model can easily encourage people to sit in judgment of others' capabilities or readiness. If training styles don't mesh or a trainer finds fault with a trainee, such judgment could be compromised. It may encourage an "I know something you don't" mentality, and subtly imply that someone is not capable of finding one's own wisdom to improve others' lives in one's own way. It carries a higher price tag than the first two options.

Option # 4. The Modello Model: Trained community-based staff

Brief Description: At least two Three Principles-trained staff are hired for every 150-200 housing units or 300-400 people, with at least ¼ time of a skilled Three Principles supervisor familiar with community work (who may or may not need to be on site). Preferably, half the staff should be from within the community. This is coupled with large community trainings for community leaders and service providers who serve the area. Staff could be hired under a new grant, or job descriptions of existing staff from agencies currently serving the area could be revised for this purpose. The staff role is to build rapport, build hope, deeply listen, provide informal counseling as needed, help out residents as needed, create vehicles to convey the understanding based on perceived community needs, assist residents in creating community change, work with schools, and provide or arrange for Three Principles-based trainings. Before hiring staff, this effort can begin with a small community group meeting once a week (with a volunteer or two facilitating) on whatever topic would attract people. This option probably is most effective when later combined with extra training for community people who have caught on most, who then help others in their community.

Rationale: Community or organizational change will most likely occur if an ongoing presence is assured. In other words, people who "live the feeling" and are trained in the Three Principles are available on an ongoing basis to help community members deal with difficulties and help them join together to improve their community.

Resources Needed: This is the most costly model because of hiring staff—*unless* existing job descriptions are revised for this purpose.

Advantages: This option ensures an ongoing staff presence in which community members (both individuals and groups) are worked with from an inside-out perspective. This option may have the greatest potential to touch the most people's lives in a community. It provides direct service to community members and guides them to make the community changes they desire from a perspective of Health.

Disadvantages: With paid staff it is easy for the community to lay the responsibility (and blame) on them and not take it themselves. It is possible that if people from within the community apply unsuccessfully for available staff positions jealousies could develop that would run counter to living the spirit of the Principles. It is also possible for jealousies to develop among other agencies if they see this program as competition. It is potentially the costliest option.

Again, combinations of these options are common, and the situation will determine which is most appropriate. There may also be other options that I, personally, have not experienced.

3. THE EXPERIENCE OF PARTICIPANTS AFTER THREE PRINCIPLES TRAINING

[Excerpts from my Doctoral Dissertation][17]

(only the interesting parts)

One day in October 1996 I received a call from Mary Marchel of the Violence Prevention Action Team in Bemidji, Minnesota, inquiring about my book *Prevention: The Critical Need*[18]. She had been searching the Internet for material on prevention for juveniles, found my book through the Texas Catalogue of Youth Programs and managed somehow to track me down.

The Violence Prevention Action Team had formed in Bemidji in May 1996 to "serve as a catalyst to initiate collaboration of community wide primary and secondary violence prevention efforts." In October of that year the Team worked with the local Family Services Collaborative to bring Arun Gandhi to Bemidji to speak on nonviolence. As a follow-up, Mary Marchel, Director of Beltrami County Public Health Nursing Service, volunteered to search for resource material to aid in writing a grant. I sent her my book.

After reading it Mary called me back to ask if I would be interested in conducting some prevention training in Bemidji. I listened to what she wanted and suggested Health Realization training might meet their needs even better than a traditional prevention training.

"What's Health Realization?" she asked.

I tried to explain it briefly and sent her an article I had written called "Moving Prevention to a Higher Plane"[19].

---

[17] Pransky, J. (1999). The experience of participants after Health Realization training: A one-year follow-up phenomenological study. Doctoral dissertation/Project Demonstrating Excellence prepared for The Union Institute, Cincinnati, Ohio.

[18] Pransky, J. (1991). *Prevention: The Critical Need.* Bloomington, IN: AuthorHouse

[19] Pransky, J. (1994). Can prevention be moved to a higher plane? *New designs for youth development*. Tucson, AZ: Development Associates. (11:2).

Mary called back again. The Action Team decided to take a chance on the training, even though they did not really understand what it was. Apparently they decided to try it because both Mary and Susan Smith, a local psychotherapist and another key member of the Action Team, had found the *Prevention* book to be "really impressive," particularly the chapter on "Spirituality in Prevention," so they decided to trust my suggestion.

Mary set up a training and invited Action Team members and other key community leaders to attend. I conducted a three-day Health Realization training in Bemidji on May 6-8, 1997. Both Mary and Susan were so impressed with the training they arranged for another to be held in October 1998 for other community members. This time I co-facilitated two-thirds of the training with Cynthia Stennis, former resident and staff member of the Modello/Homestead Gardens project.

The Bemidji trainings came to my mind for study because initially they had no idea what Health Realization was, nor what to expect. I called Mary Marchel to ask if she would be willing to have me conduct follow-up research on the results of the training. She agreed.

The Study

For my doctoral dissertation for The Union Institute & University, I decided on a qualitative phenomenological research design[20] because I was interested in participants' detailed perceptions of *how* their lives had changed as a result of Health Realization training. I also wanted to know whether any effects lasted longitudinally (over time), in this case approximately one year after the two Bemidji trainings.

My study question was, "How do people perceive and describe their experience following Health Realization training?" I wanted participants' own descriptions of any major changes they had observed in their thoughts, feelings, and behaviors since the training. I wanted to know to what did they attribute those changes, what meaning it had for their lives, and what they were now doing with the understandings gained from that experience.

---

[20] I won't even define it here. Too academic. If you're interested you can Google it.

A total of 41 participants (mostly white, middle-class professionals in the helping professions) attended two separate three-day Health Realization trainings. Of these, 37 were found eligible to participate in the study, which occurred approximately one year after the two trainings. Of these, 23 returned survey questionnaires (11 from the May 1997 training, and 12 from October 1997), and 13 agreed to be interviewed extensively.

Results

Through a rigorous examination of the interviews and clustering these data I found that, one year after the three-day Health Realization training, participants experienced:

a. *more calm and comfort in life*
b. *more lightheartedness, or a lighter feeling*
c. *fewer and less intense emotional reactions*
d. *less stress*
e. *better, higher quality relationships*

Included here are one or two interview excerpts in each category.

a. *More calm and comfort in life*

DD: It has made me more secure. It's made me calmer. It's made me...feel better about things... Everything. Everything. Just my life…, my life at home and my family. All my relationships... It's just much calmer. It's more secure. It's more happy. It has a better feeling. There's more love. It's more peaceful. It feels healthier… This is my thoughts, creating my reality.

MM: I don't know any other way to describe it but...to use the words "calm at my core." That's a new feeling for me. And it was amazing to me that regardless of what else is going on in my life or outside in the environment, that sense of peacefulness and calm like I've never known before... I guess the word that just kind of pops into my head...is relief..., in the sense of, I don't have to know all the answers, I don't have to take on all the burdens that I previously had, whether it's at work or home. That's been big for me. It's obviously increased the quality of my life.

b. *More lightheartedness or a lighter feeling*

SS: I don't know, it's lighter, light, it feels lighter, more interesting, more fun [laughs]. I don't have the words. It's just more available... There are just so many more possibilities and opportunities than I would have acknowledged before... When I would get involved with thinking in limited ways I would feel discouraged, or I would feel lack of hope, or I would feel stuck, or those kinds of things... So I feel hopeful more of the time, and like, Whoa, why not try that?... Because it makes so much sense...I feel like my own personal growth just has been accelerated... Another thing is feeling more able to take risks, and that feels like another lighter thing. Not taking risks before was based in fear, and so there's not that fear...

c. *Fewer and less intense emotional reactions*

CA: When I use Health Realization I respond differently to things that happen between [my son] and I, because I don't just get this instant hurt, and I tend to look at it differently, look at him and where he's coming from...

d. *Less stress*

MM: It's been definitely more of a recognition that I'm creating my own stress, and that's been pretty nice to just know that I do it to myself and where that comes from. So I would say definitely my stress is lessened much since going through this, and again...it doesn't mean I never get stressed because I certainly do, but I noticed that I visit there less often, I don't stay there as long, and…and backing up from it and sometimes thinking to myself, "This too shall pass," I would say it's…much less stress. And I recognize myself as the creator of that stress.

e. *Better, higher quality relationships* *(with spouses/partners, children, at work, people they found difficult):*

MN: … this is some of the best training that I've ever had in my life, and I can't really pinpoint huge ways that it's changed my life, but in a lot of little ways it has—particularly at work. It's just been incredible in dealing with employees one-on-one, helping resolve disputes between employers and employees, and supervisors, etc. etc. It's been really helpful. A lot of their disagreements are just sort of disappearing now, where they used to continue fighting and dragging things out... The way I've been able to use the training is the indicator of its success. But I've also been through eighteen-and-a-half years of various human resources trainings, how to be a supervisor, how to train supervisors to be supervisors, how to deal with conflicts and all of those kinds of trainings, and I have never, with all the techniques I have learned, had anything that worked anywhere as well as this does... Since I've had the training I haven't tried to be so controlling. And the amazing thing is that they are much more receptive...[and] what I end up saying afterwards is usually more appropriate to the situation than much of what I would have said previously.

1. Why are they experiencing these results in their lives?

a. *They realized their own power of creation—of their life experience*
b. *They realized a source of "health" within, and to trust it*
c. *They realized the pathway to their health, and what blocks it*
d. *They recognized the signals that show whether or not they are in their health, so they could self-monitor*
e. *They saw their choice to live in an outside, personal world or in an inside, nonpersonal world*
f. *They saw their own habitual thinking patterns that kept them stuck, and their ability to transcend them by raising their level of understanding*

a. *Realizing the source of creation of their life experience: Thought*

MM: The whole idea of really seeing myself as the thinker...was huge, and in particular seeing myself coming to understand about my choices I make, and also...about changing my mind. That was particularly big. …when you came a year ago, at that time...I was in the process of a divorce…and we were literally days away from having that happen. And I can remember one morning taking a walk and thinking—and this was...

about a month after the Health Realization [training]—thinking to myself…, "I don't love this man. Can I ever love him again?" And that's the point where I could see about changing my mind, and that I change my mind all the time, and that our feelings are a result of our thinking, and really seeing that and knowing that, "Yes, I can change my mind." And as I was able to change my mind from loving him to not loving him,...I could also reverse that... It was only the recognition to me that it was thought, that it's thought behind the feeling, the feeling of love... I don't think I went out of my way to change my mind. I saw some things that I hadn't seen before. I saw humility in this man that I hadn't seen before...and what those choices were in not taking things so personally... It was a relief to really see that that was all coming from my thinking... It was pretty incredible... So, you came in May and [my husband] was back home at the end of July… We [had been] all set, ready to go, and everything had been decided upon, agreed upon, …just waiting for the court date...

DD: What's changed is my understanding that it's my thinking about what's going on out there that either makes me angry or uncomfortable, or however it is that I feel... It's not that stuff out there, but I can think differently, and it makes me feel differently...

b. *Realizing their unlimited capacity for innate "wisdom" or "health"*

SS: One of the pieces of truth is that when people are calm, they know what to do... That's a difference that I see is, in the...more common realm of psychology...when we get into that messy thought content like defensiveness or shame or guilt, you have to figure it out in order to get out of it… Health Realization shows another way. Figuring it out just keeps you there longer… But that I have—we all have—a healthier thought process that's just natural if we don't try to figure this out. If we just let it go and trust that we know what we'll need to know about it if we need to know something, and by letting it go we have better access to that understanding… I can remember a time in my life where…I would write out affirmations and read them and remember to tell myself these things and start to believe them. When the piece that Health Realization offers is that I don't have to do any of that stuff. It is already there!... I just have to let...that...feeling come. There is no work to it. And that's a lot of work to take twenty minutes a day to visualize the perfect personality [laughs]. That's a lot of time—when it is already there! I don't have to do it, because it's in there. …

c. *Realizing the pathway to their health, and what blocks it: A calm and clear mind*

WP: Well, I guess the biggest thing is that I can enjoy the moment more... At one point in my life I could sit out on the deck and look out over the pasture and the pond and the flower bed, and I would see flowers to be weeded, a pond that needed cleaning out and needed fixing, I could see horses that needed their hooves trimmed, cockleburs taken out of their manes, and I'm sure they need shots again... Or you walk out through the garage and you see, "Oh man, I have to do this, this and this," and "that should have been taken care of," and "that has to be put away." And so you can either spend moment-to-moment getting stressed even in the most enjoyable moments on your deck, looking out over [these] beautiful… acres… You can clear away all this junk, and you just see more, and you see more beautiful, and the view is more grand. And I guess in a way that's kind of what's happened, is that you can sit out there, and you can enjoy the moment and you don't have to think about all that has to be done or should be done or could be done or would be done if I wasn't sitting here enjoying the moment. And so that's been big for me, too, is that moment—that must have been in the training, something about the moment... Clear your mind, and that works, and I think the more you do it, the faster it works and the better it works.

d. *Recognizing the signals of whether or not they are in their health, so they could self-monitor*

SS: The piece that was entirely new to me from the training was the whole revelation about moods…in spite of all of the background that I've got in mental health and family relationships, I had never heard talked about in that way. And…I was fascinated by it. And that was one of the first things that I began to look at for myself in all my relationships...[and] the first thing that I started to help people with was my understanding of moods... And then at another level I seem to gain a greater ability to just be self-observant, so I would notice myself in low moods more often than I used to. I used to ignore and deny that I was in a low mood. So I think I've noticed myself there more often. I wouldn't say that I go there more often, I probably go there less often, but I see myself—I'm more aware of it, and at times get caught in it, but I still know that I'm caught in it. I'm aware of it now—almost invariably I know when I'm in it.

BC: Last fall BY was just in a...bad mood,...growling...like a rabid grizzly, and then all of a sudden he walked back into the room and he said, "You know, I'm just in a low mood, and I've taken it out on you, and it's not fair." And I went, "Awwww, [sigh]" [laughter]. And then everything was just fine. And he's really done that a couple of times, just stopped, and that's been wonderful.

e. *Seeing their choice to live in an outside, personal world or in an inside, nonpersonal world*

JF: When I first came back to the office after the training...there's a person there that always bugs me... We just don't really click. But when I came back from the training, she did the same stuff...to me, and it was like I had this shield... I could just see her, and...I didn't take it personally... It was, like, "Oh, you must be really insecure." ...I mean, I could see so much clearer. [Before]...I was more into reacting. I was more into taking it personally…but...one of the thoughts that came to me is, "I wonder what it would be like to live with herself," so then I felt more compassion. Poor thing! [laughs] I should bring her brownies... I guess what I see now is...I don't have to get caught up—…there's just more perspectives and ways of looking at the experience of the moment than just one... It moves you into a different perspective where you can look at the situation from a different angle...

CJ: Something just this past week...challenged me to this personal-nonpersonal thing... I have a son who has diabetes. He's been having a lot of low blood sugar lately. Now, the key symptoms of low blood sugar is irritability and not really being in your right mind, and some of these are in the middle of the night. And the other night at three a.m. he says to me, "You're the worst thing that's ever happened to me!" Now, I left his bedroom thinking, "Okay, CJ—that's about the worst thing that I could hear." I know he has low blood sugar...but I was faced with…what am I going to do? Am I going to sit here and dwell on that and start tearing up on that? No,...that would be the stupidest thing for me to do. There's no rationality into that. And then a couple of days later something else came out of his mouth. He had a 34-blood sugar—really low—and so I've just more really realized how here's a situation where in anybody's right mind they should never take that kind of thing personally. And so in my daily life when things happen to me...I have a choice... When you were a kid...people would say, "Don't take it personally." It's like, "Well then, tell me how else to take it! You know?" And I think that the training gave me that...

SS: The first snowstorm this year, I was going to go out to the store to get some groceries, and I went out to get in the car and I had to scrape all the windows. And as I went around the car scraping the windows one by one I somehow broke off all the windshield wipers, so by the time I got done scraping my windshield I had no windshield wipers on my car. And I just got progressively more upset and more upset, and by the time I got done I thought, "All I wanted to do was go to the store, get some groceries, and here I have my windshield wipers in my hand and I can't go anywhere because I can't see out the windows!" And all of a sudden it dawned on me that I was taking this personally, and I burst out laughing. And it was the first time it occurred to me that I could take something personally from an inanimate object, in that I would just get stuck in that way of thinking and get upset. And that was just an element of my deeper understanding of personal and impersonal, and that it had more to do with personalizing something, and it had to do with just the kind of thought that I was going into—those two different kinds of thought that I could find myself in. The minute I started to laugh at the windshield wipers all coming off my car, I switched out of personal thought into that lighter, freer thought that doesn't take things personally.

f. *Seeing their habitual thinking patterns, and transcending them by raising their level of understanding*

JL: I put on a really nice party for my daughter's graduation at a distance in Minneapolis, so I had to do a lot of the planning in Bemidji and go down there early to my mother's and try to get everything together and figure out how many people were coming. This is not a big deal, but in the past I would have had quite a bit of sense of stress about, "Am I going to get everything done?" and, "Are there going to be enough chairs?" [laughs]. Just all those things. But every time I found myself thinking that maybe I would get a little bit worried about something, I would just say to myself, "It's going to work out. Just enjoy the fact that right now you're cutting up celery. You're with your ninety-three-year-old old mom here, it's not going to be much longer." So every time I found myself wanting to fall into an old habit of fretting, I would instead say, "However it works out, it's going to be okay." So people will have a nice time. And it was the most relaxed getting ready and the most comfortably relaxed party that I've ever had. We had enough chairs, and it was supposed to be a bonfire-wienie roast-veggie burger cookout, and it was raining. Actually everything went perfectly...

BC: You...realize, all of a sudden…I could be one thought away from health... I was all upset about something one day, and we had just gone through the training, and I thought, "I'm frickin' twenty-nine ideas away from health!" [laughter] I mowed the whole damn yard, and it was October [laughter], because [my husband] was going to tie the handle on the lawn mower to let it run at of gas, and I thought, "I'll go out and mow the lawn." Then I felt much better because the lawn was mowed and I got my exercise and then blew off some steam. And I kind of knew…while I was doing it, "...Okay, so maybe I'm twenty-eight thoughts away from health [laughter]. But it's just the thought! And the real thought is, "Oh, I'm in a low mood." That's your one thought away from health...is that recognition. And then just go, "Oh, maybe now isn't the time to [take care of] everything, because I'm low mood."

2. How did they come to have this new experience in life?

a. *Something "just clicked"*

JF: The first day...when I went to the training, I was like, "So?" But the second day it started to sink in. And by the third day I remember a moment where it just all came together, where I had that place of understanding, where all the pieces kind of came together... I remember tears came to my eyes, I remember that feeling of, "Oop, I'm going to cry." I remember just a real sense of peace and understanding...It was the third day and...people were talking. I don't remember exactly. I just remember this sense of "Ahhh, I see it now. I see it now." You know, it's been kind of like to me...those pictures that you can look at at the science center, and you can't see it and you can't see, and where's the...[3D] horse or whatever in the picture? And all of a sudden, "Whooo, I see it!" ... That to me is what this Health Realization is about, I mean the way that you learn it. It's not like people see it just because you said it... They had to see it in their own insight, and at their own time. And so when it comes up for you, it's going to be a different time than it comes up for me. But I remember that experience of, "Ahhhh, I see it now." I can see it with my own insight.

b. *They gained new understanding or knowledge about their psychological functioning*

BY: One of the contributions of the training is that I have that notion in my repertoire now, and I didn't have it before... that most of the time, or all the time, people are doing the best they can, given where they are and what they're thinking. And that's a real state-of-grace statement in words...and it's happened to me a couple of times. You really feel it. There's a shift there, and I think that's part of the truth, that seems to feel like truth…

c. *They gained new tools*

MM: I hadn't realized before what an awful listener I was, and how wonderful it is to feel the closeness in really listening to somebody explore their own thoughts, come up with their own answers, and that's kind of hand-in-hand with relief... I don't have to come up with your answers. And I know that if I listen, that that's still of help to you... Sometimes I visit my dad, and he's eighty-five, and I have heard some of the same stories for years and years and years—I thought! And suddenly...I decided, well, it might be just a good time to practice deep listening. And...I heard the same story, but it wasn't the same story. And I heard something I never heard before. And it was amazing to me to see that, and have that happen, and go away with a much deeper sense and closeness to him, of somebody that I love so much. And so just with the quality of what that can bring to the quality of my life, it's really exciting to think about

3. What meaning did this have for their lives?

JF: I have more hope because until this came along there just didn't seem to be any hope for society's ills. I hate to say that this is the panacea for all of society's ills, but it has a hopeful quality... It gives me a sense that my life has meaning and purpose… Health Realization has done a lot for me... What this has done for me is woke me up more. I think of Health Realization as a spiritual experience, I would say, and an awakening. And it does help the quality of my life a lot. And when I bring it back to my

Christianity, it just fits so beautifully into my journey there, so it integrates into my whole spirituality so beautifully. And I think it makes me better able to become who I was created to become, you know? And get the barriers out of the way. And then that just springs out into the family and to friends and to people, and so it's been really great.

BY: I can just share a comment with you that…one of my colleagues said at one of our gatherings... She's recovering, and she said after going through Health Realization..., "Yup, that AA destroyed my drinking, and Health Realization destroyed my thinking." [laughter]

4. What have they done with this newfound understanding?

a. *They naturally used their own understanding within their own families and primary relationships to improve those relationships.*
b. *They used it at work to improve relationships and effectiveness.*
c. *Some then helped their friends gain new understandings.*
d. *Some conducted their own Health Realization training for others in Bemidji.*
e. *Many continued to meet periodically to work for community change.*

JF: [My daughter] just is strong-willed, and I think I was trying to really, like, make her not strong-willed, and then that would make me a good parent. So once I kind of let her be who she is and validated that "you already are perfect inside somewhere"—you know, it just kind of validated her and made our relationship a lot better... We had just kind of been struggling a lot. We just fought about little things, you know, not being nice to her sister. And I'm always, kind of, like, you know, yelling at her..., "I'm sick and tired of—knock it off!"...because...every time I'd see her it was like she was...doing something...that I didn't like, so I was always pointing that out to her. So I was always kind of in this struggle with her for a long time. And so when I just came home and came up to her and said, "You know, I think maybe I've been kind of doing this wrong. I mean I really feel like...maybe you already have it, and I just...need to help bring that out in you." And she just lit up...and she said, "I told you!" And...she was so glad I finally was enlightened... So it just made the parenting thing like a whole lot easier.

MM: There's...people all over the place [as a result of these sessions]… on the continuum of...seeing little bits and pieces to people who have been kind of hit over the head with a two-by-four, really, and seeing it in a huge way... I had one other experience that...was pretty profound... CJ and I were doing a group of fifty kids,...so we spent quite a bit of time talking about moods. And at the end of this three hours around a circle of fifty kids we asked them each to go around, if they were willing, to share if they learned something new or had some insight about something that we had said...and there was this girl—I think she was probably a senior—she started to get a little teary. And she said, "You know, I've been on antidepressants for several years, and...this is the first time anybody has ever told me that moods were normal, that other people had moods, and that all it was was a mood. And...it makes me feel so hopeful that someday I won't have to be on medicine, and it's normal, and the rest of you here have moods just like me, and...that's okay." And...I thought, every second that we have spent talking and thinking and preparing and whatever, was worth it for me in that instant. I thought, "Yes, that's what it's all about!"

Summary

SS: The really clear piece that's different for me is, in the general realm of psychology, it almost always deals with what people are thinking, what people are feeling…and...on why people think what they think…and oftentimes there's not even a connection made between thoughts and feelings in that whole realm… Psychology stays in the personal thought system…trying to understand the way someone thinks and analyze it and pick it apart, make meaning out of it in some way. And this differs for me in that I don't even have to go there... And I think as I learned more from that first impetus of the training...because I don't think I grasped that immediately at the training,...and that stuff's phenomenal, understanding that. The other part that I need more of an understanding of is the natural intelligence of our impersonal thought or our innate health or wisdom, and that I can trust it, that it's there, and I don't have to think about it [laughs], and that I can have all kinds of messy thought content, and be upset and annoyed, and I don't have to figure that out to get...myself out of it. …Health Realization shows another way. Figuring it out just keeps you there longer…but…we all have a healthier thought process that's just natural if we don't try to figure this out. If we just let it go and trust that we know what we'll need to know about it if we need to know something, and by letting it go we have better access to that understanding.

FINAL NOTE

If you are either involved with a community project or would like to start one and would like further consultation on how to do this work from the inside-out via the Three Principles, you may contact Jack Pransky through his website: **www.insideoutunderstanding.com**.

ABOUT THE AUTHOR

Jack Pransky, Ph.D. is founder/director of the Center for Inside-Out Understanding and an internationally recognized trainer, coach, counselor and consultant who since 1992 has been studying and teaching "The Three Principles," an inside-out, spiritually-based model and approach. Dr. Pransky is one of the most widely-published authors of Three Principles-based books, including, ***Seduced by Consciousness; Somebody Should Have Told Us!***; ***Modello: A Story of Hope for the Inner City and Beyond; Parenting from the Heart; Paradigm Shift; Prevention from the Inside-Out***; and coauthoring the children's picture books, ***What Is a Thought? (A Thought is A Lot)*** and ***What is Wisdom (and Where Do I find It?),*** and the ***Healthy Thinking/ Feeling/Doing from the Inside-Out*** prevention curriculum for middle school students. Jack has worked in the field of prevention since 1968 in a wide variety of capacities and now provides training and consultation internationally. He was instrumental in creating the first state law (Vermont) requiring state agencies to plan for and conduct prevention practices, and he worked on developing national prevention policy. He also cofounded and codirected Prevention Unlimited which created the Spirituality of Prevention Conference. In 2001 his book, ***Modello*** received the Martin Luther King Storyteller's Award for the book best exemplifying Dr. King's vision of "the beloved community," and in 2004 Jack won the Vermont Prevention Pioneer's Award.

OTHER BOOKS BY JACK PRANSKY

Somebody Should Have Told Us!

Seduced by Consciousness

Paradigm Shift: A History of the Three Principles

Modello: A Story of Hope for the Inner City and Beyond

Parenting from the Heart

Prevention from the Inside-Out

What is a Thought? (A Thought is a Lot), co-authored with Amy Kahofer - a children's picture book

What is Wisdom (and Where Do I Find It)?, co-authored with Amy Kahofer - a children's picture book

Healthy Thinking/Feeling/Doing from the Inside-Out, co-authored with Lori Carpenos - a prevention curriculum for middle school students

Prevention: The Critical Need [Note: Not a Three Principles book]

CPSIA information can be obtained
at www.ICGtesting.com
Printed in the USA
BVHW080945030121
596829BV00005B/319